Cub

TAP
TAP
TAP

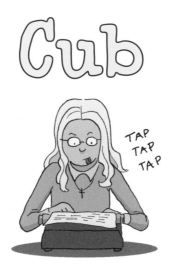

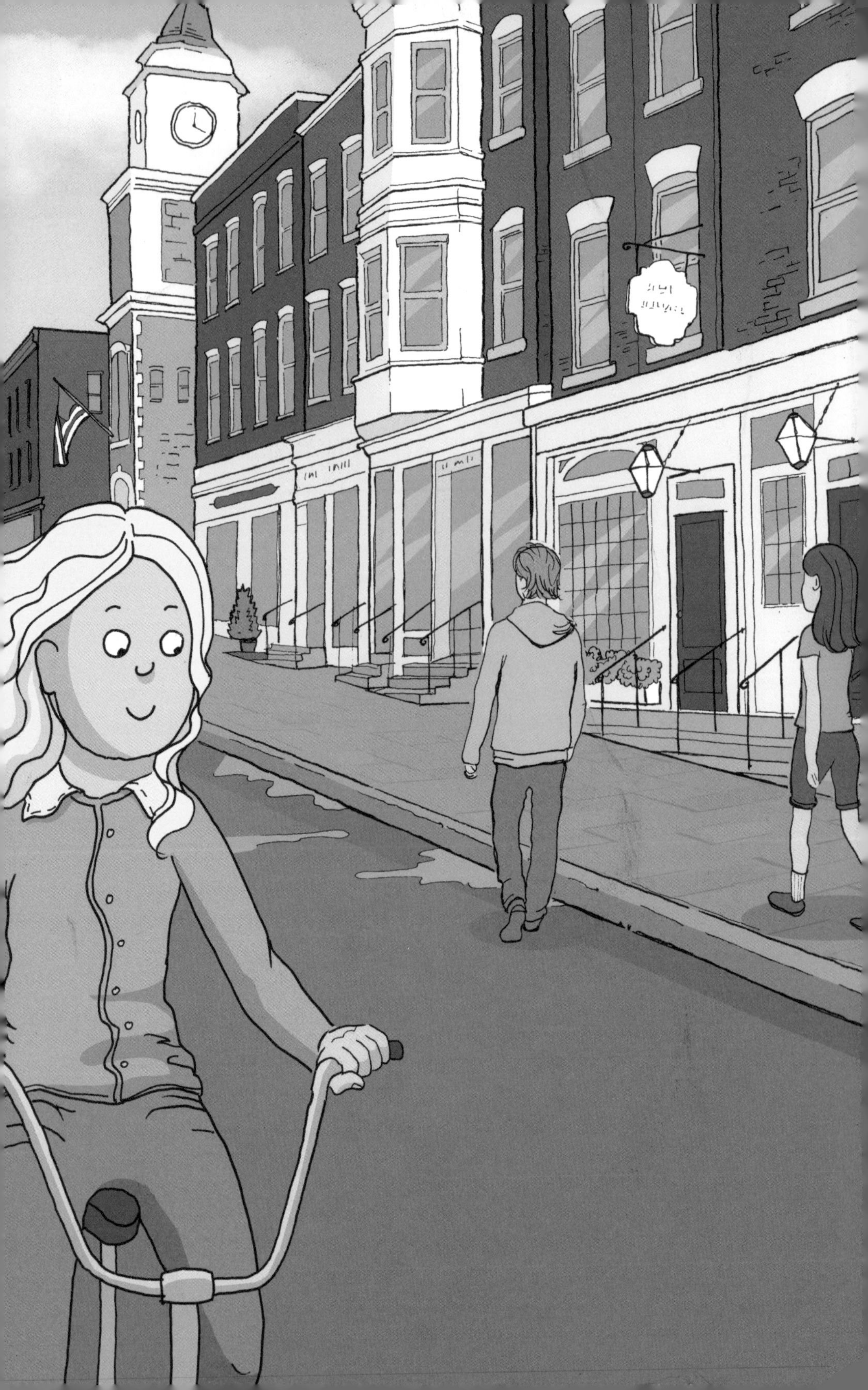

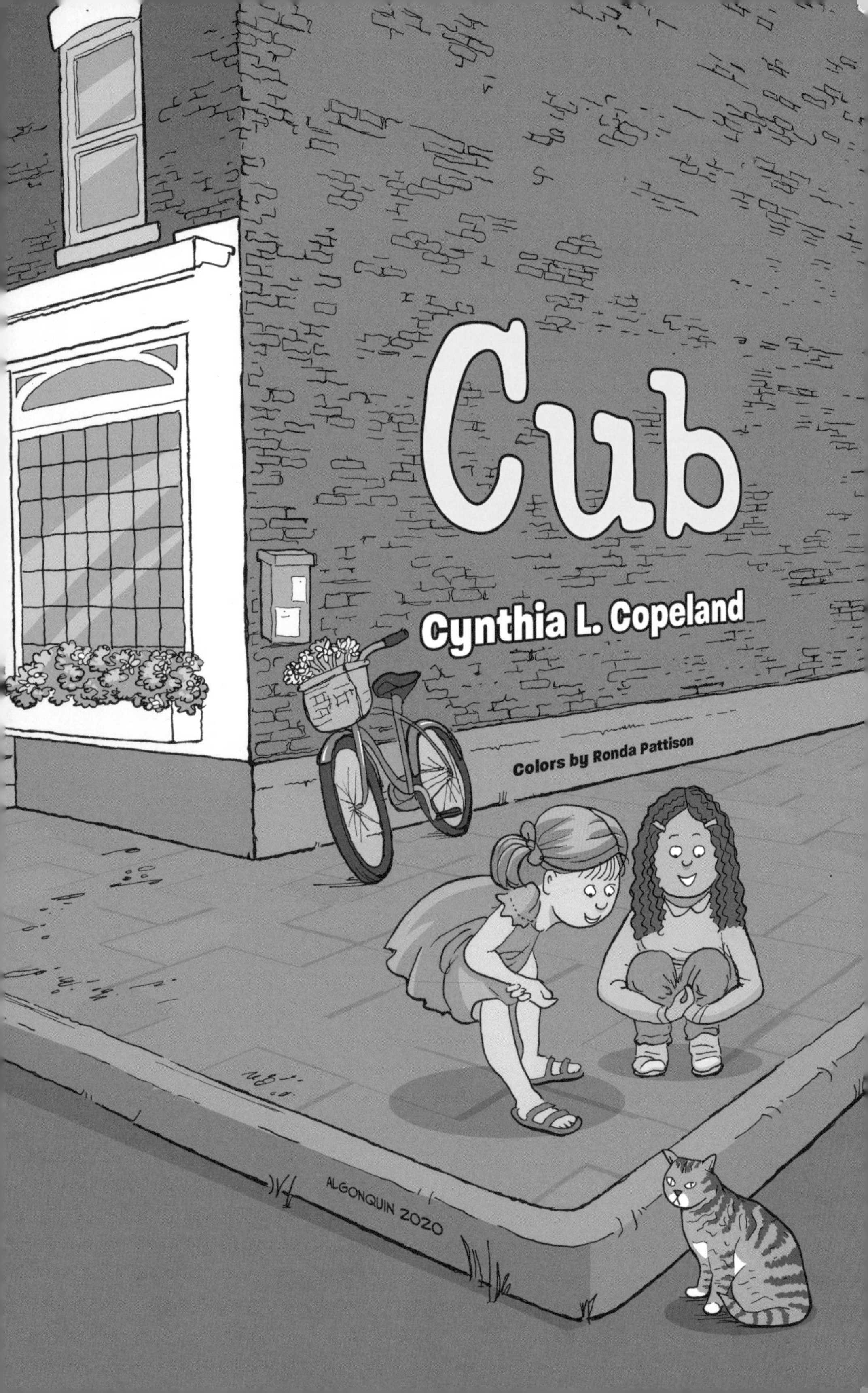
Cub
Cynthia L. Copeland
Colors by Ronda Pattison
ALGONQUIN 2020

ALSO BY CYNTHIA L. COPELAND

REALLY IMPORTANT STUFF MY DOG HAS TAUGHT ME

PUBLISHED BY ALGONQUIN YOUNG READERS

AN IMPRINT OF ALGONQUIN BOOKS OF CHAPEL HILL

POST OFFICE BOX 2225

CHAPEL HILL, NORTH CAROLINA 27515-2225

A DIVISION OF WORKMAN PUBLISHING

225 VARICK STREET

NEW YORK, NEW YORK 10014

PRINTED IN SOUTH KOREA.

PUBLISHED SIMULTANEOUSLY IN CANADA BY THOMAS ALLEN & SON LIMITED.

DESIGN BY NEIL SWAAB.

CATALOGING-IN-PUBLICATION DATA FOR THIS BOOK

IS ON FILE AT THE LIBRARY OF CONGRESS.

10 9 8 7 6 5 4 3 2 1

FIRST EDITION

FOR MY DAD

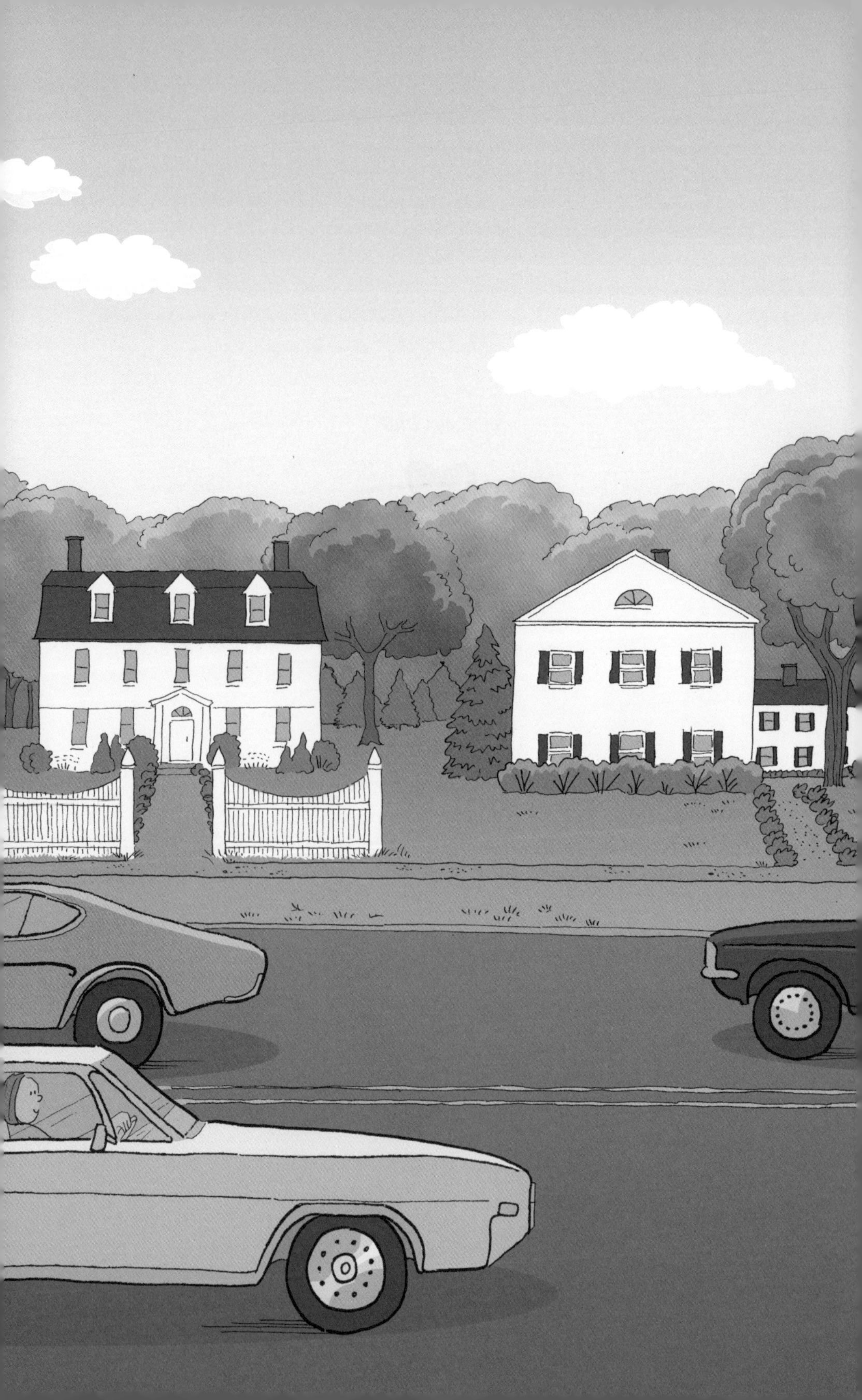

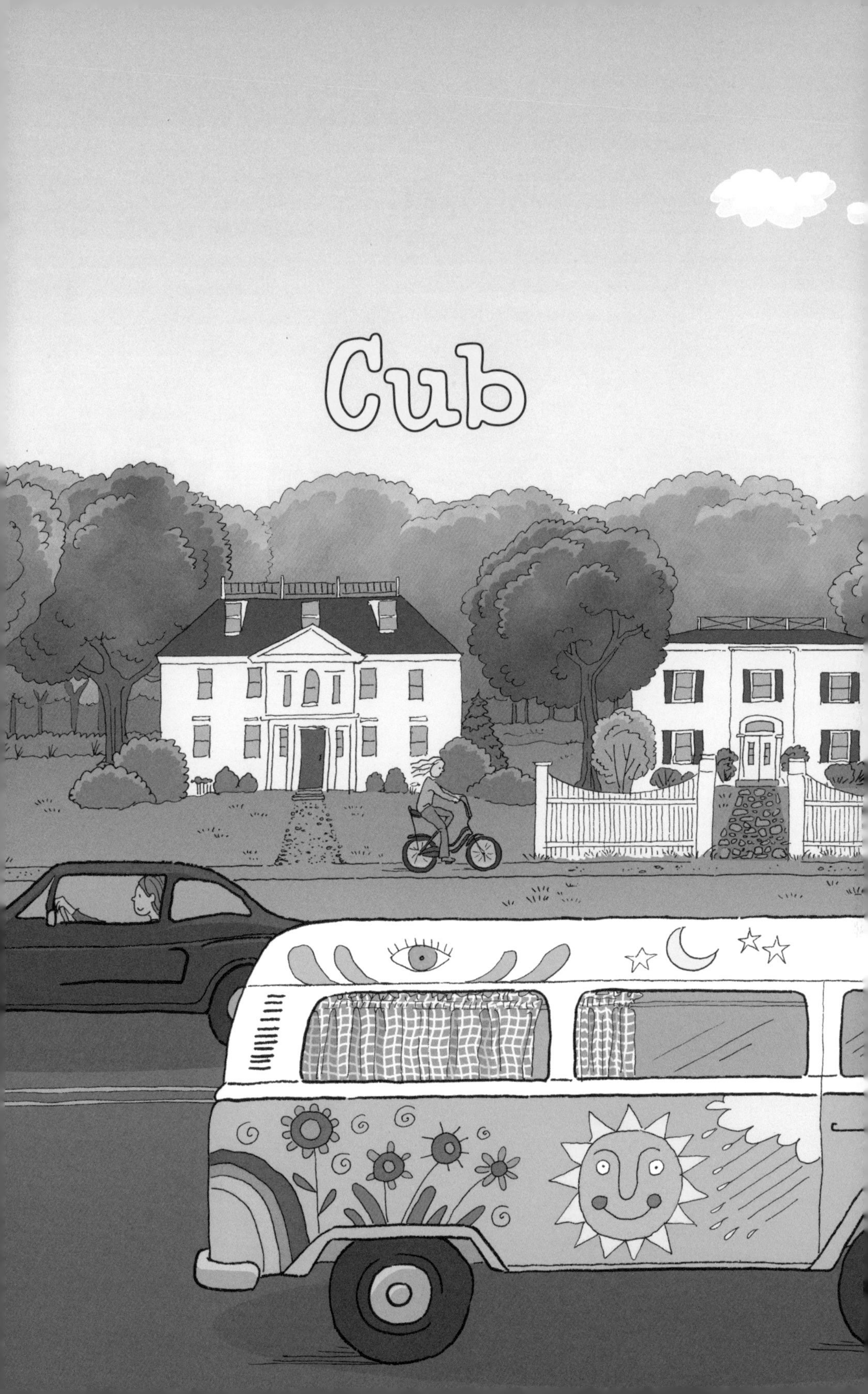
Cub

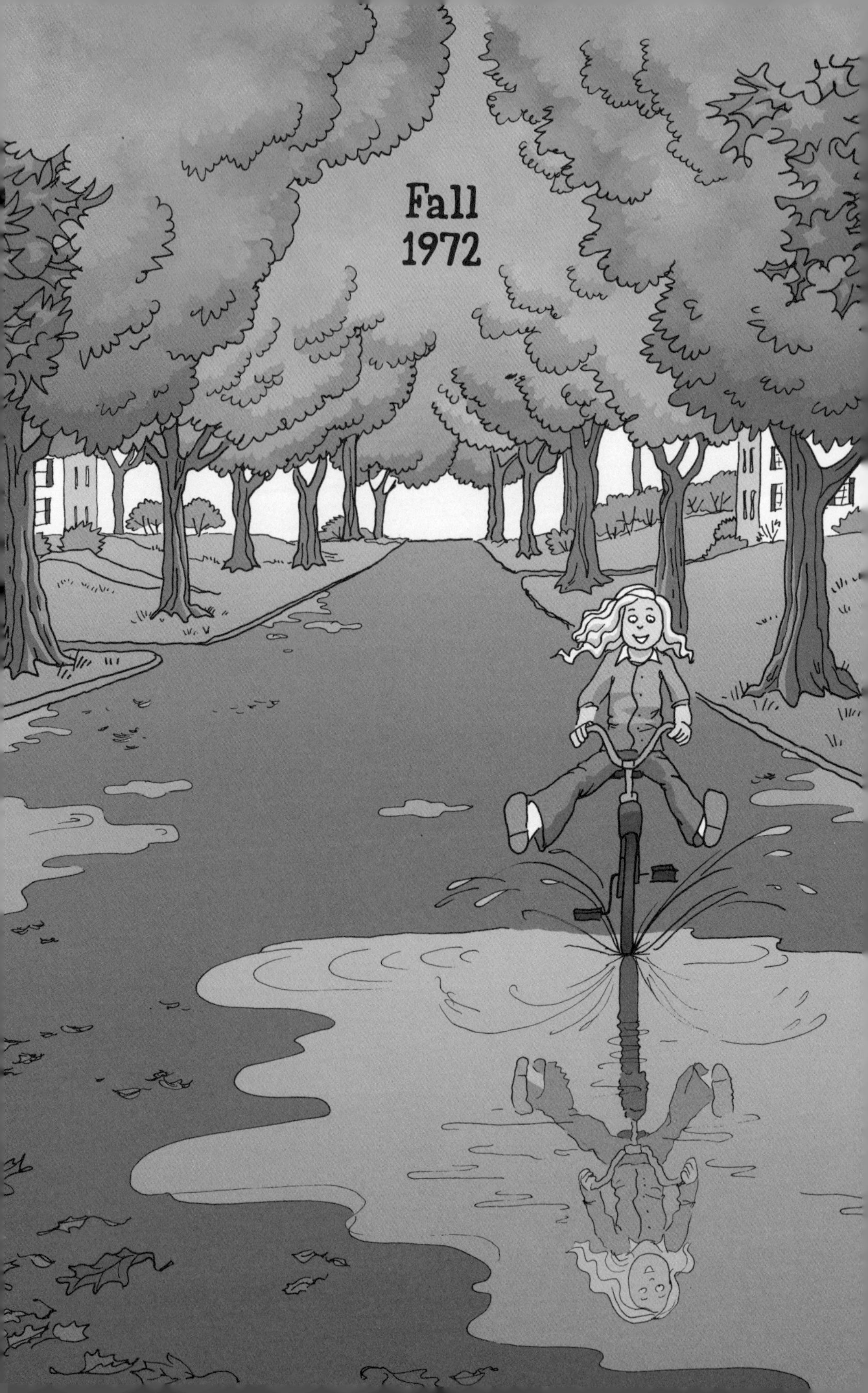
Fall
1972

Chapter 1

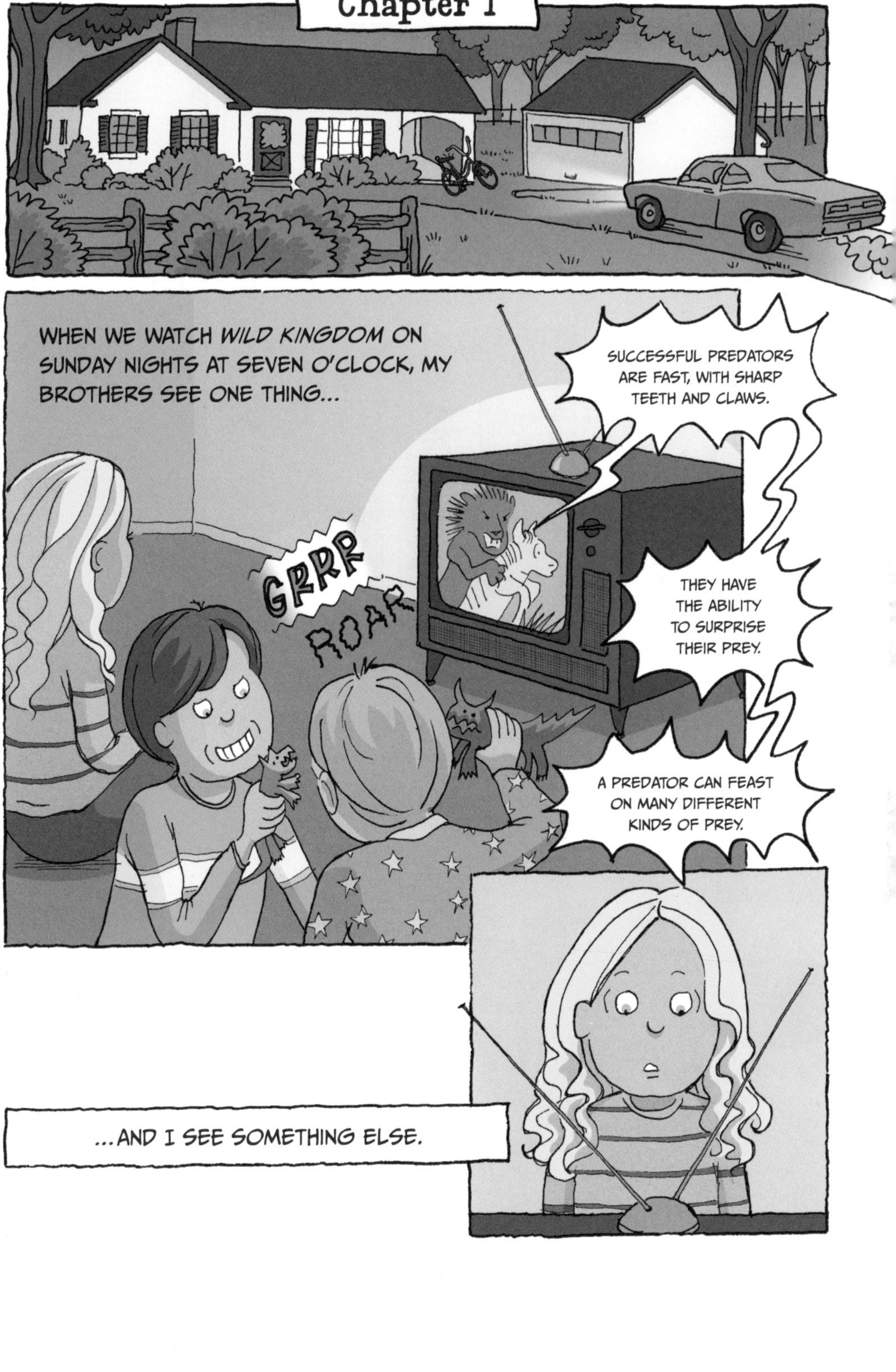
WHEN WE WATCH *WILD KINGDOM* ON SUNDAY NIGHTS AT SEVEN O'CLOCK, MY BROTHERS SEE ONE THING...
SUCCESSFUL PREDATORS ARE FAST, WITH SHARP TEETH AND CLAWS.
GRRR
ROAR
THEY HAVE THE ABILITY TO SURPRISE THEIR PREY.
A PREDATOR CAN FEAST ON MANY DIFFERENT KINDS OF PREY.
...AND I SEE SOMETHING ELSE.

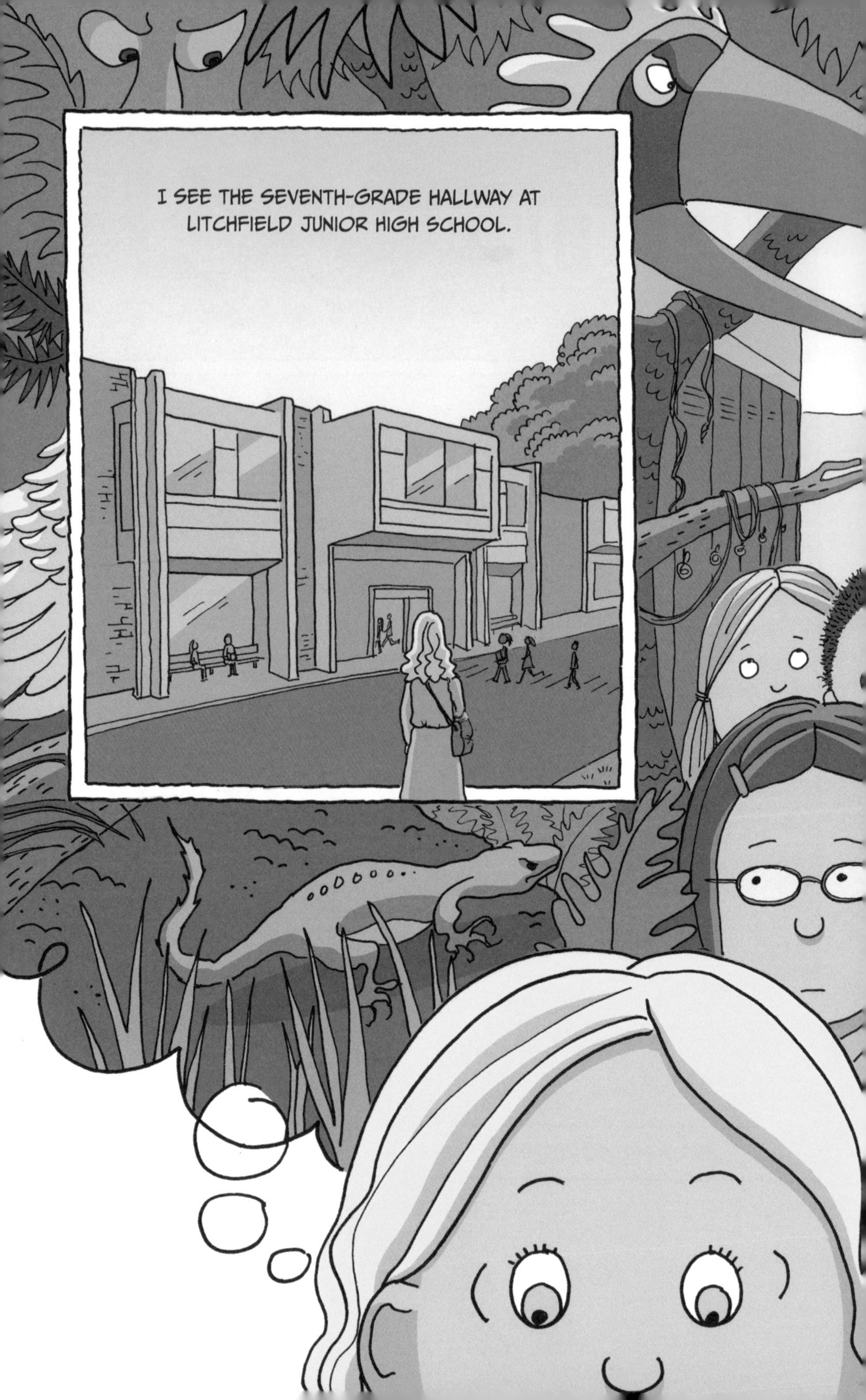
I SEE THE SEVENTH-GRADE HALLWAY AT LITCHFIELD JUNIOR HIGH SCHOOL.

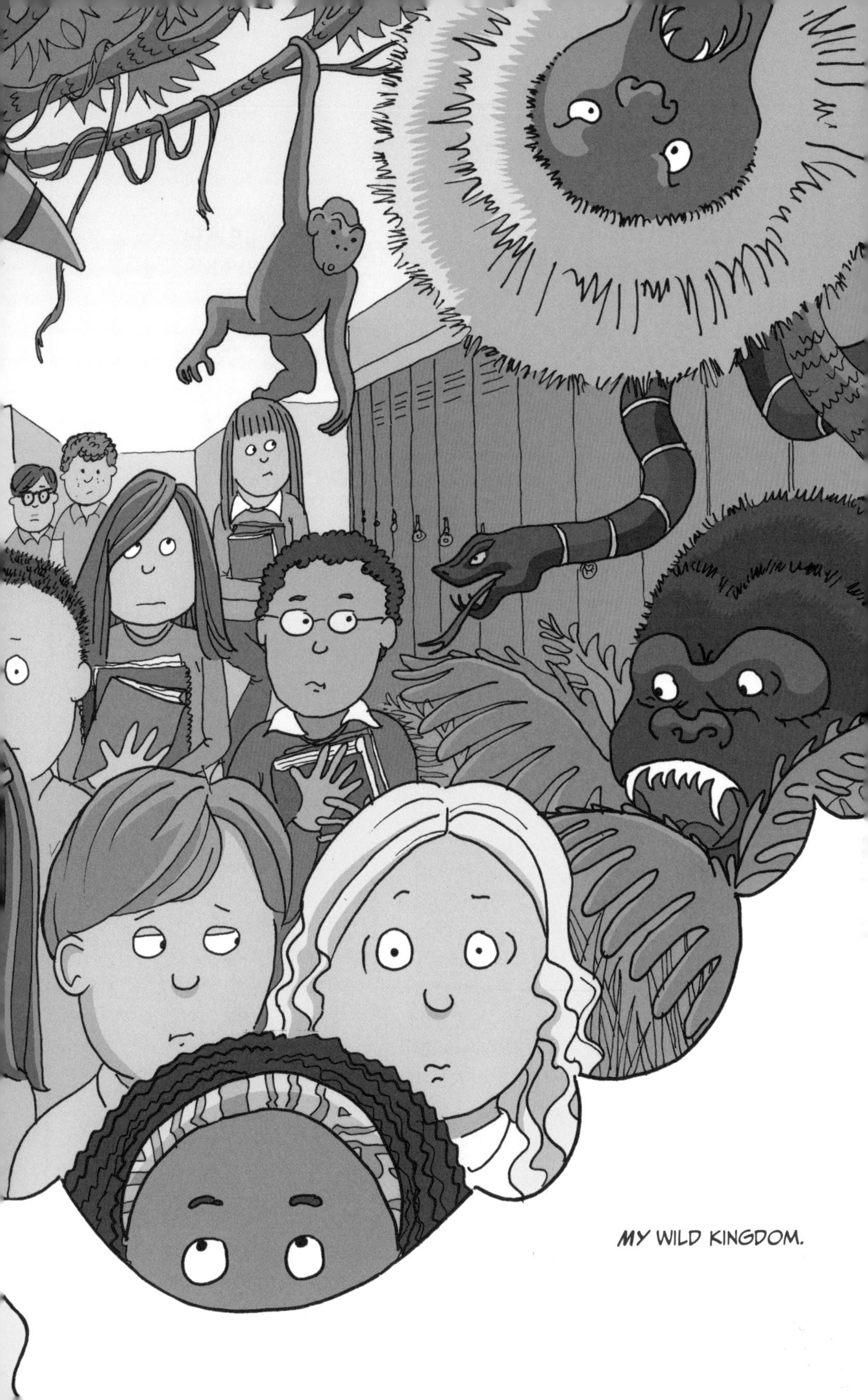

MY WILD KINGDOM.

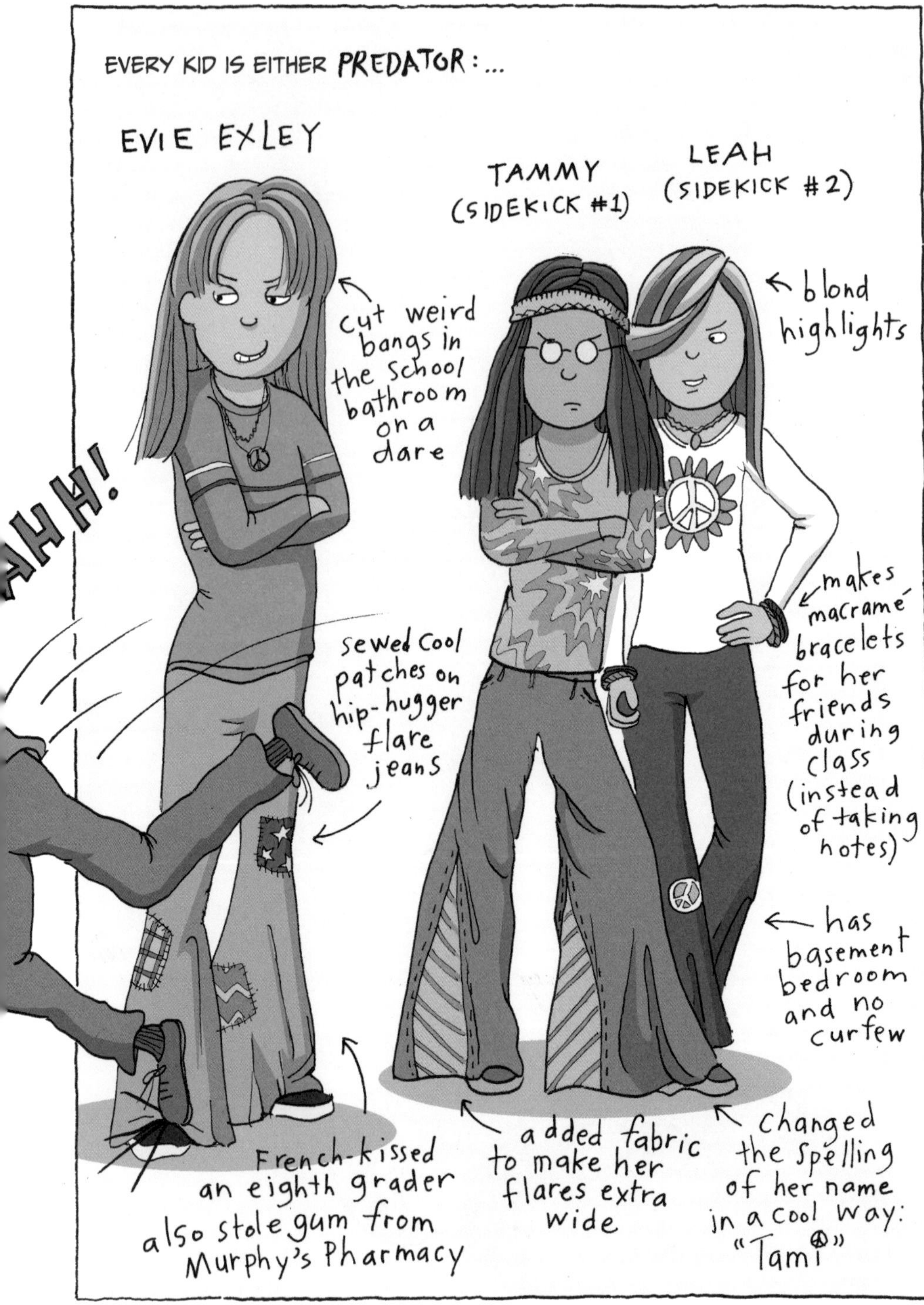

EVERY KID IS EITHER PREDATOR: ...
EVIE EXLEY
TAMMY (SIDEKICK #1)
LEAH (SIDEKICK #2)
AHH!
cut weird bangs in the school bathroom on a dare
sewed cool patches on hip-hugger flare jeans
French-kissed an eighth grader also stole gum from Murphy's Pharmacy
blond highlights
makes macramé bracelets for her friends during class (instead of taking notes)
has basement bedroom and no curfew
added fabric to make her flares extra wide
Changed the spelling of her name in a cool way: "Tami☮"

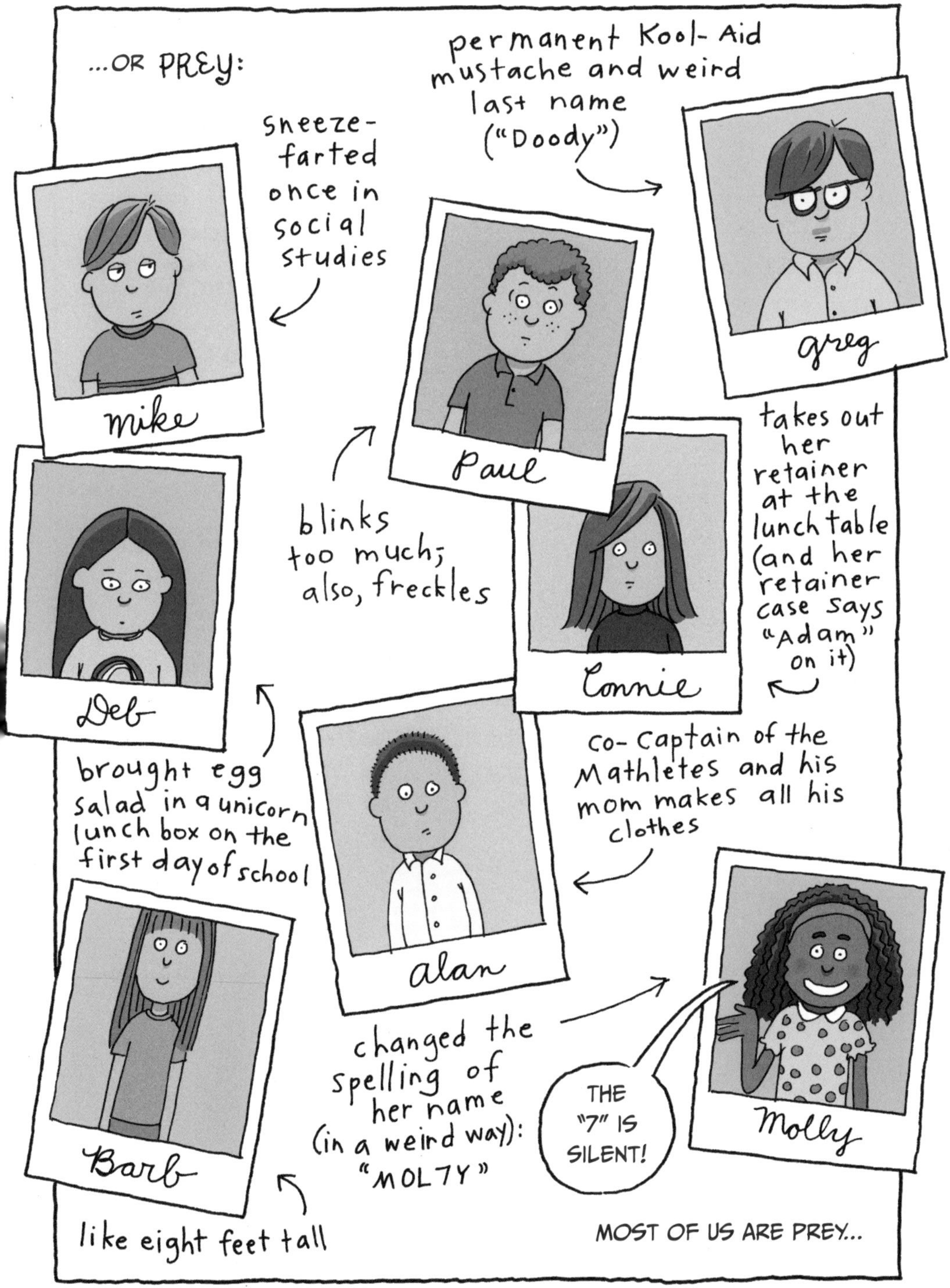
...OR PREY:
permanent Kool-Aid mustache and weird last name ("Doody")
sneeze-farted once in social studies
mike
Paul
greg
takes out her retainer at the lunch table (and her retainer case says "Adam" on it)
blinks too much; also, freckles
Deb
Connie
brought egg salad in a unicorn lunch box on the first day of school
co-captain of the Mathletes and his mom makes all his clothes
alan
Barb
changed the spelling of her name (in a weird way): "MOL7Y"
THE "7" IS SILENT!
Molly
like eight feet tall
MOST OF US ARE PREY...

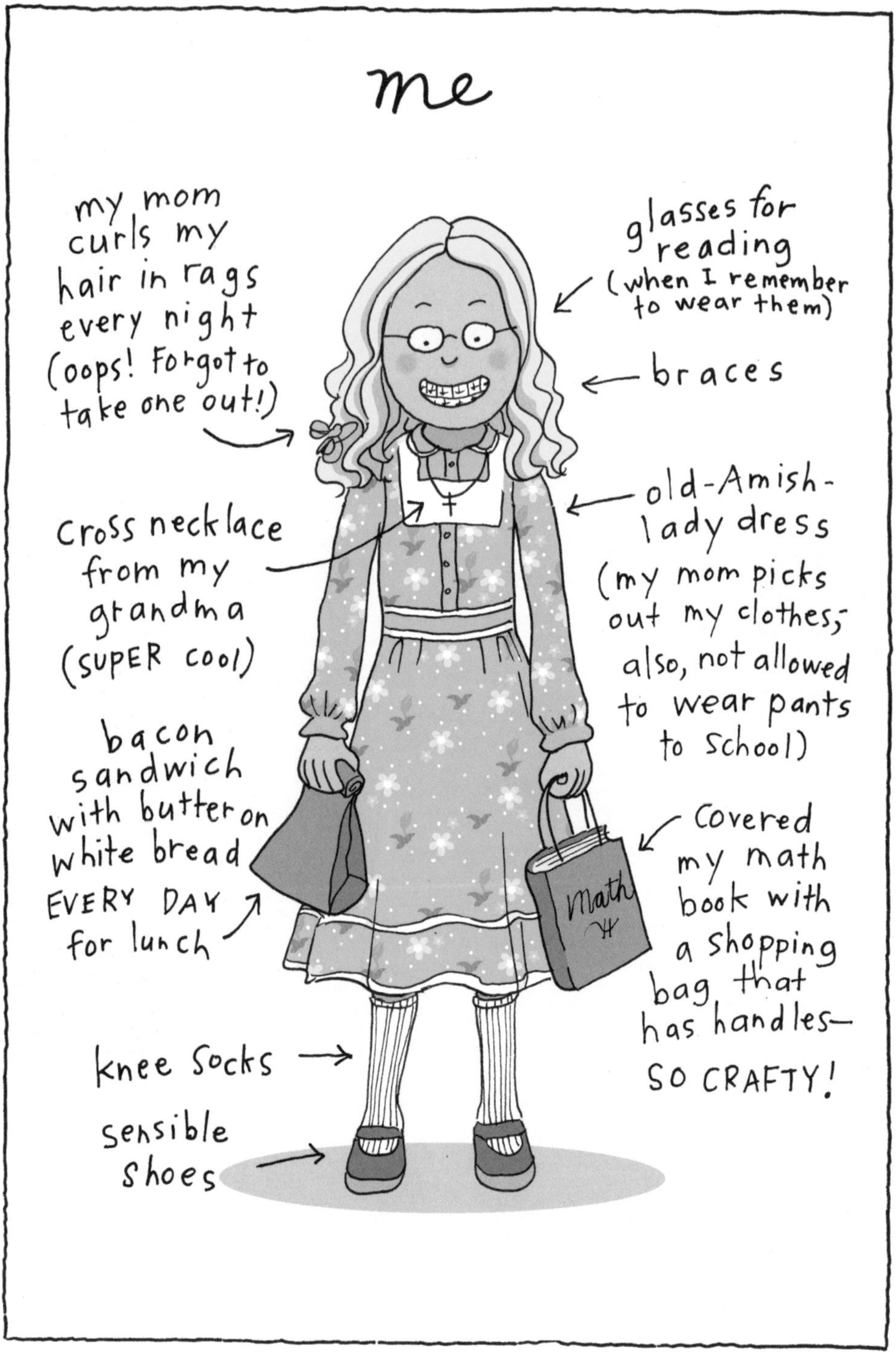
me
my mom curls my hair in rags every night (oops! Forgot to take one out!)
glasses for reading (when I remember to wear them)
braces
cross necklace from my grandma (SUPER cool)
old-Amish-lady dress (my mom picks out my clothes; also, not allowed to wear pants to school)
bacon sandwich with butter on white bread EVERY DAY for lunch
covered my math book with a shopping bag that has handles—SO CRAFTY!
Math
knee socks
sensible shoes

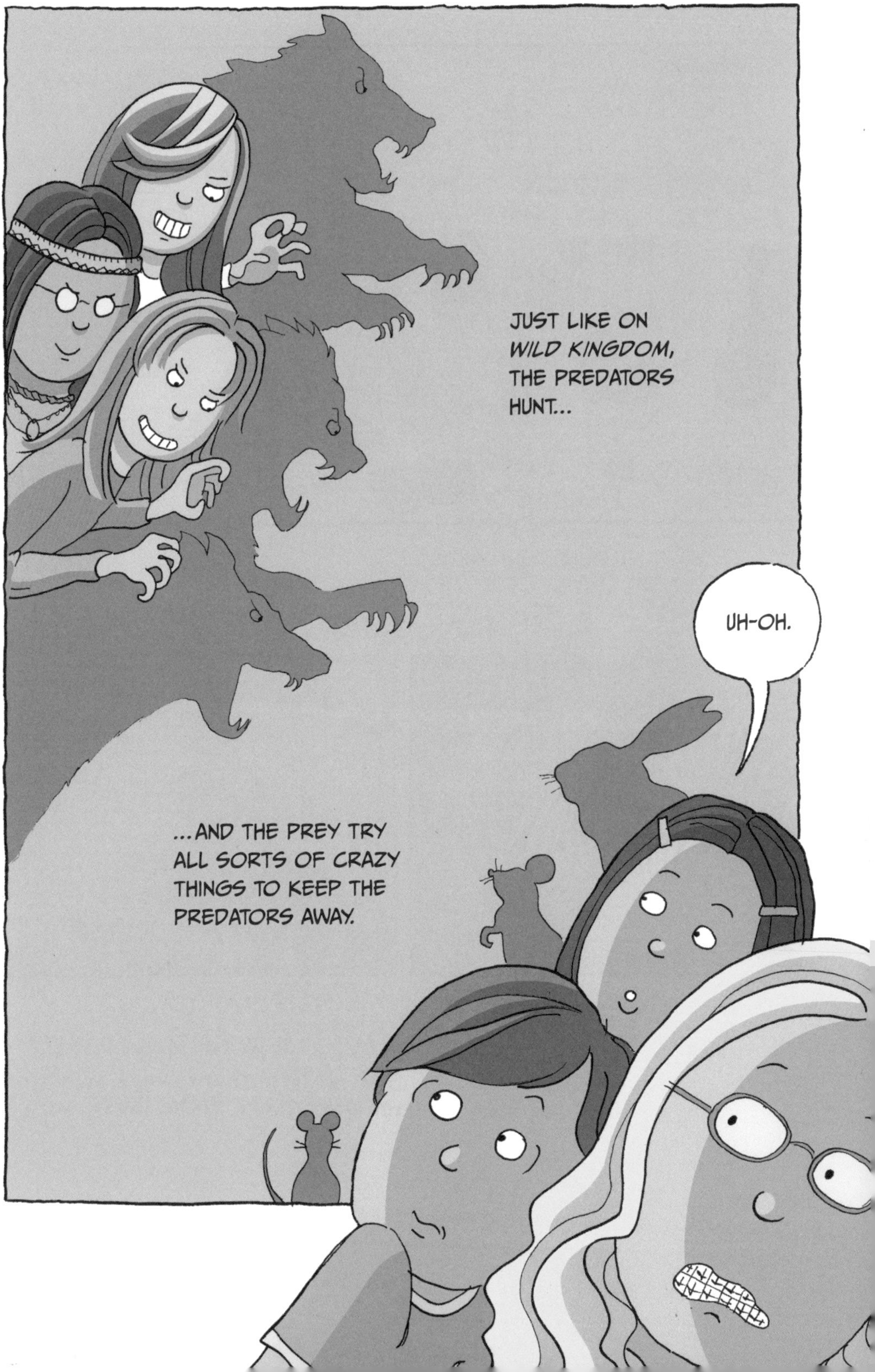
JUST LIKE ON *WILD KINGDOM*, THE PREDATORS HUNT...
...AND THE PREY TRY ALL SORTS OF CRAZY THINGS TO KEEP THE PREDATORS AWAY.
UH-OH.

SOME USE CAMOUFLAGE.

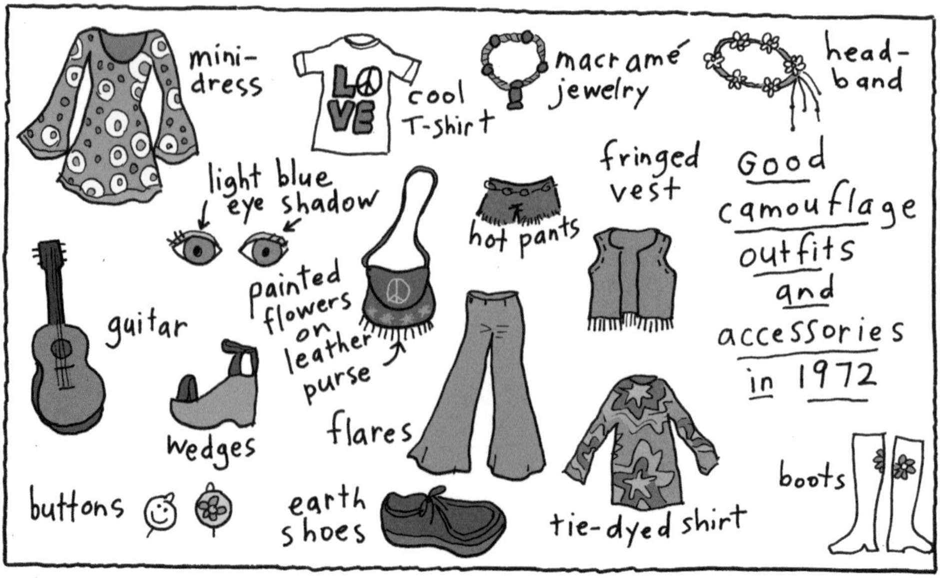
mini-dress
LOVE
cool T-shirt
macramé jewelry
head-band
light blue eye shadow
fringed vest
Good camouflage outfits and accessories in 1972
hot pants
guitar
painted flowers on leather purse
wedges
flares
buttons
earth shoes
tie-dyed shirt
boots

OTHERS USE PREDATOR CONFUSION.*

How it works in the wild:

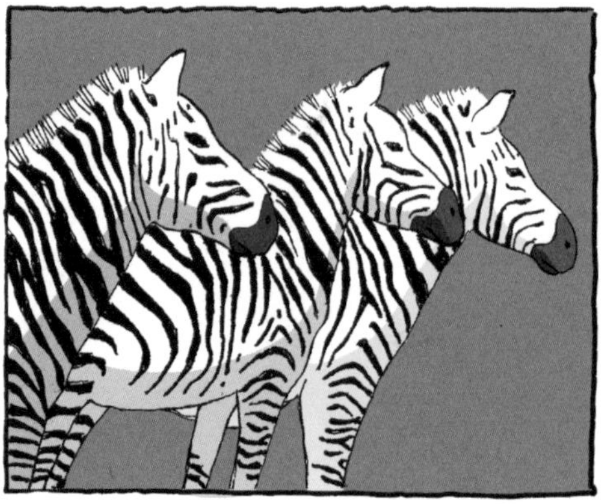

Zebras

How it works in school:

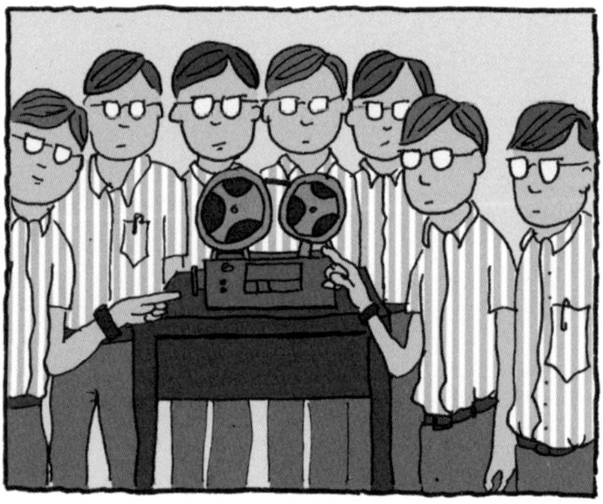

The AV Club

("AV" stands for "Audio visual." Like, before there were computer geniuses, there were these guys.)

*WHEN PREY LOOK THE SAME, THE PREDATORS CAN'T SINGLE OUT JUST ONE TO ATTACK.

SOMETIMES, TO ESCAPE, THEY STARTLE THE PREDATORS...

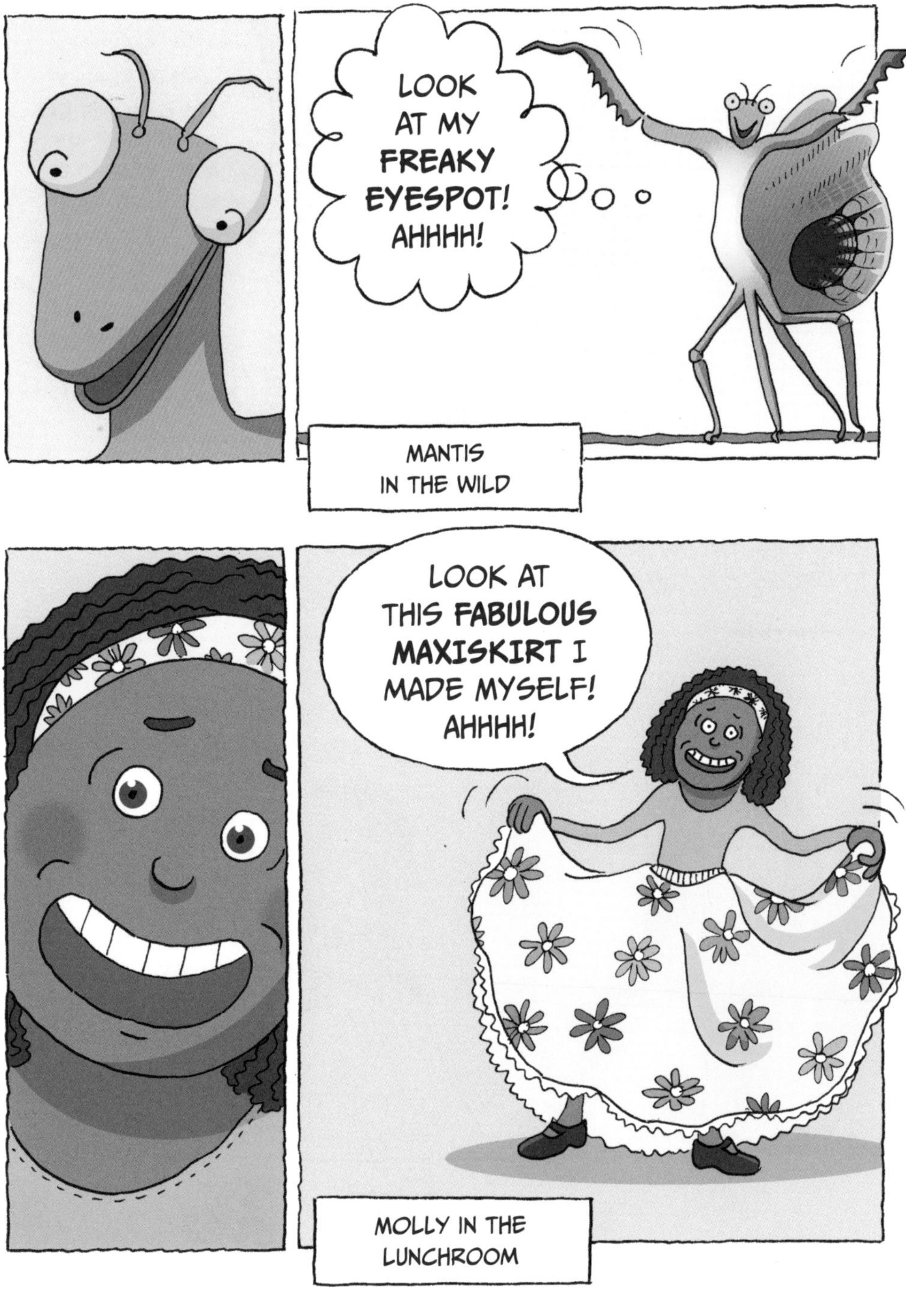
LOOK AT MY **FREAKY EYESPOT!** AHHHH!
MANTIS IN THE WILD
LOOK AT THIS **FABULOUS MAXISKIRT** I MADE MYSELF! AHHHH!
MOLLY IN THE LUNCHROOM

...OR DISTRACT THEM.

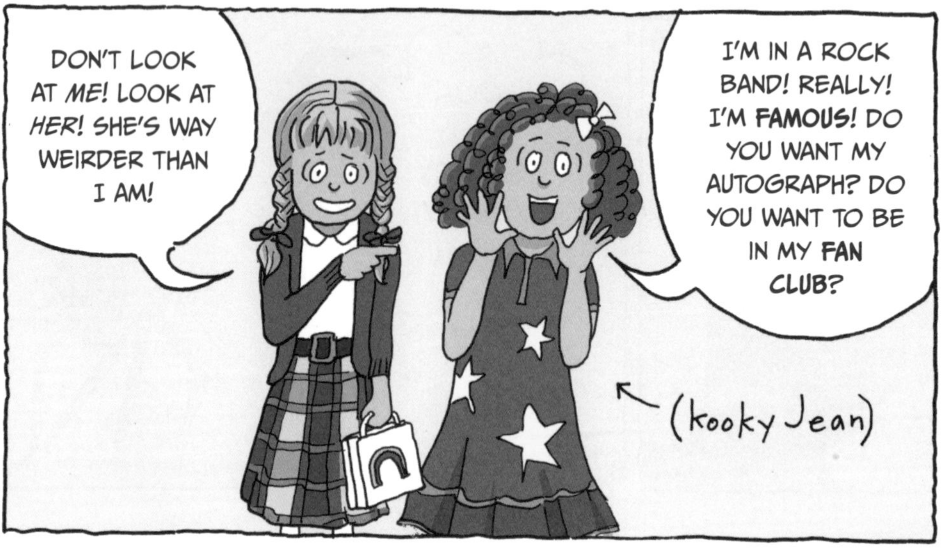
DON'T LOOK AT *ME*! LOOK AT *HER*! SHE'S WAY WEIRDER THAN I AM!
I'M IN A ROCK BAND! REALLY! I'M **FAMOUS!** DO YOU WANT MY AUTOGRAPH? DO YOU WANT TO BE IN MY **FAN** CLUB?
(kooky Jean)

SOME EVEN THROW UP WHEN THEY'RE SCARED (TO GROSS OUT THE PREDATORS).

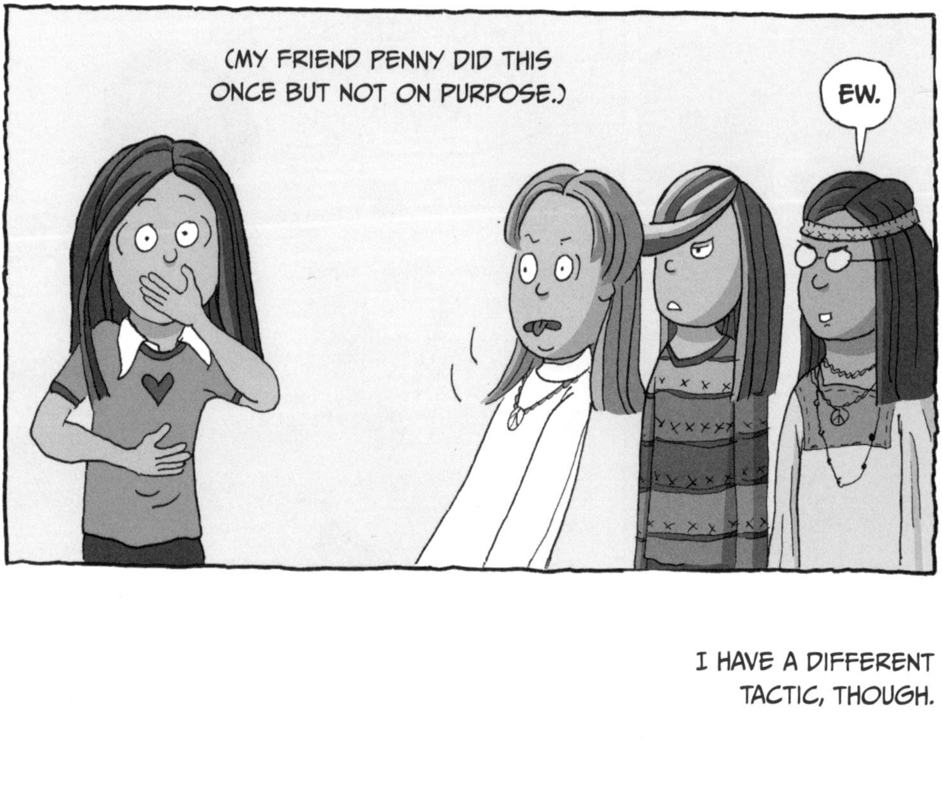
(MY FRIEND PENNY DID THIS ONCE BUT NOT ON PURPOSE.)
EW.

I HAVE A DIFFERENT TACTIC, THOUGH.

I PLAY DEAD.
NOT DEAD LIKE
BUT DEADISH.
I JUST ACT SO BORING,
THE PREDATORS LOSE INTEREST IN
ME AND GO AFTER SOMEONE ELSE.

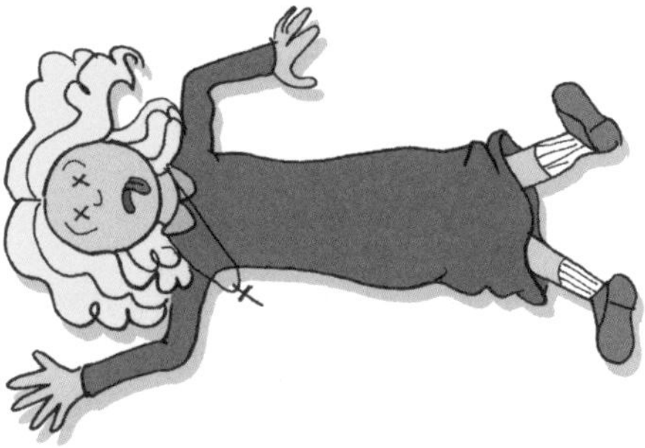

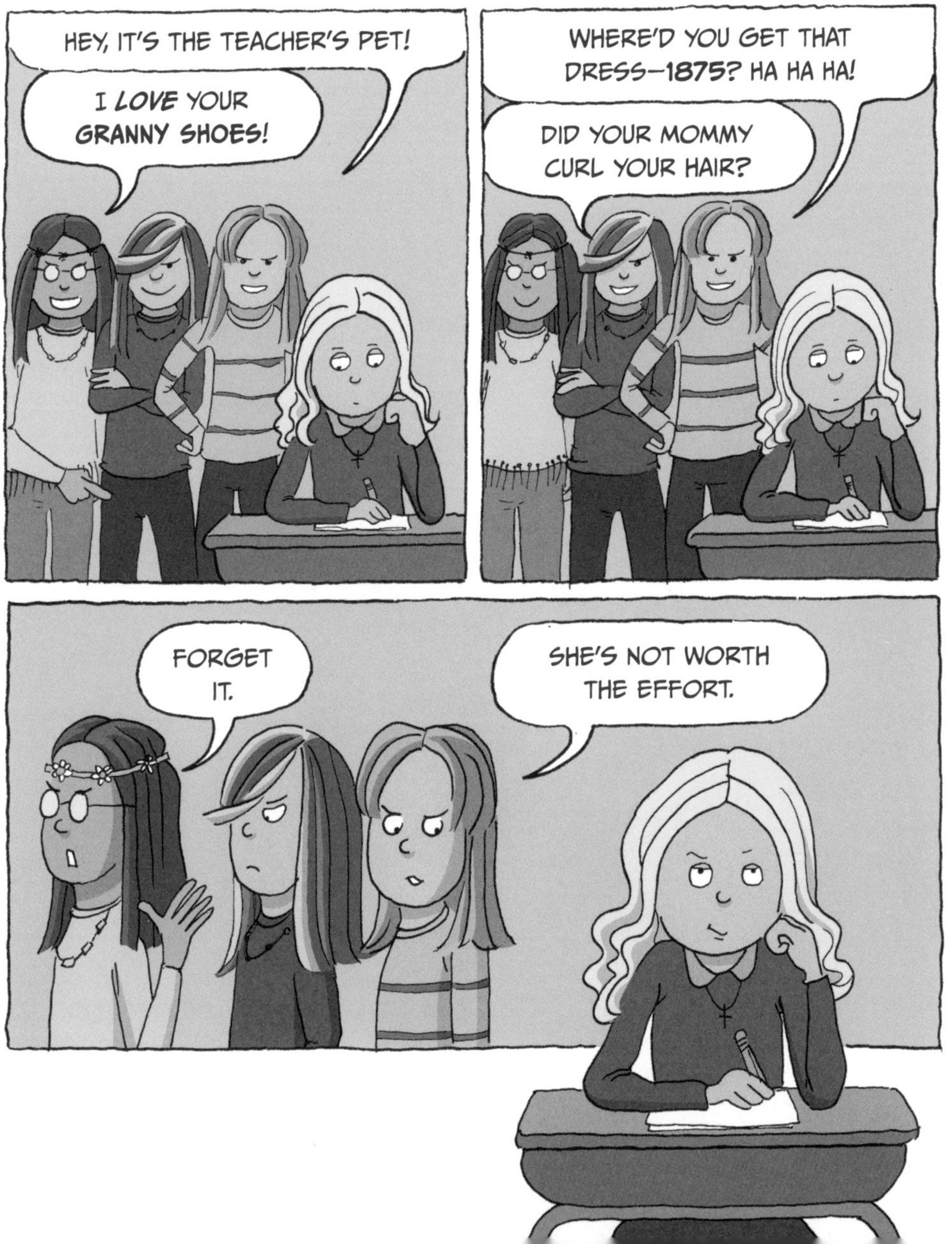

HEY, IT'S THE TEACHER'S PET!
I *LOVE* YOUR **GRANNY SHOES!**
WHERE'D YOU GET THAT DRESS—**1875**? HA HA HA!
DID YOUR MOMMY CURL YOUR HAIR?
FORGET IT.
SHE'S NOT WORTH THE EFFORT.

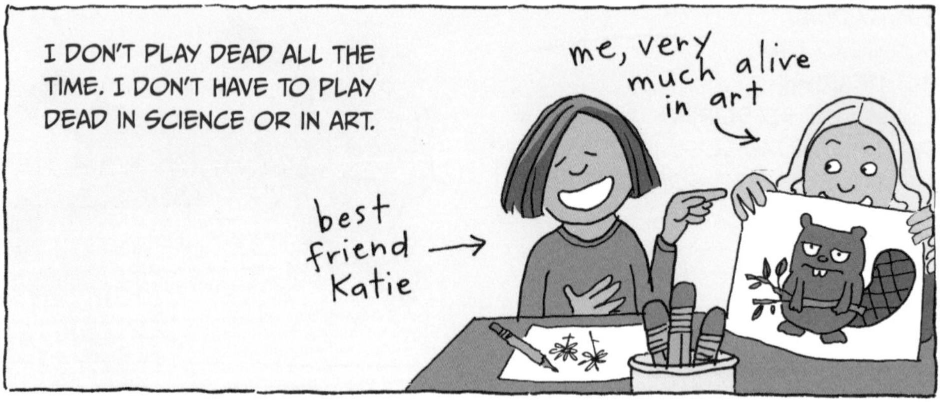
I DON'T PLAY DEAD ALL THE TIME. I DON'T HAVE TO PLAY DEAD IN SCIENCE OR IN ART.
me, very much alive in art
best friend Katie

MOST IMPORTANT OF ALL, I DON'T HAVE TO PLAY DEAD IN ENGLISH: MY VERY FAVORITE CLASS WITH MY VERY FAVORITE TEACHER, MRS. SCHULZ.

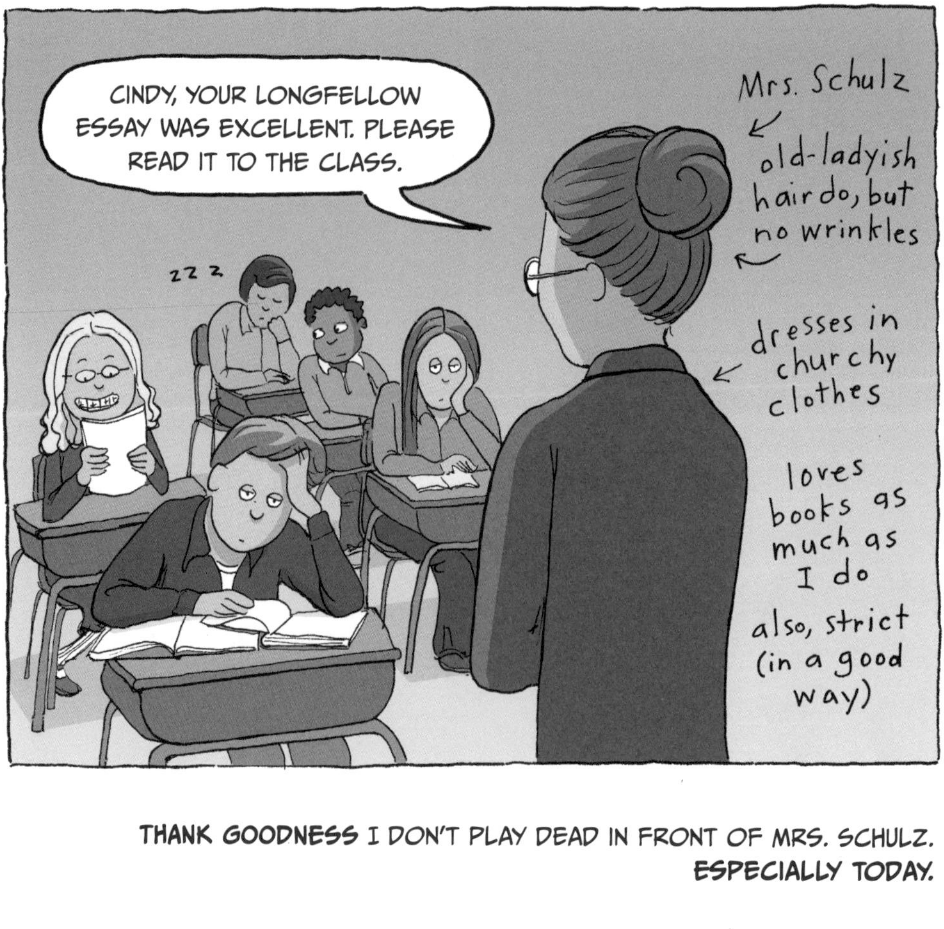
CINDY, YOUR LONGFELLOW ESSAY WAS EXCELLENT. PLEASE READ IT TO THE CLASS.
Mrs. Schulz
old-ladyish hairdo, but no wrinkles
dresses in churchy clothes
loves books as much as I do
also, strict (in a good way)
zzz

THANK GOODNESS I DON'T PLAY DEAD IN FRONT OF MRS. SCHULZ.
ESPECIALLY TODAY.

Chapter 2

I HAVE AN ORTHODONTIST APPOINTMENT. MY MOM SAYS SHE'LL PICK ME UP RIGHT AFTER SCHOOL.

SHE WON'T. SHE'LL BE LATE.

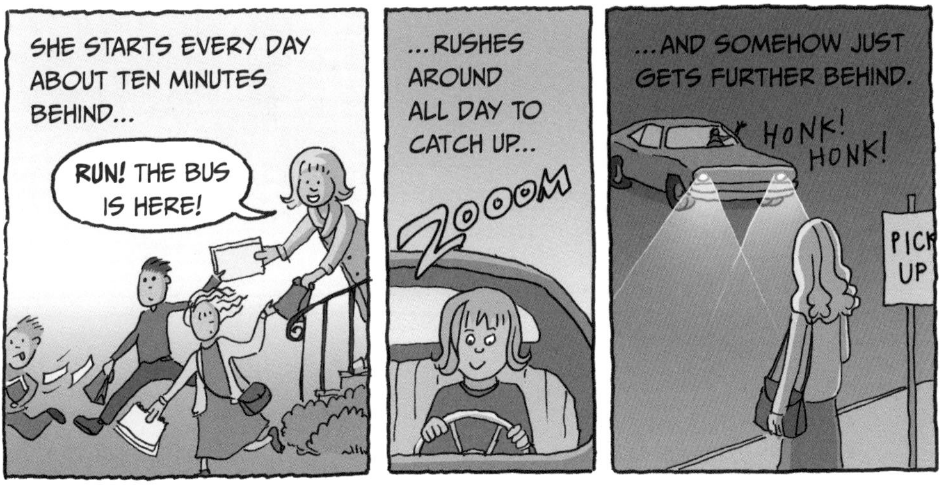

SHE STARTS EVERY DAY ABOUT TEN MINUTES BEHIND...
RUN! THE BUS IS HERE!
...RUSHES AROUND ALL DAY TO CATCH UP...
ZOOOM
...AND SOMEHOW JUST GETS FURTHER BEHIND.
HONK! HONK!
PICK UP

BUT MOST OF THE TIME, BEING THE LAST KID TO GET PICKED UP ISN'T THAT BAD.

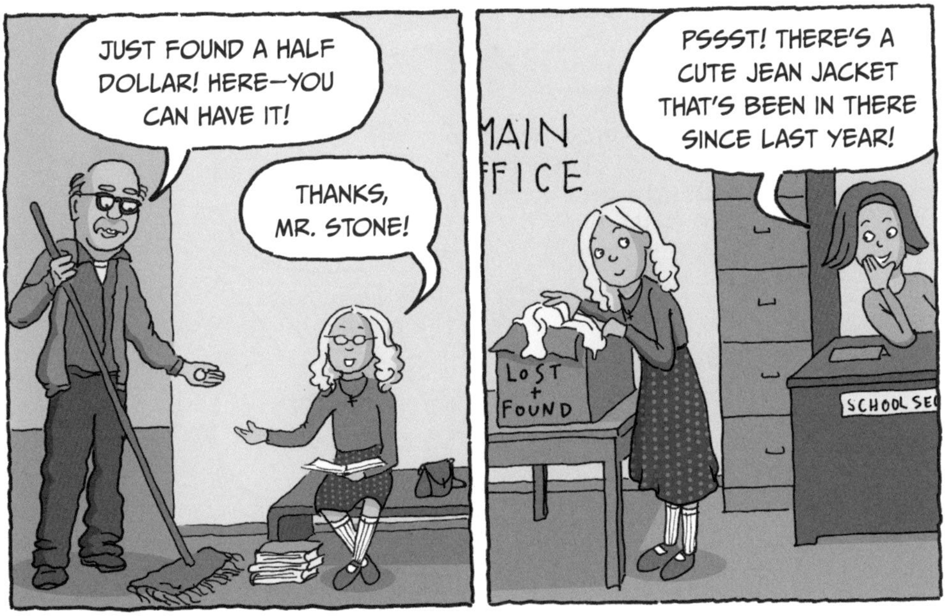

JUST FOUND A HALF DOLLAR! HERE—YOU CAN HAVE IT!
THANKS, MR. STONE!
PSSST! THERE'S A CUTE JEAN JACKET THAT'S BEEN IN THERE SINCE LAST YEAR!
LOST + FOUND

TODAY, IT JUST MIGHT BE THE BEST THING THAT'S EVER HAPPENED TO ME.

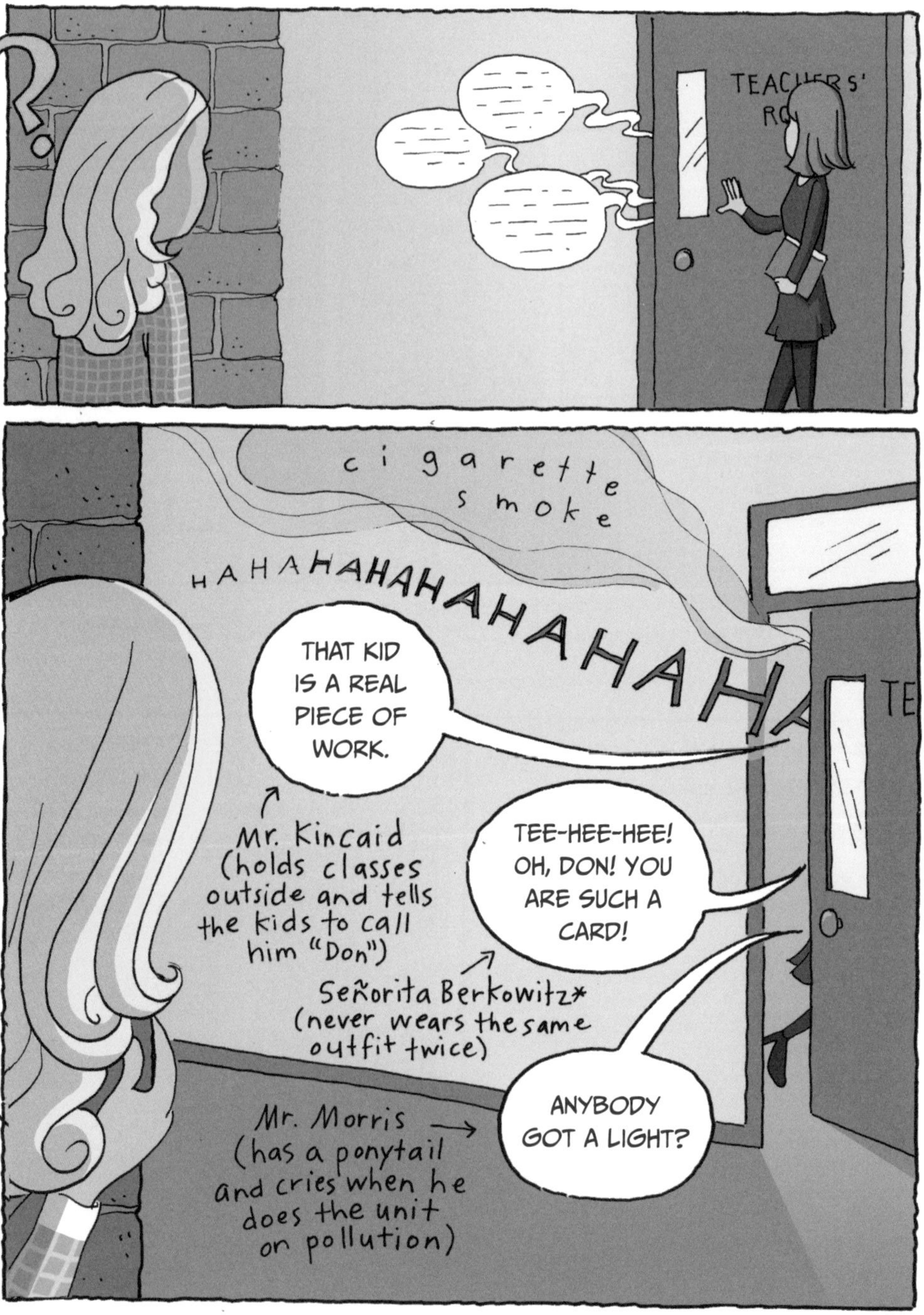
cigarette smoke
HAHAHAHAHAHAHAHAHA
THAT KID IS A REAL PIECE OF WORK.
Mr. Kincaid (holds classes outside and tells the kids to call him "Don")
TEE-HEE-HEE! OH, DON! YOU ARE SUCH A CARD!
Señorita Berkowitz* (never wears the same outfit twice)
Mr. Morris (has a ponytail and cries when he does the unit on pollution)
ANYBODY GOT A LIGHT?

*OR MADEMOISELLE BERKOWITZ IF YOU TAKE FRENCH

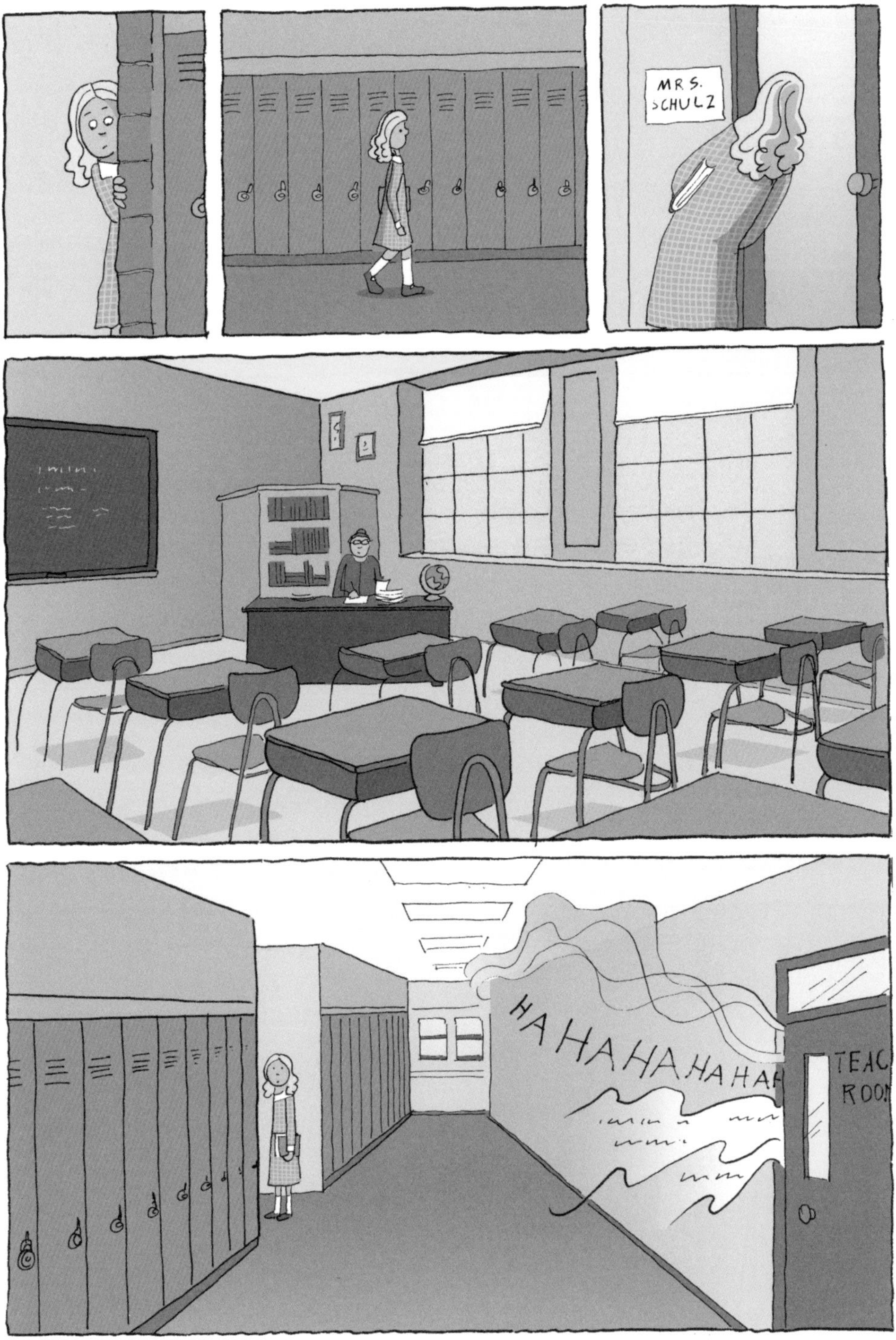
MRS. SCHULZ
HAHAHAHAHAHA
TEAC
ROO

HELLO.

OH! HELLO, CINDY!

I WANT TO TELL MRS. SCHULZ THAT SHE IS MY VERY FAVORITE TEACHER.
THAT ENGLISH IS THE BEST PART OF EVERY DAY.

THAT I LOVE MADELEINE L'ENGLE AS MUCH AS SHE DOES.
THAT I MEMORIZE ALL THE SUPER NICE COMMENTS SHE WRITES ON MY PAPERS.

BUT I DON'T TELL HER ANY OF THOSE THINGS.
I JUST STAND THERE FEELING WEIRD.

SAYING NOTHING.

COME IN! I'M NOT BUSY!

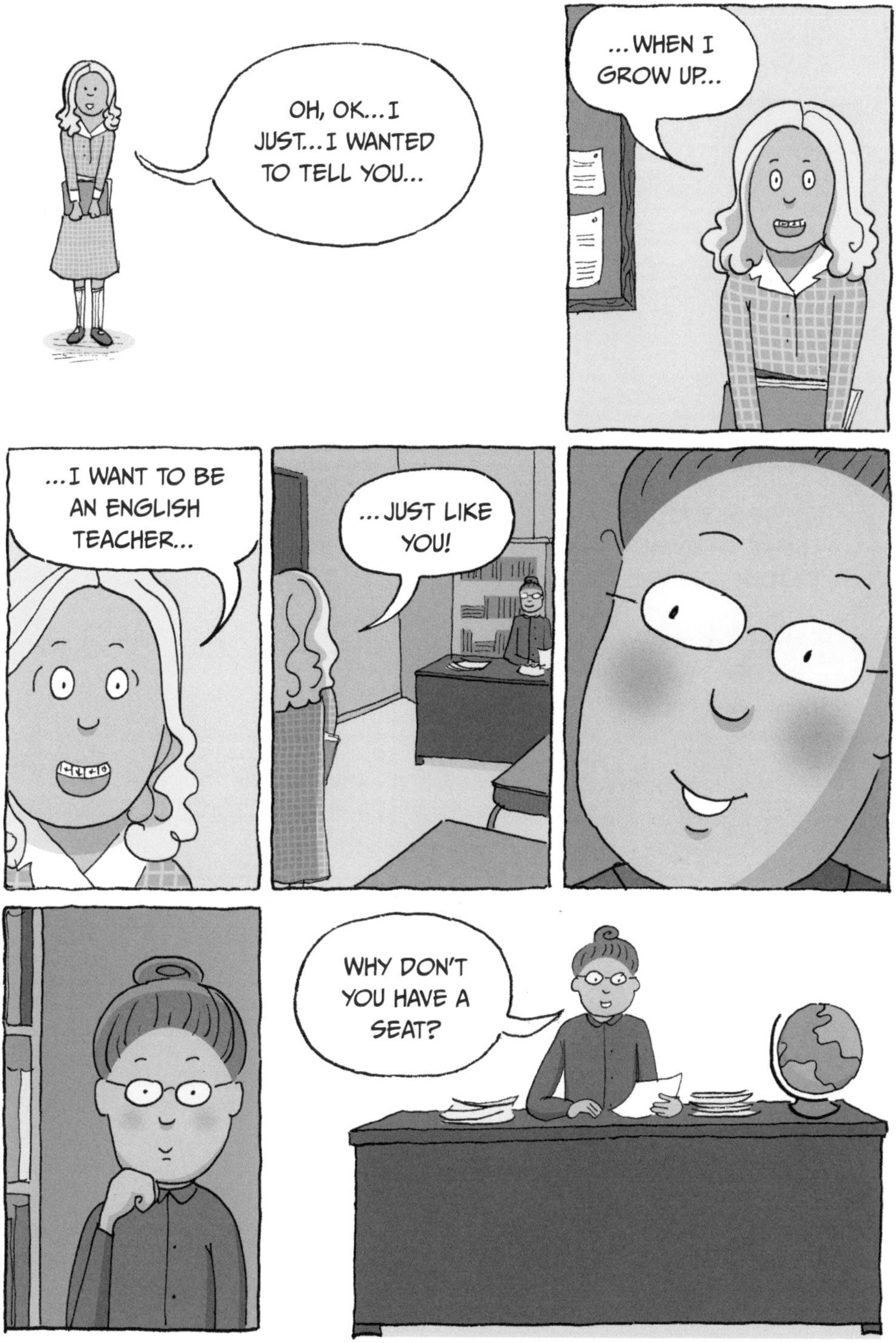
OH, OK...I JUST...I WANTED TO TELL YOU...
...WHEN I GROW UP...
...I WANT TO BE AN ENGLISH TEACHER...
...JUST LIKE YOU!
WHY DON'T YOU HAVE A SEAT?

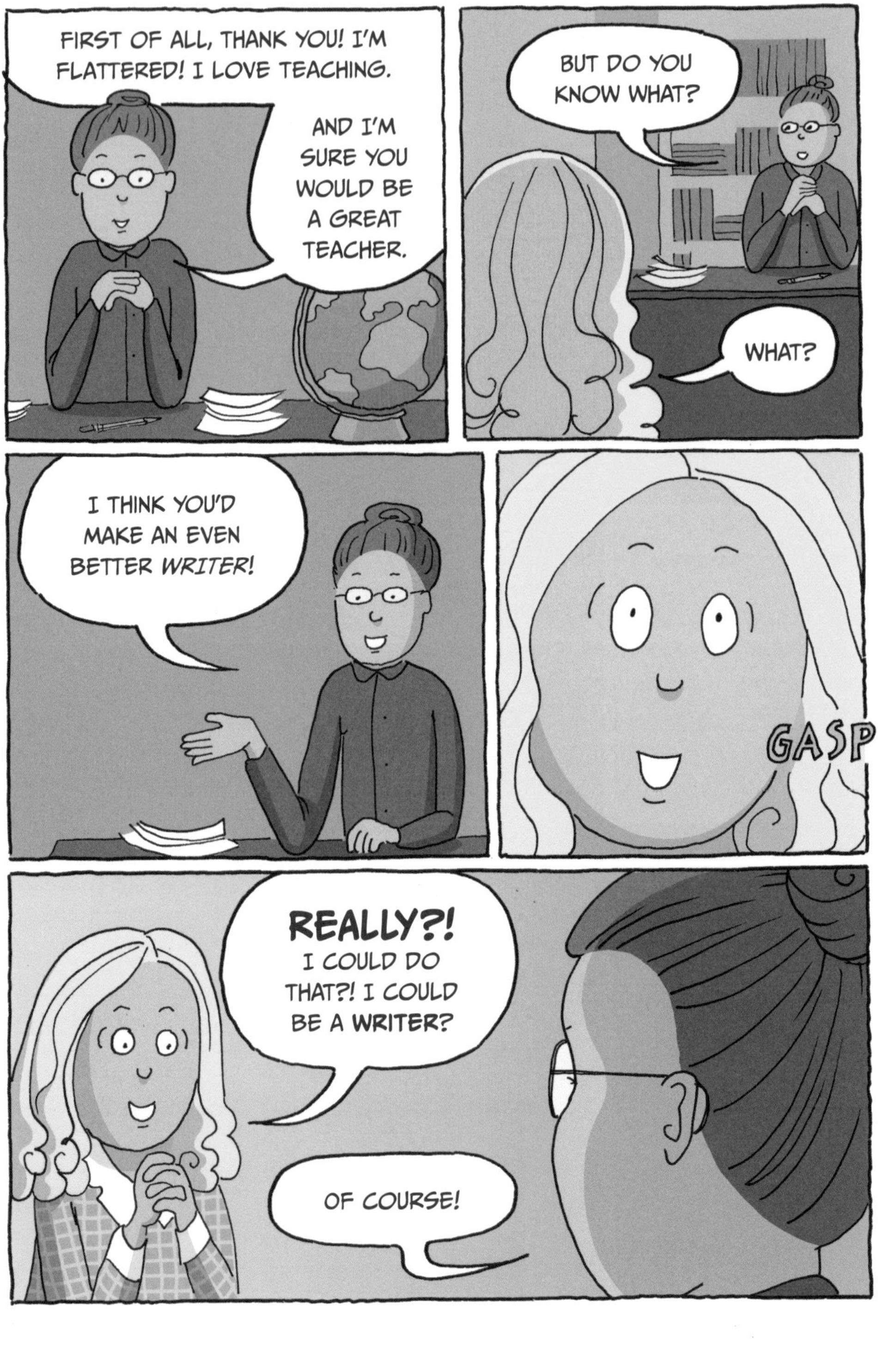
FIRST OF ALL, THANK YOU! I'M FLATTERED! I LOVE TEACHING.
AND I'M SURE YOU WOULD BE A GREAT TEACHER.
BUT DO YOU KNOW WHAT?
WHAT?
I THINK YOU'D MAKE AN EVEN BETTER *WRITER*!
GASP
REALLY?! I COULD DO THAT?! I COULD BE A **WRITER**?
OF COURSE!

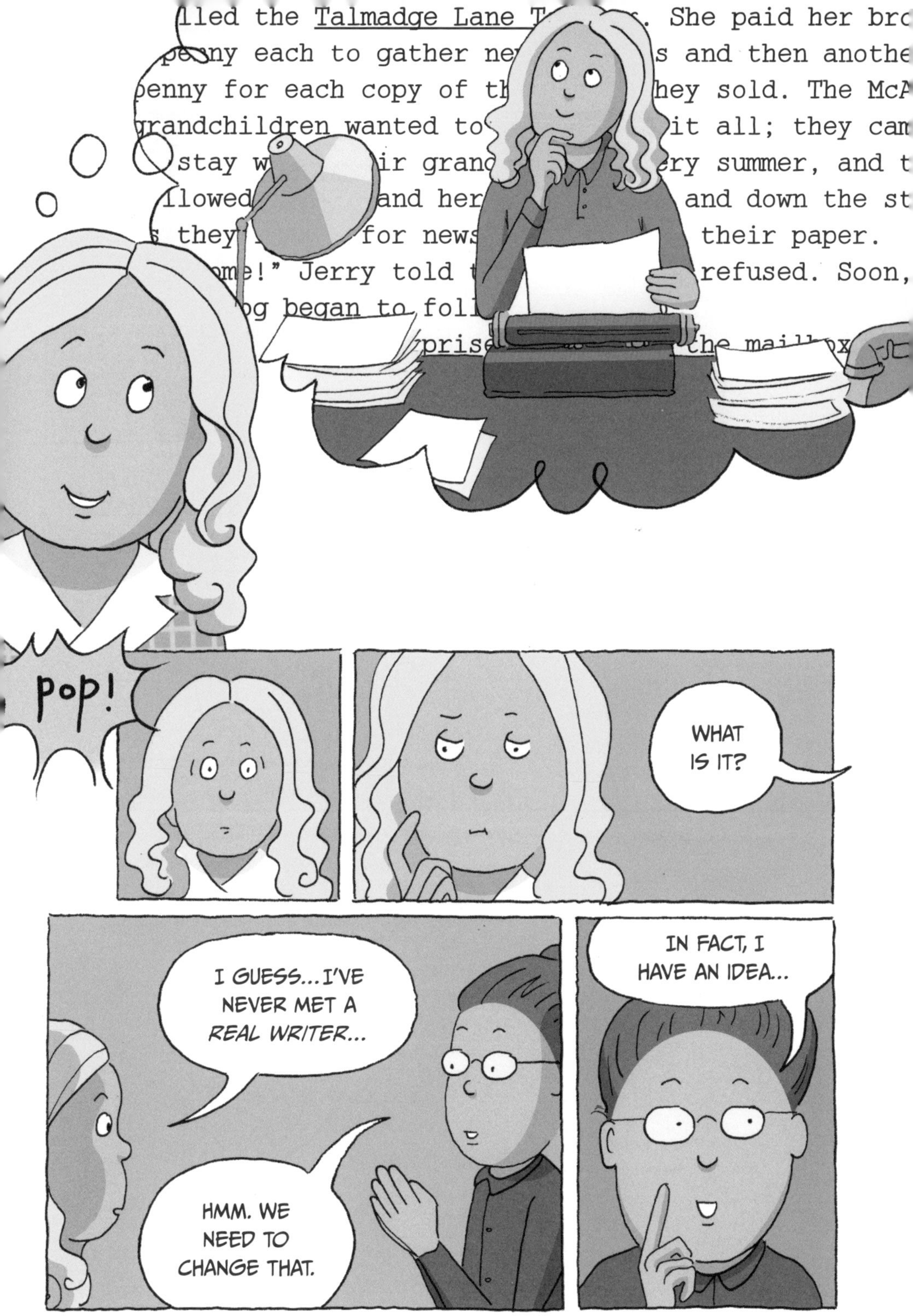
lled the Talmadge Lane T . She paid her bro
penny each to gather ne s and then anothe
penny for each copy of th hey sold. The McA
grandchildren wanted to it all; they cam
stay w ir grand ery summer, and t
llowed and her and down the st
they for news their paper.
me!" Jerry told t refused. Soon,
og began to fol
prise the mailbox
pop!
WHAT IS IT?
I GUESS...I'VE NEVER MET A *REAL WRITER*...
HMM. WE NEED TO CHANGE THAT.
IN FACT, I HAVE AN IDEA...

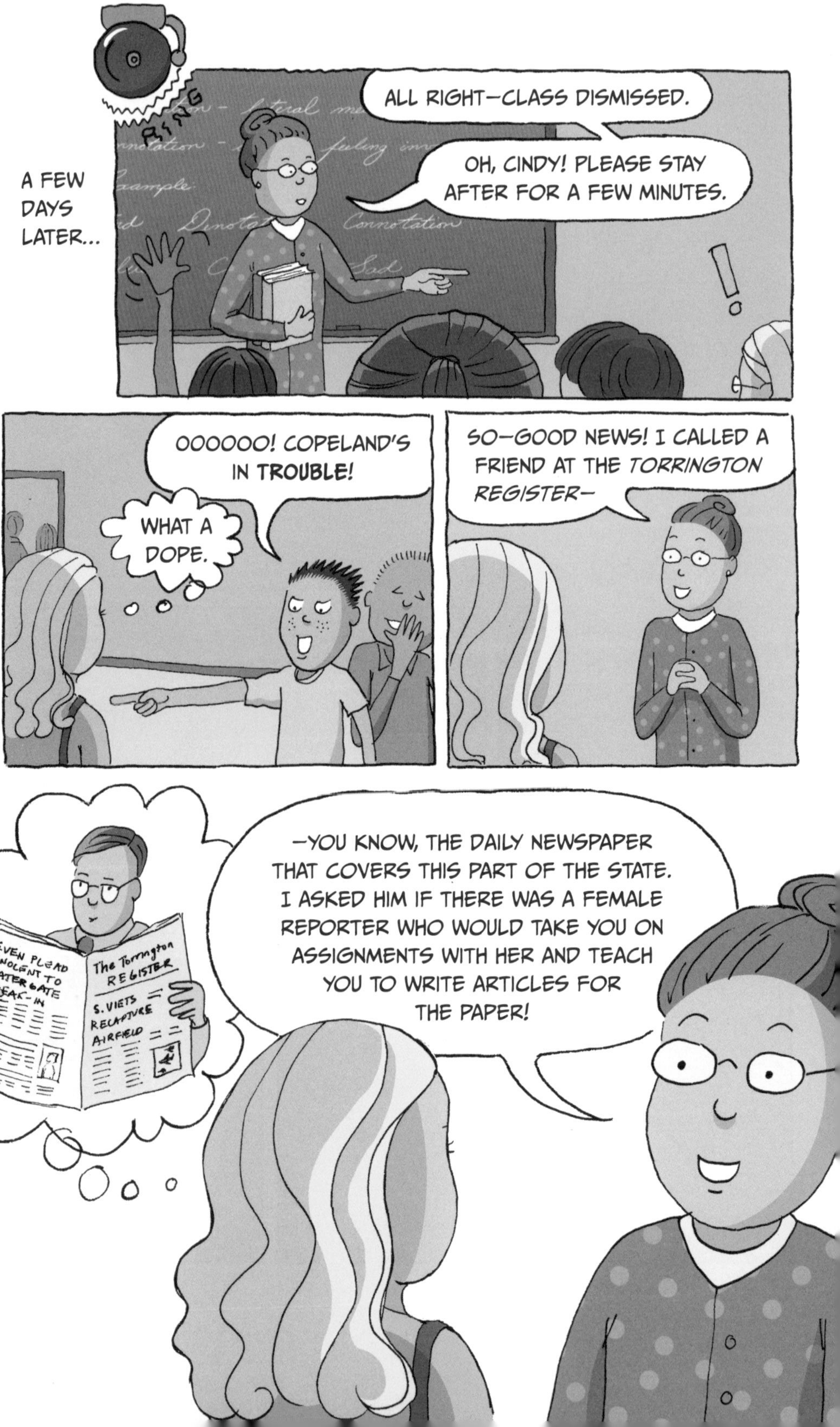
A FEW DAYS LATER...
RING
ALL RIGHT—CLASS DISMISSED.
OH, CINDY! PLEASE STAY AFTER FOR A FEW MINUTES.
!
OOOOOO! COPELAND'S IN **TROUBLE!**
WHAT A DOPE.
SO—GOOD NEWS! I CALLED A FRIEND AT THE *TORRINGTON REGISTER*—
SEVEN PLEAD INNOCENT TO WATERGATE BREAK-IN
The Torrington REGISTER
S. VIETS RECAPTURE AIRFIELD
—YOU KNOW, THE DAILY NEWSPAPER THAT COVERS THIS PART OF THE STATE. I ASKED HIM IF THERE WAS A FEMALE REPORTER WHO WOULD TAKE YOU ON ASSIGNMENTS WITH HER AND TEACH YOU TO WRITE ARTICLES FOR THE PAPER!

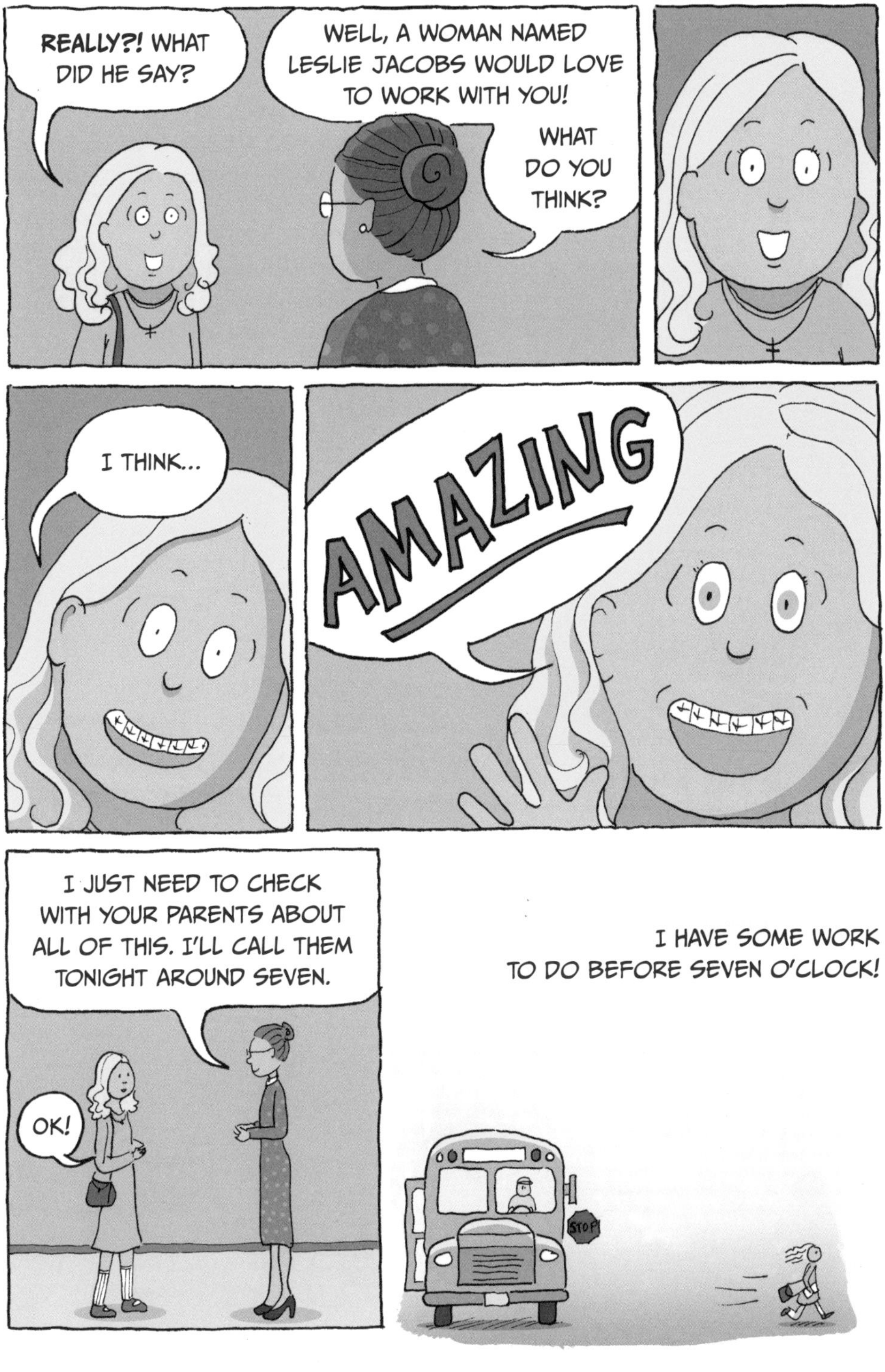
REALLY?! WHAT DID HE SAY?
WELL, A WOMAN NAMED LESLIE JACOBS WOULD LOVE TO WORK WITH YOU!
WHAT DO YOU THINK?
I THINK...
AMAZING
I JUST NEED TO CHECK WITH YOUR PARENTS ABOUT ALL OF THIS. I'LL CALL THEM TONIGHT AROUND SEVEN.
OK!
I HAVE SOME WORK TO DO BEFORE SEVEN O'CLOCK!
STOP

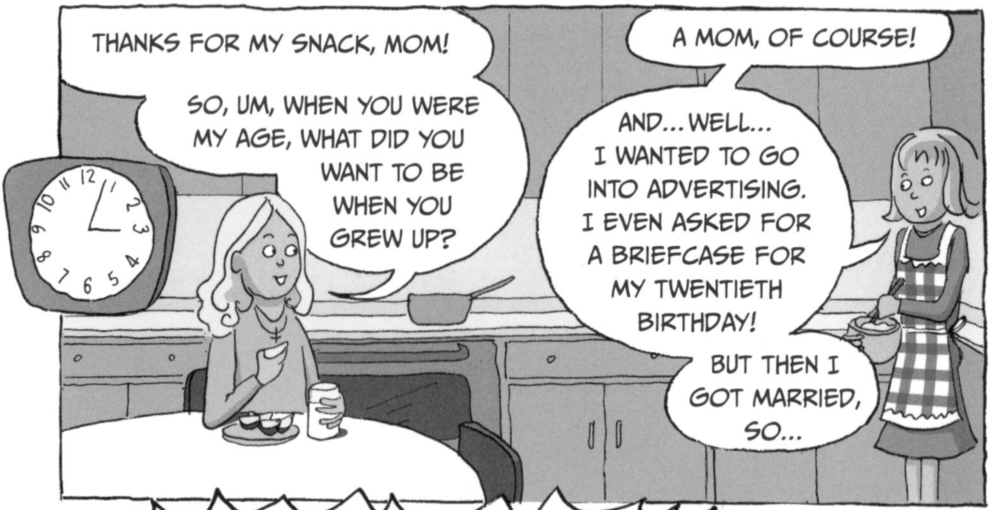
THANKS FOR MY SNACK, MOM!
SO, UM, WHEN YOU WERE MY AGE, WHAT DID YOU WANT TO BE WHEN YOU GREW UP?
A MOM, OF COURSE!
AND...WELL... I WANTED TO GO INTO ADVERTISING. I EVEN ASKED FOR A BRIEFCASE FOR MY TWENTIETH BIRTHDAY!
BUT THEN I GOT MARRIED, SO...

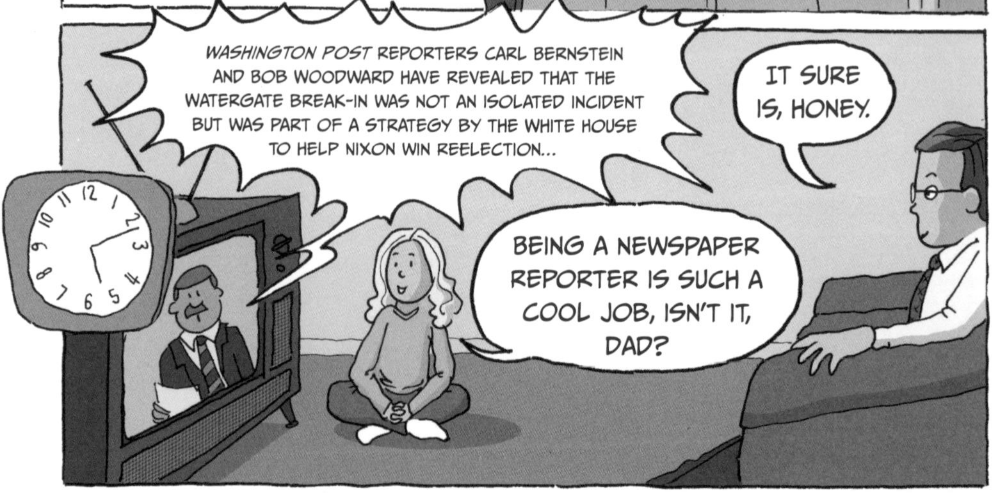
WASHINGTON POST REPORTERS CARL BERNSTEIN AND BOB WOODWARD HAVE REVEALED THAT THE WATERGATE BREAK-IN WAS NOT AN ISOLATED INCIDENT BUT WAS PART OF A STRATEGY BY THE WHITE HOUSE TO HELP NIXON WIN REELECTION...
BEING A NEWSPAPER REPORTER IS SUCH A COOL JOB, ISN'T IT, DAD?
IT SURE IS, HONEY.

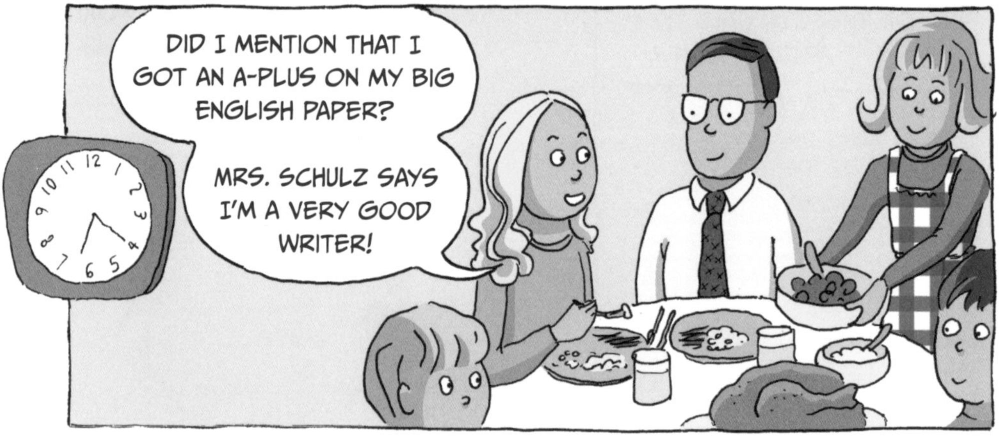
DID I MENTION THAT I GOT AN A-PLUS ON MY BIG ENGLISH PAPER?
MRS. SCHULZ SAYS I'M A VERY GOOD WRITER!

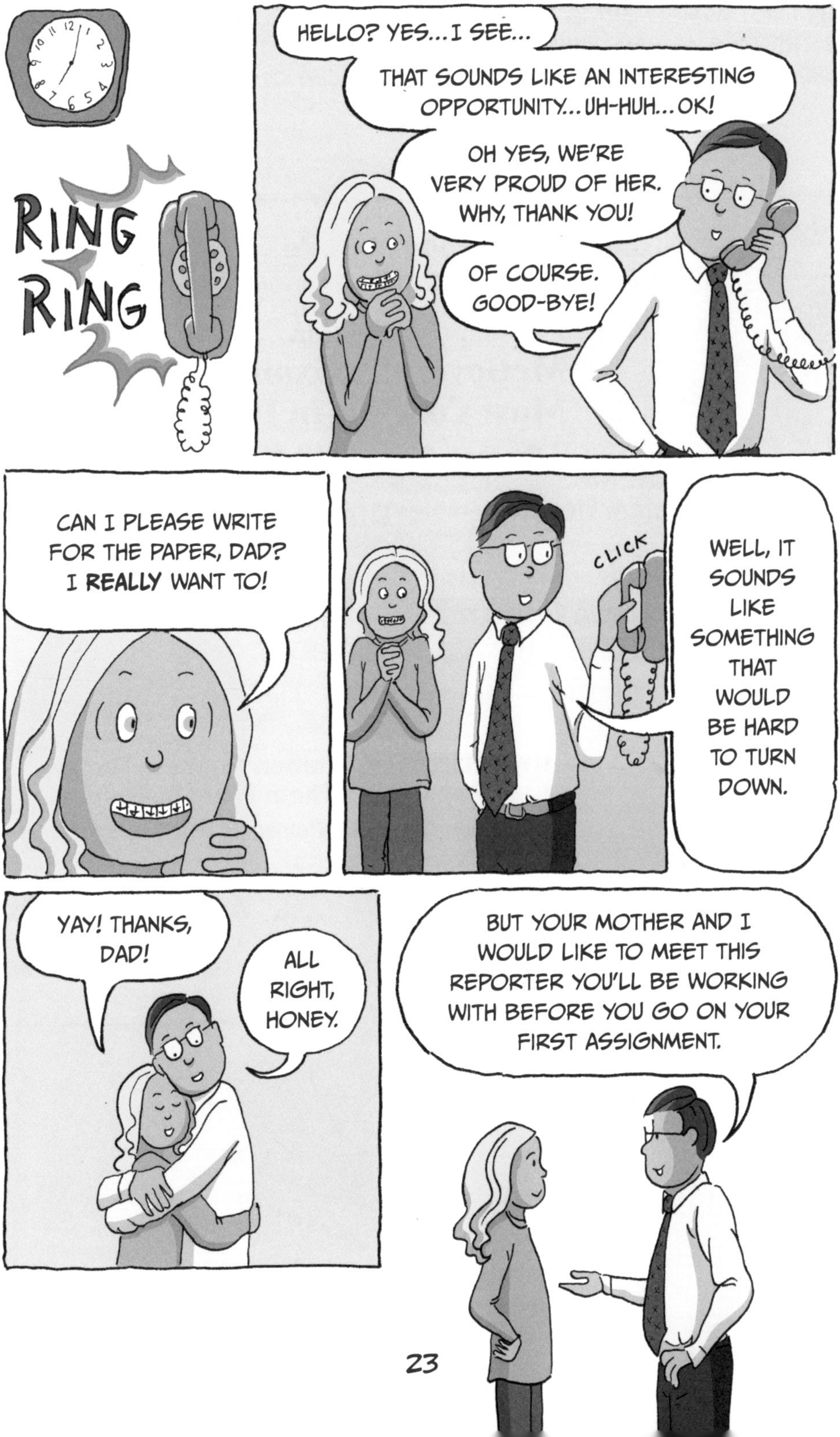
RING
RING
HELLO? YES... I SEE...
THAT SOUNDS LIKE AN INTERESTING OPPORTUNITY... UH-HUH... OK!
OH YES, WE'RE VERY PROUD OF HER. WHY, THANK YOU!
OF COURSE. GOOD-BYE!
CAN I PLEASE WRITE FOR THE PAPER, DAD? I **REALLY** WANT TO!
CLICK
WELL, IT SOUNDS LIKE SOMETHING THAT WOULD BE HARD TO TURN DOWN.
YAY! THANKS, DAD!
ALL RIGHT, HONEY.
BUT YOUR MOTHER AND I WOULD LIKE TO MEET THIS REPORTER YOU'LL BE WORKING WITH BEFORE YOU GO ON YOUR FIRST ASSIGNMENT.

MY FIRST ASSIGNMENT IS **SIX ENTIRE DAYS** AWAY! SO I TRY TO GET READY BY READING AS MANY NEWSPAPERS AS I CAN... EVEN THOUGH I DON'T UNDERSTAND *EVERYTHING* I READ. (OR EVEN MOST OF IT.)

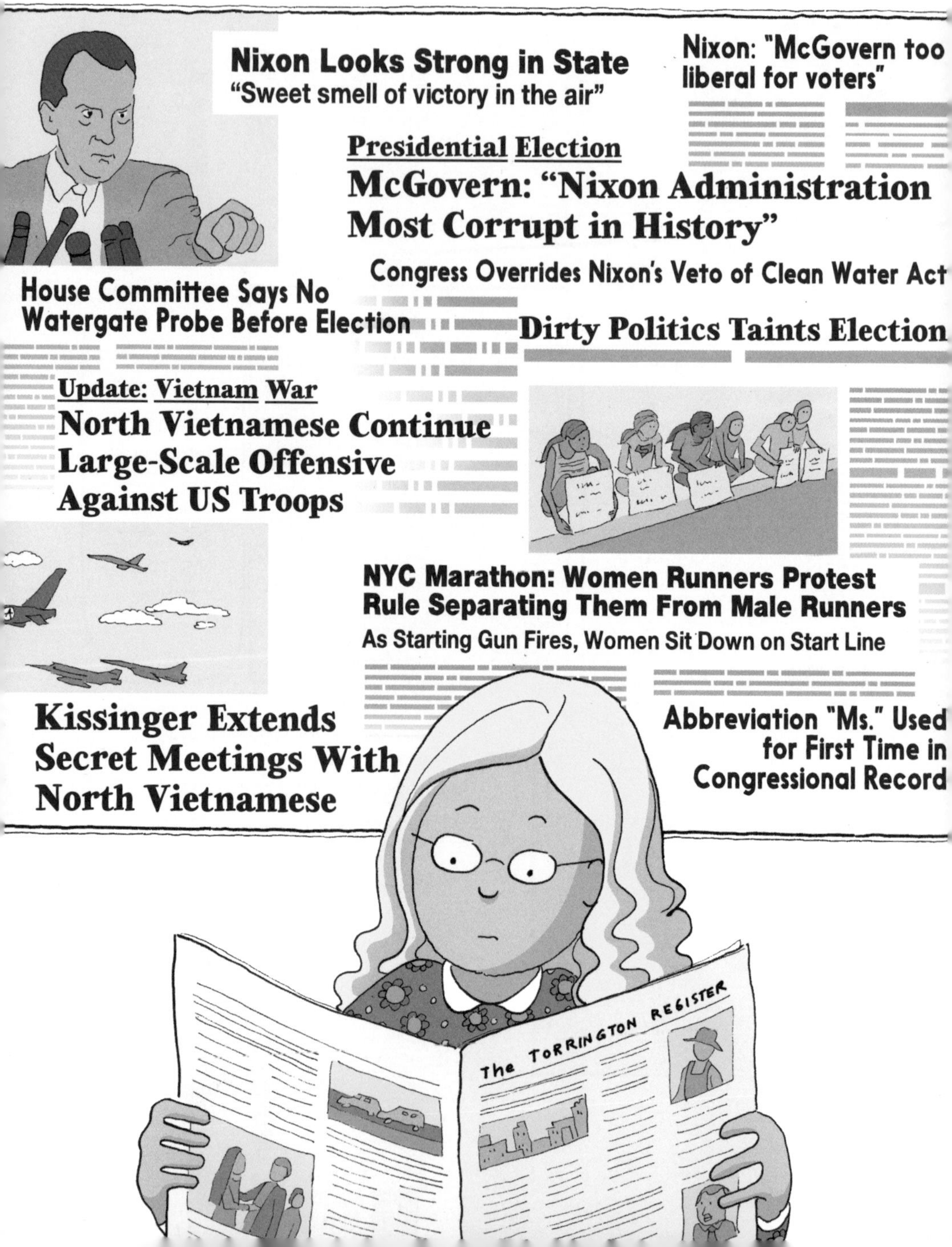

Nixon Looks Strong in State
"Sweet smell of victory in the air"
Nixon: "McGovern too liberal for voters"
Presidential Election
McGovern: "Nixon Administration Most Corrupt in History"
Congress Overrides Nixon's Veto of Clean Water Act
House Committee Says No Watergate Probe Before Election
Dirty Politics Taints Election
Update: Vietnam War
North Vietnamese Continue Large-Scale Offensive Against US Troops
NYC Marathon: Women Runners Protest Rule Separating Them From Male Runners
As Starting Gun Fires, Women Sit Down on Start Line
Kissinger Extends Secret Meetings With North Vietnamese
Abbreviation "Ms." Used for First Time in Congressional Record
The TORRINGTON REGISTER

FINALLY... THE BIG DAY IS HERE!

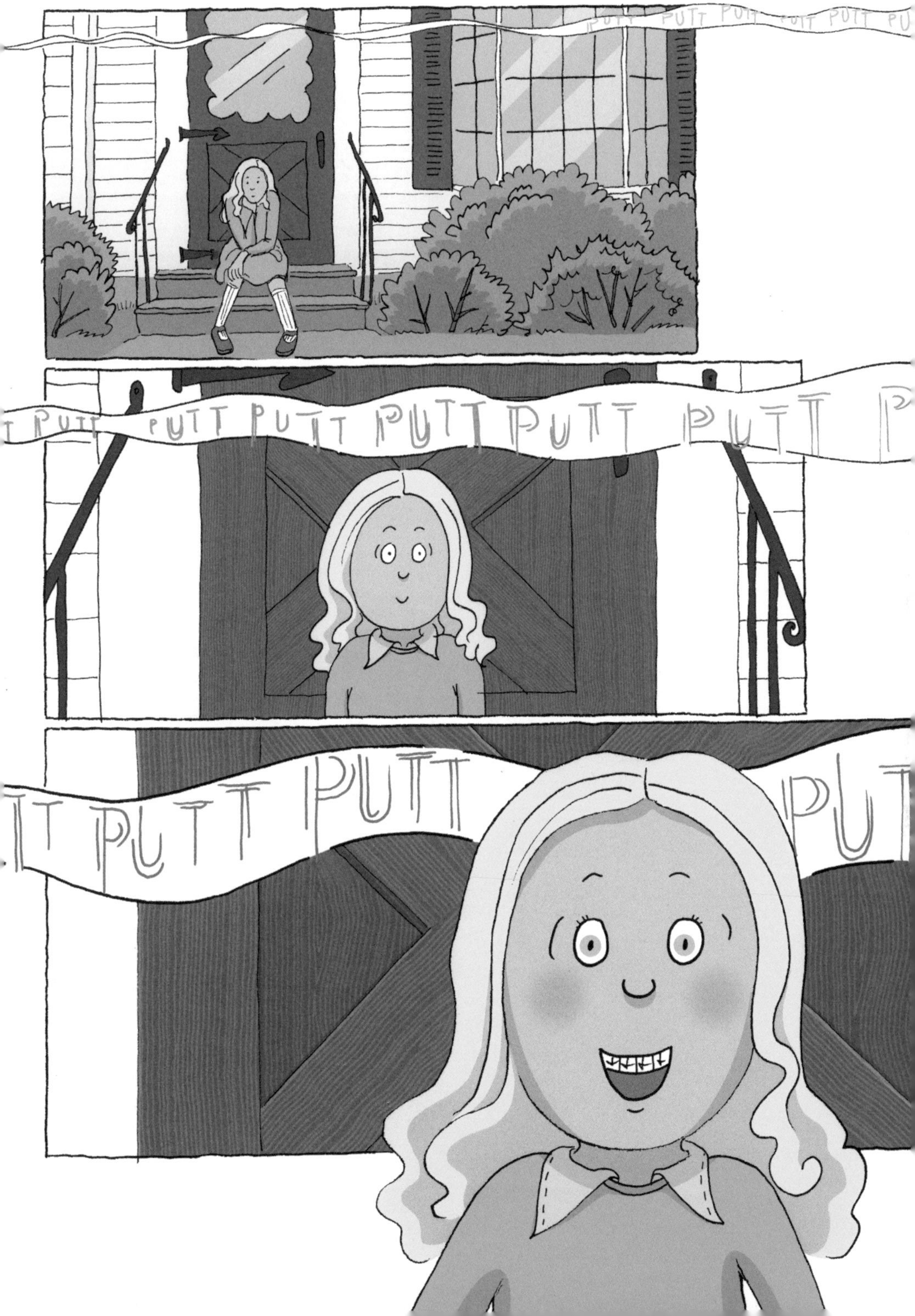
PUTT PUTT PUTT
PUTT PUTT PUTT PUTT
PUTT PUTT

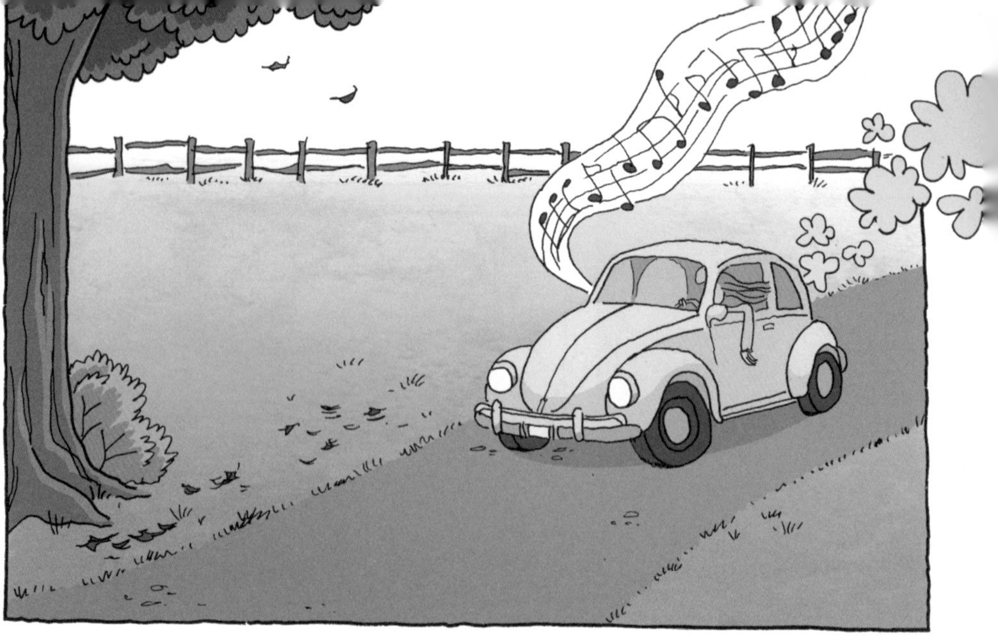

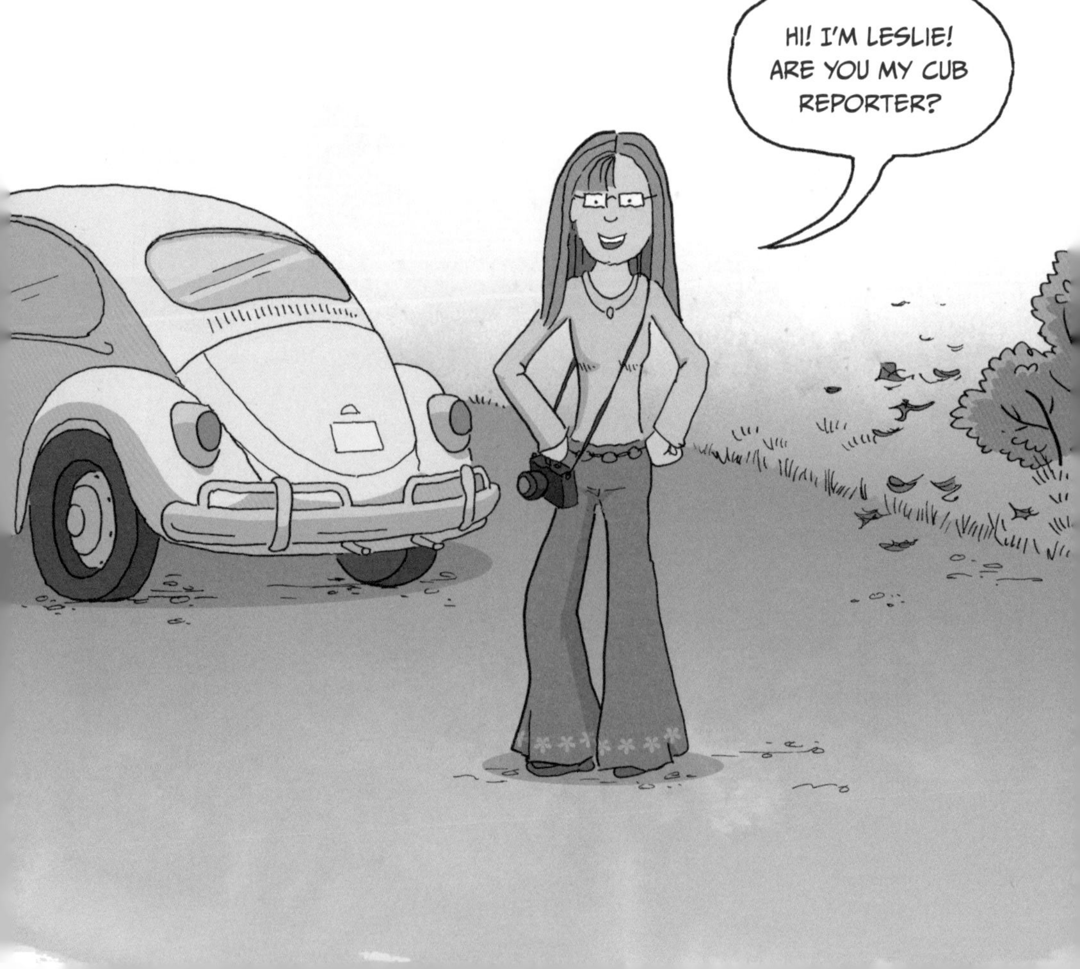
HI! I'M LESLIE! ARE YOU MY CUB REPORTER?

Chapter 3

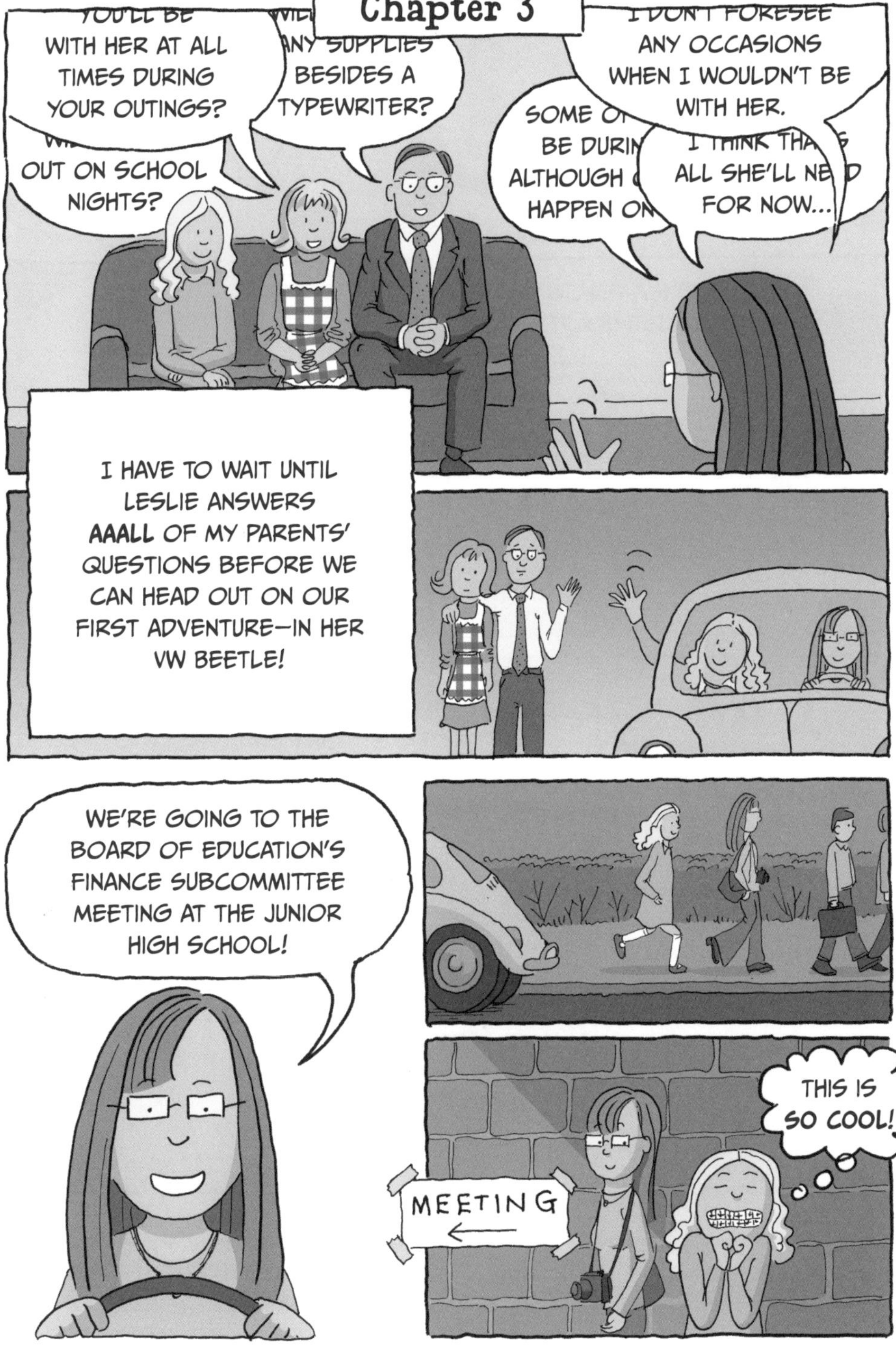
OUT ON SCHOOL NIGHTS?
YOU'LL BE WITH HER AT ALL TIMES DURING YOUR OUTINGS?
ANY SUPPLIES BESIDES A TYPEWRITER?
SOME OF
BE DURIN
ALTHOUGH
HAPPEN ON
I DON'T FORESEE ANY OCCASIONS WHEN I WOULDN'T BE WITH HER.
I THINK THA S ALL SHE'LL NE D FOR NOW...
I HAVE TO WAIT UNTIL LESLIE ANSWERS **AAALL** OF MY PARENTS' QUESTIONS BEFORE WE CAN HEAD OUT ON OUR FIRST ADVENTURE—IN HER VW BEETLE!
WE'RE GOING TO THE BOARD OF EDUCATION'S FINANCE SUBCOMMITTEE MEETING AT THE JUNIOR HIGH SCHOOL!
MEETING
THIS IS SO COOL!

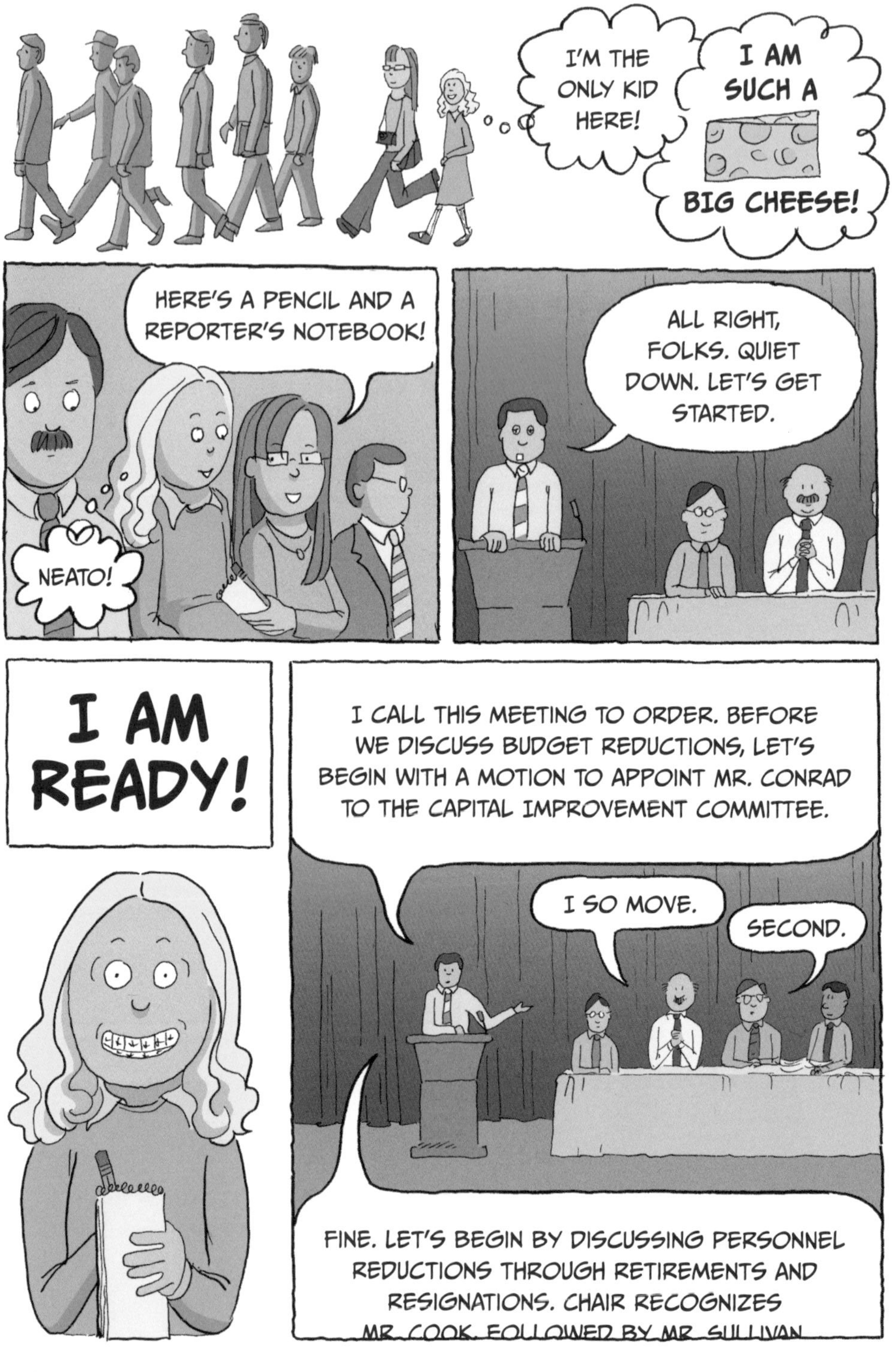
I'M THE ONLY KID HERE!
I AM SUCH A BIG CHEESE!
HERE'S A PENCIL AND A REPORTER'S NOTEBOOK!
NEATO!
ALL RIGHT, FOLKS. QUIET DOWN. LET'S GET STARTED.
I AM READY!
I CALL THIS MEETING TO ORDER. BEFORE WE DISCUSS BUDGET REDUCTIONS, LET'S BEGIN WITH A MOTION TO APPOINT MR. CONRAD TO THE CAPITAL IMPROVEMENT COMMITTEE.
I SO MOVE.
SECOND.
FINE. LET'S BEGIN BY DISCUSSING PERSONNEL REDUCTIONS THROUGH RETIREMENTS AND RESIGNATIONS. CHAIR RECOGNIZES

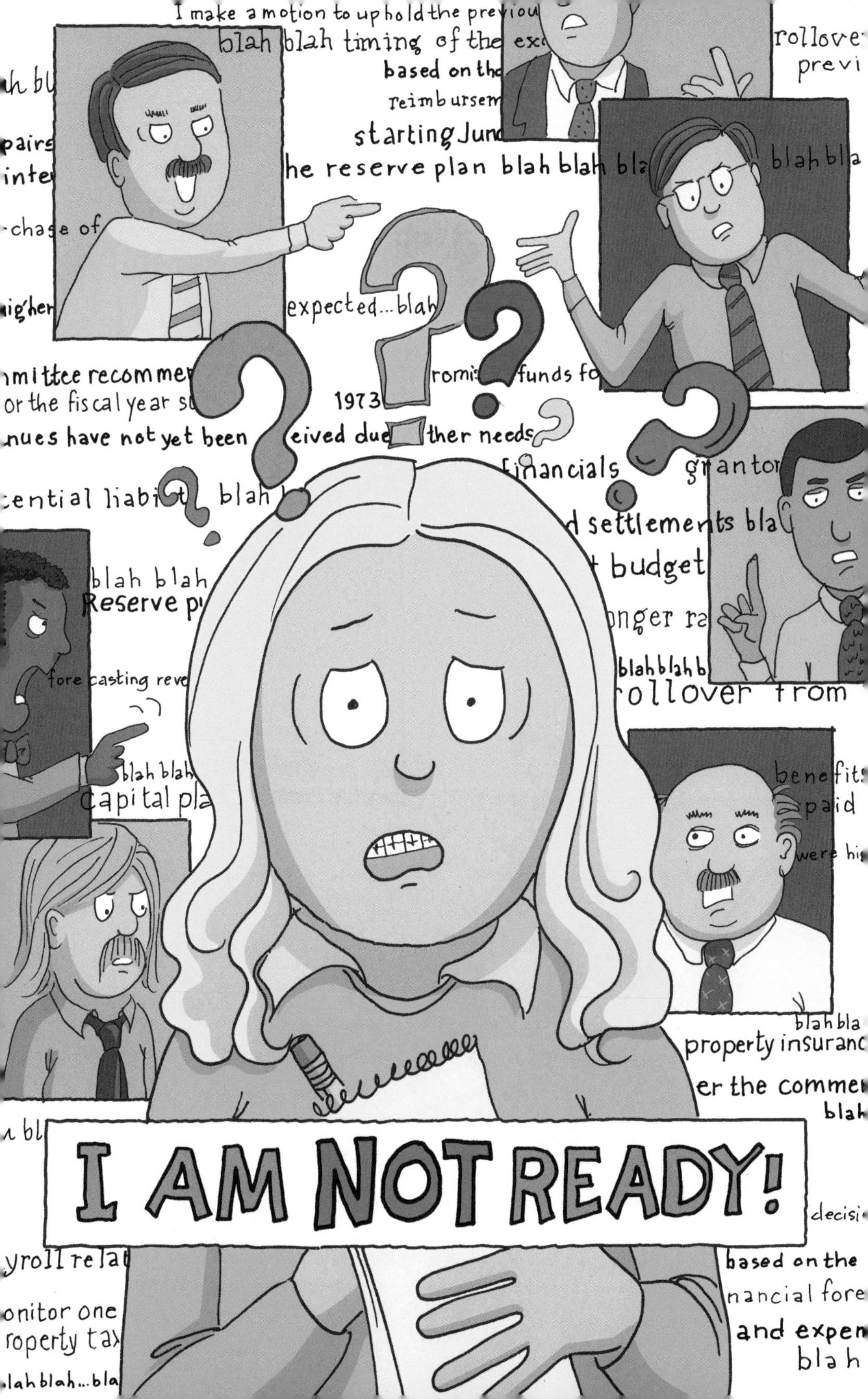

I make a motion to uphold the pre
blah blah timing of the
based on the
reimbursem
starting Jun
he reserve plan blah blah
blah bla
rollove
previ
chase of
expected...blah
mittee recomme
or the fiscal year s
1973
funds fo
nues have not yet been
eived due
ther needs
financials
gran tor
ential liabi
blah
settlements bla
budget
blah blah
Reserve p
nger ra
fore casting reve
blahblahb
ollover from
blah blah
capital pla
benefits
paid
were hi
blahbla
property insuranc
er the comme
blah
I AM NOT READY!
decisi
yroll rela
based on the
nancial fore
onitor one
roperty ta
and expen
blah
lahblah...bla

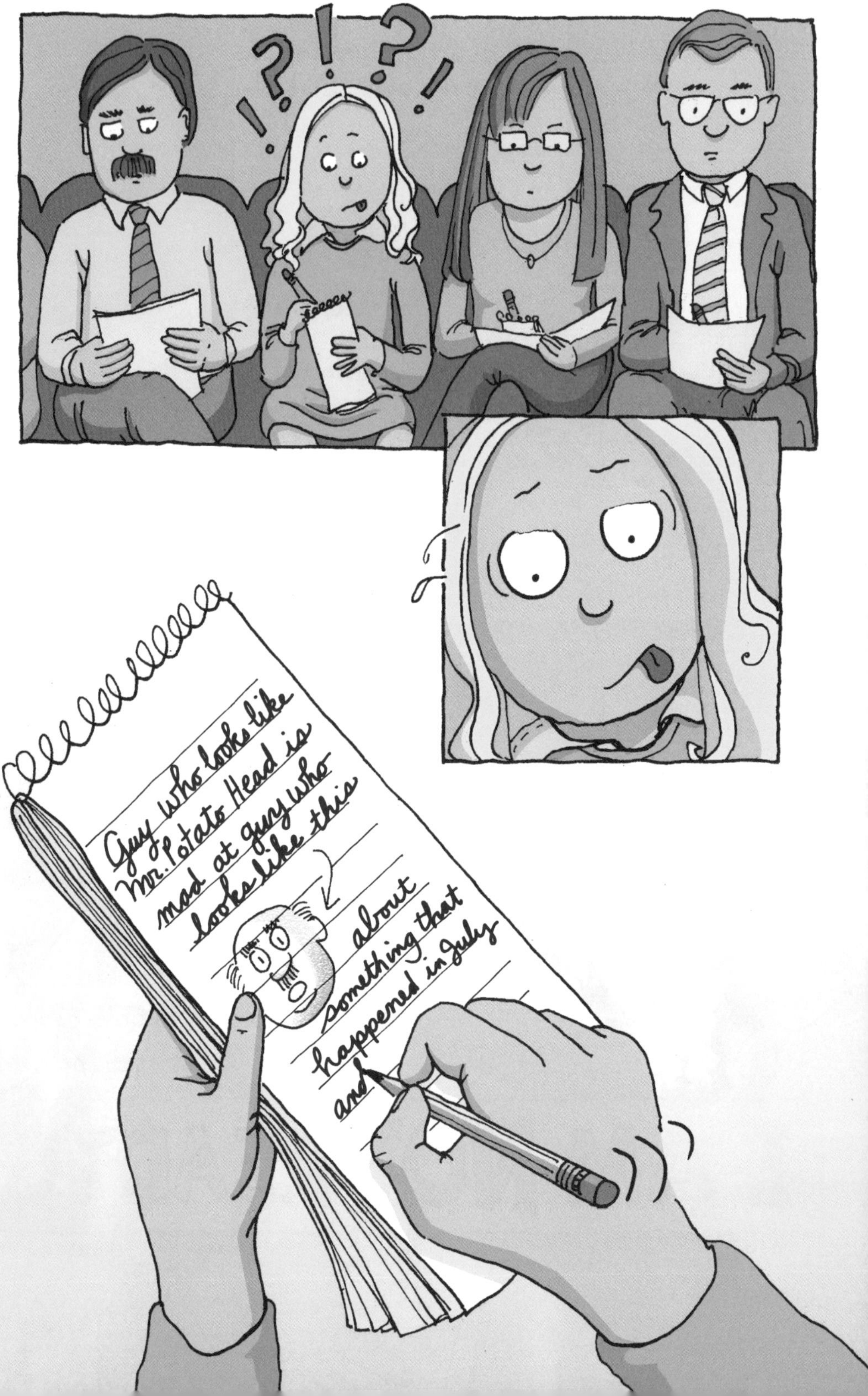
Guy who looks like Mr. Potato Head is mad at guy who looks like this
about something that happened in July
and

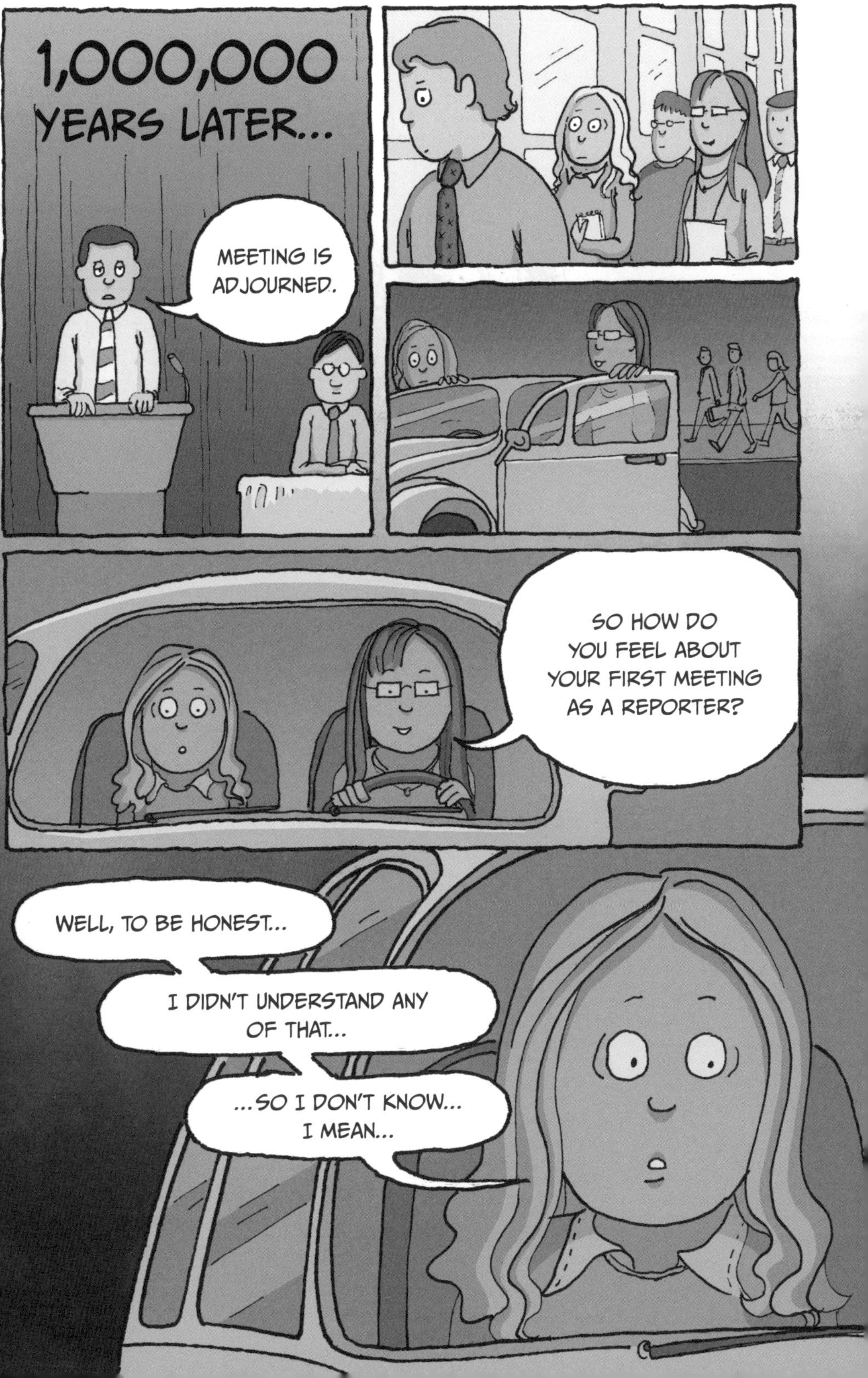
1,000,000 YEARS LATER...
MEETING IS ADJOURNED.
SO HOW DO YOU FEEL ABOUT YOUR FIRST MEETING AS A REPORTER?
WELL, TO BE HONEST...
I DIDN'T UNDERSTAND ANY OF THAT...
...SO I DON'T KNOW... I MEAN...

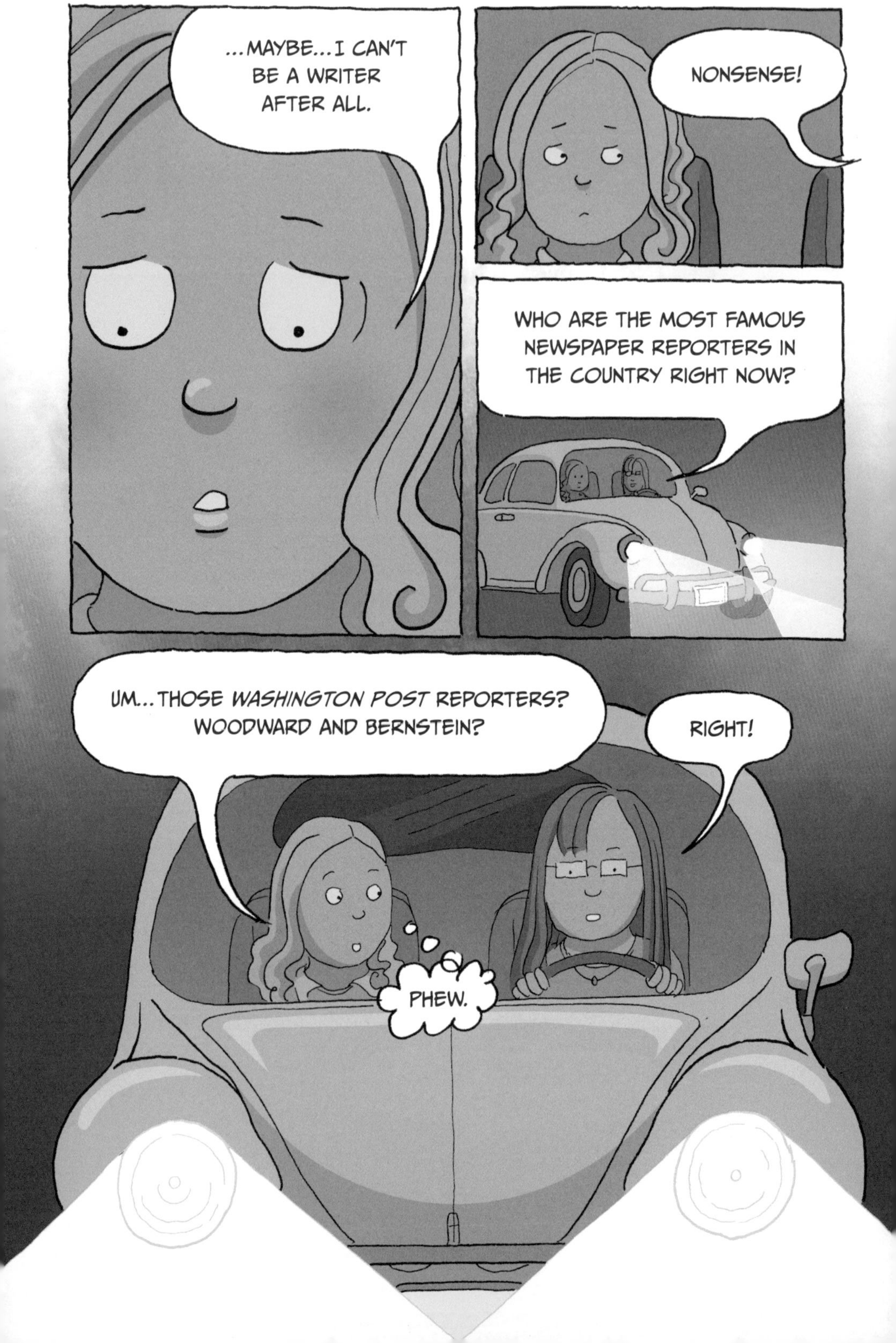
...MAYBE...I CAN'T BE A WRITER AFTER ALL.
NONSENSE!
WHO ARE THE MOST FAMOUS NEWSPAPER REPORTERS IN THE COUNTRY RIGHT NOW?
UM...THOSE *WASHINGTON POST* REPORTERS? WOODWARD AND BERNSTEIN?
RIGHT!
PHEW.

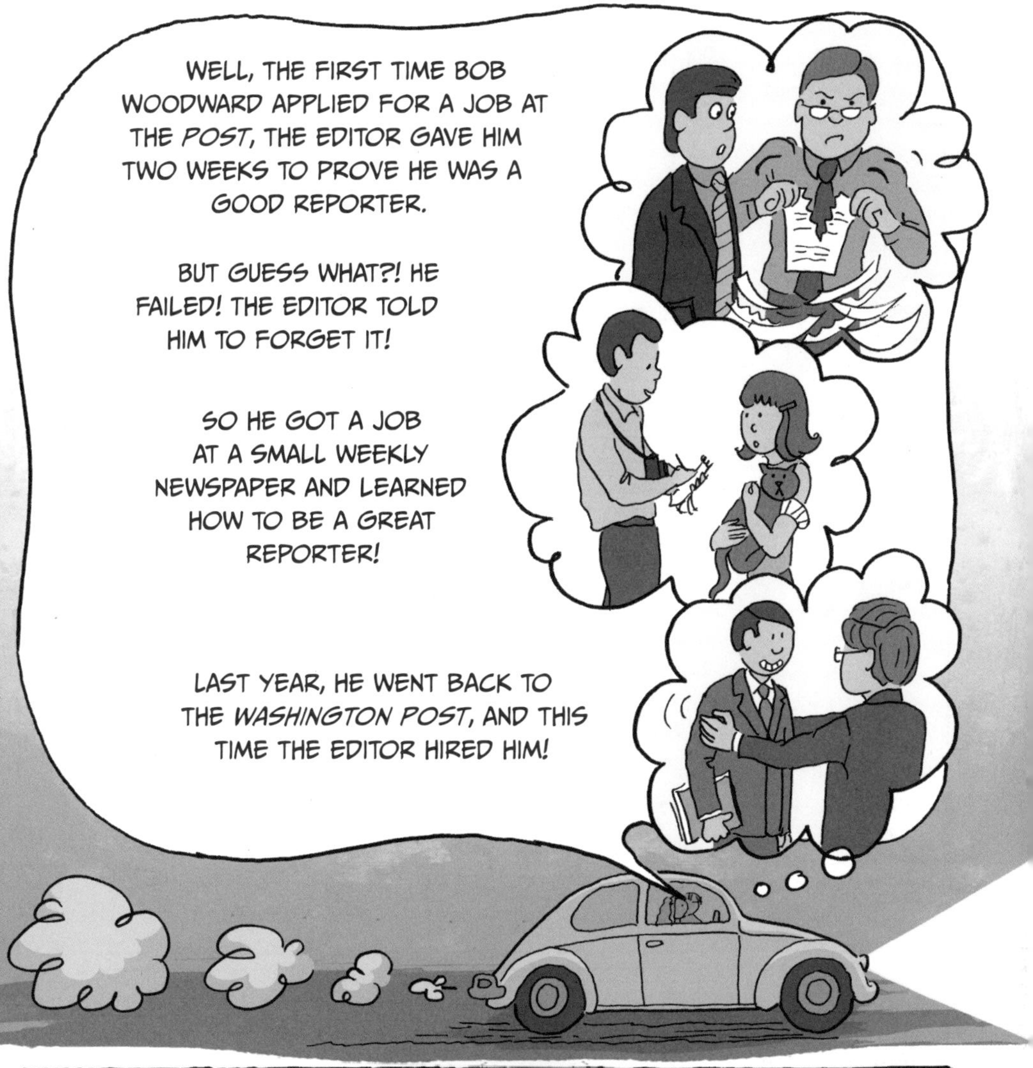
WELL, THE FIRST TIME BOB WOODWARD APPLIED FOR A JOB AT THE *POST*, THE EDITOR GAVE HIM TWO WEEKS TO PROVE HE WAS A GOOD REPORTER.
BUT GUESS WHAT?! HE FAILED! THE EDITOR TOLD HIM TO FORGET IT!
SO HE GOT A JOB AT A SMALL WEEKLY NEWSPAPER AND LEARNED HOW TO BE A GREAT REPORTER!
LAST YEAR, HE WENT BACK TO THE *WASHINGTON POST*, AND THIS TIME THE EDITOR HIRED HIM!

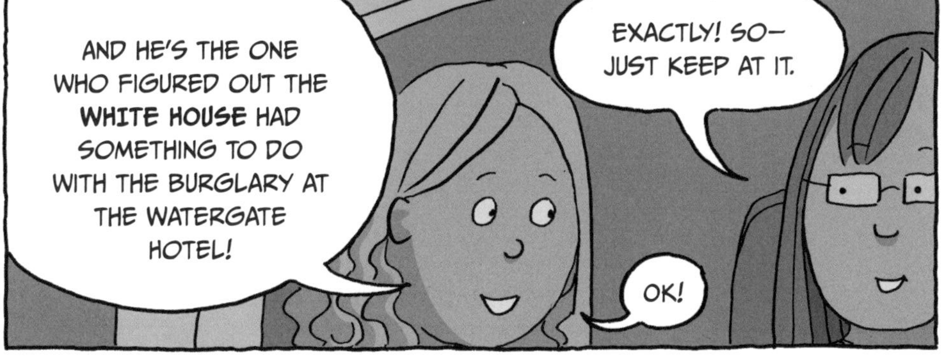
AND HE'S THE ONE WHO FIGURED OUT THE **WHITE HOUSE** HAD SOMETHING TO DO WITH THE BURGLARY AT THE WATERGATE HOTEL!
EXACTLY! SO— JUST KEEP AT IT.
OK!

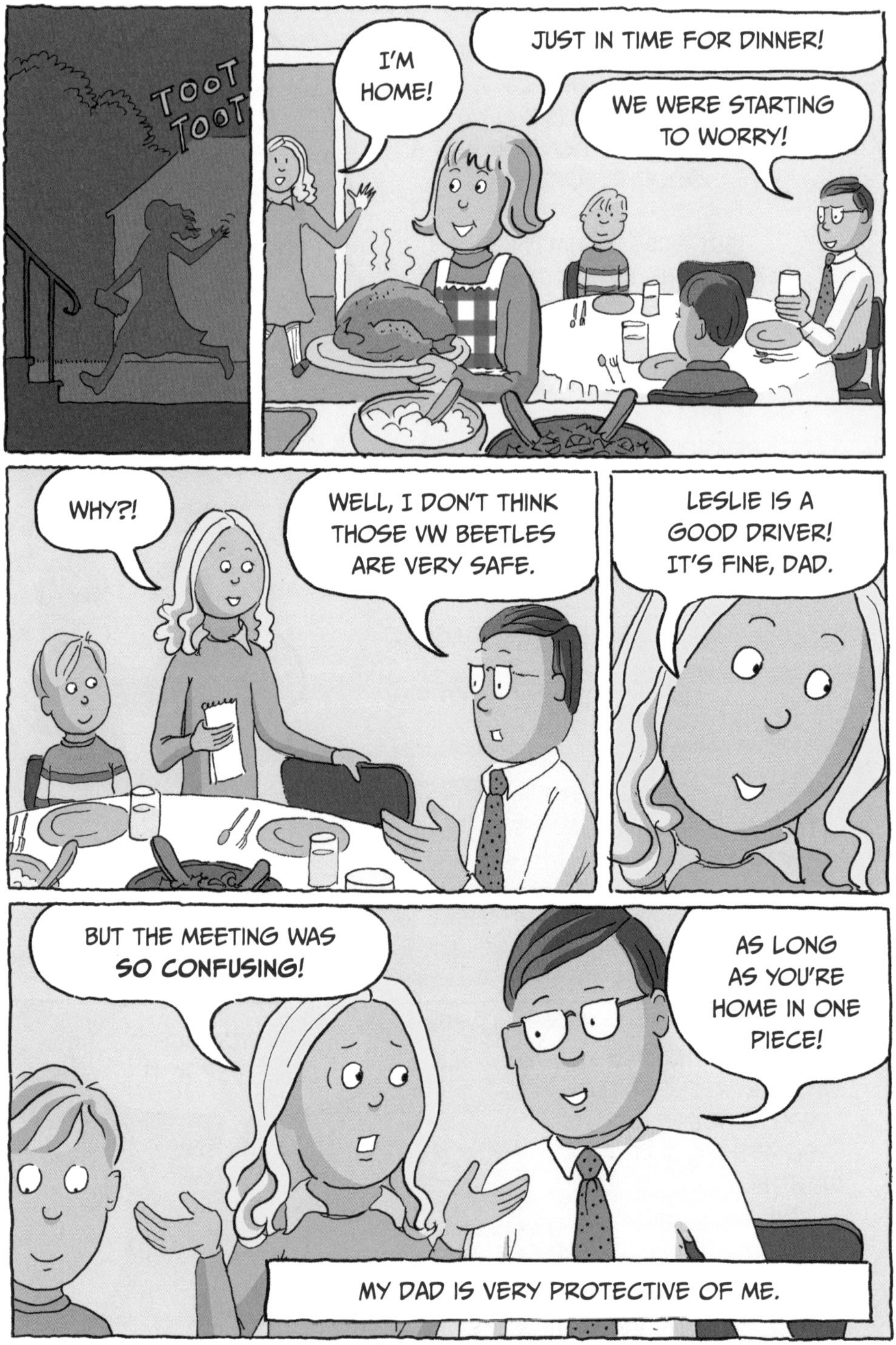
TOOT TOOT
I'M HOME!
JUST IN TIME FOR DINNER!
WE WERE STARTING TO WORRY!
WHY?!
WELL, I DON'T THINK THOSE VW BEETLES ARE VERY SAFE.
LESLIE IS A GOOD DRIVER! IT'S FINE, DAD.
BUT THE MEETING WAS SO CONFUSING!
AS LONG AS YOU'RE HOME IN ONE PIECE!
MY DAD IS VERY PROTECTIVE OF ME.

HE WANTS ME
TO BE SAFE...

...BUT HE
WANTS MY
BROTHERS
TO BE
SUCCESSFUL.

JOHN, I KNOW
1972 HAS BEEN A
GOOD YEAR FOR THE
STOCK MARKET, BUT
LET'S CHECK OUT
SOME REAL ESTATE
INVESTMENTS.

AND, GAR, THERE'S
NO REASON YOU CAN'T
PLAY PROFESSIONAL
TENNIS IN YOUR TEENS.
JIMMY CONNORS IS
TWENTY AND HE JUST
TURNED PRO!

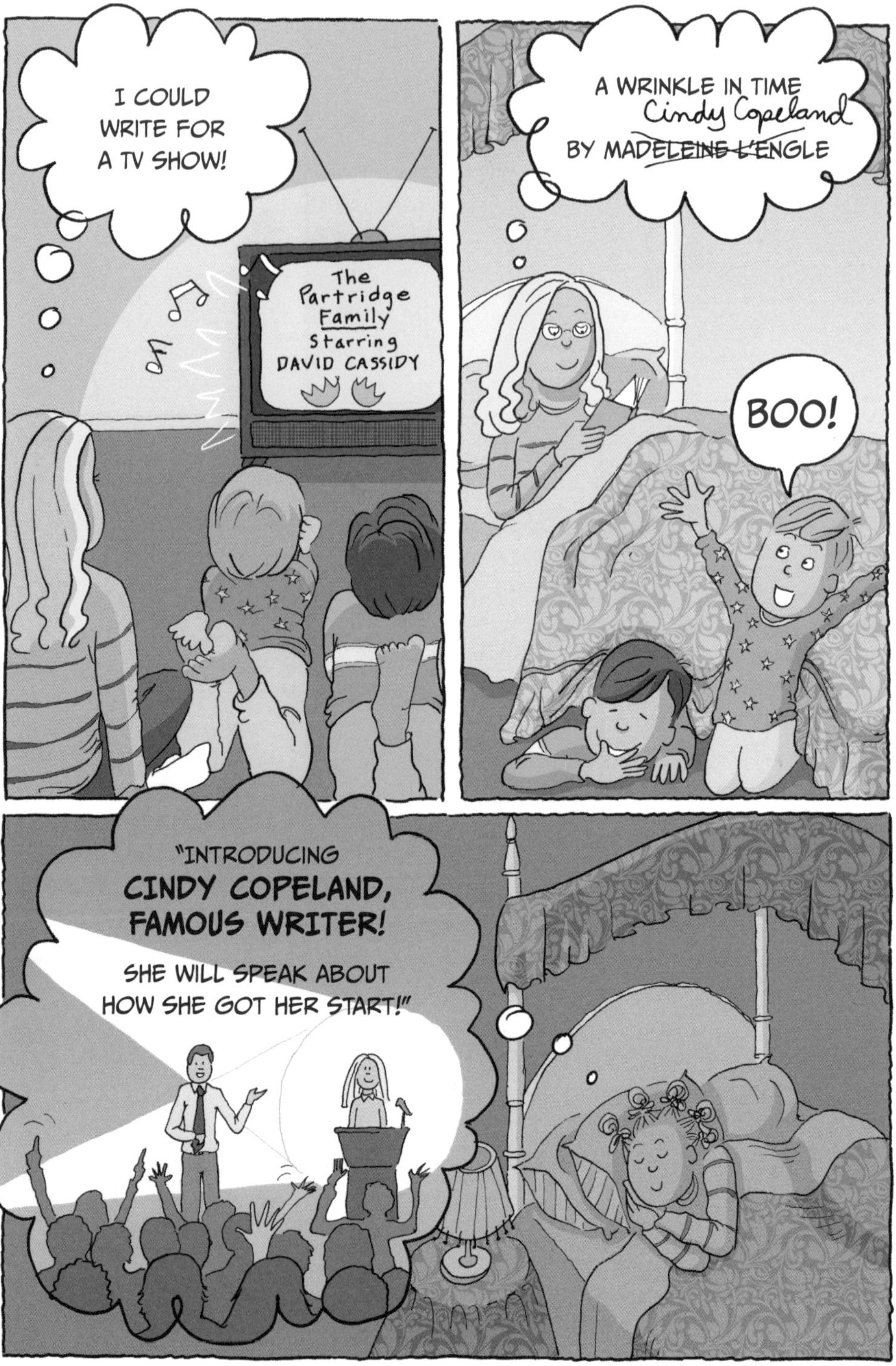
I COULD WRITE FOR A TV SHOW!
The Partridge Family Starring DAVID CASSIDY
A WRINKLE IN TIME
Cindy Copeland
BY MADELEINE L'ENGLE
BOO!
"INTRODUCING CINDY COPELAND, FAMOUS WRITER!
SHE WILL SPEAK ABOUT HOW SHE GOT HER START!"

Chapter 4

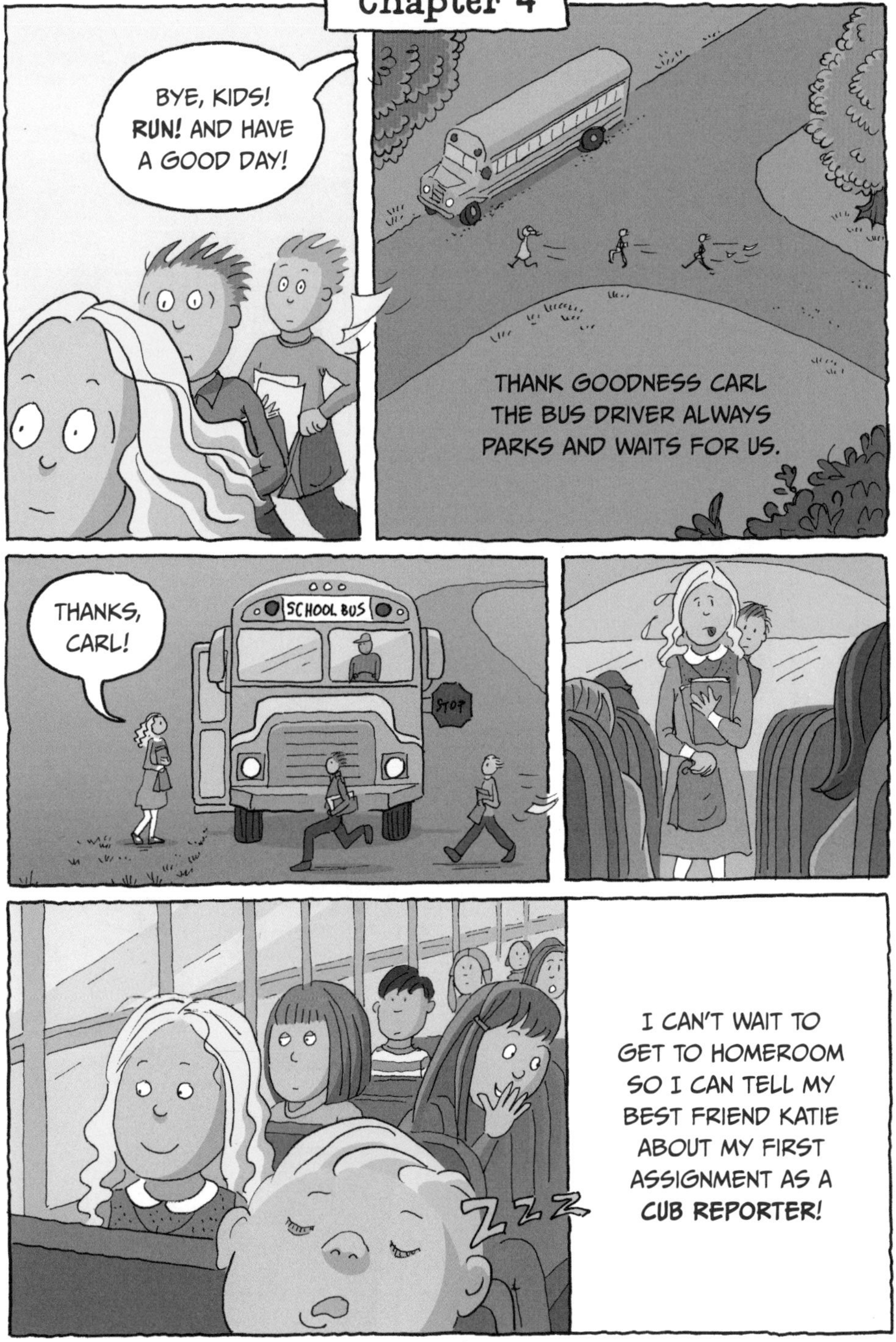
BYE, KIDS! **RUN!** AND HAVE A GOOD DAY!
THANK GOODNESS CARL THE BUS DRIVER ALWAYS PARKS AND WAITS FOR US.
THANKS, CARL!
SCHOOL BUS
STOP
ZZZ
I CAN'T WAIT TO GET TO HOMEROOM SO I CAN TELL MY BEST FRIEND KATIE ABOUT MY FIRST ASSIGNMENT AS A **CUB REPORTER!**

KATIE AND I HAVE BEEN BEST FRIENDS SINCE FIRST GRADE, WHEN OUR MOMS ARRANGED FOR US TO WALK TO SCHOOL TOGETHER.

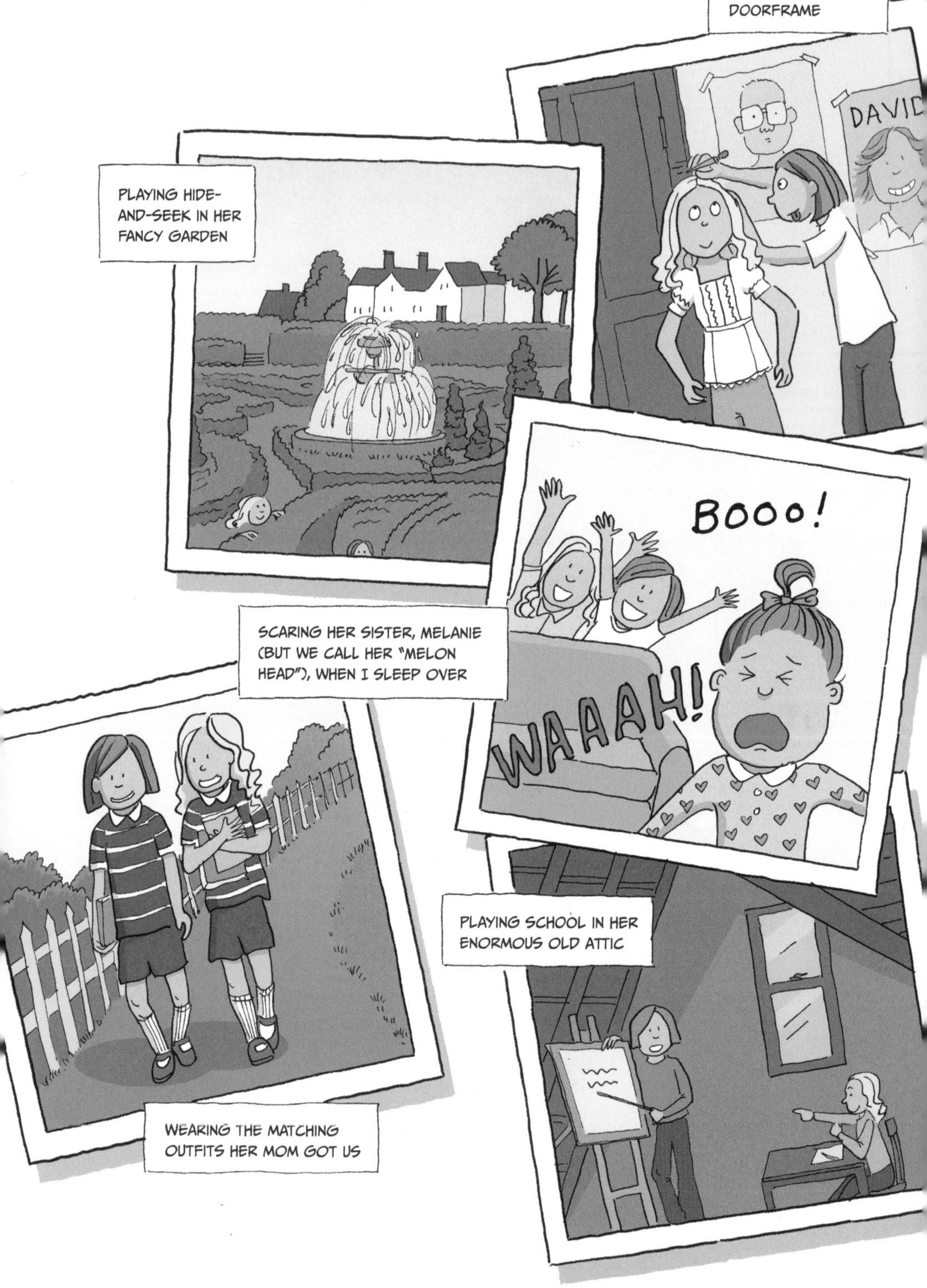
KEEPING TRACK OF HOW MUCH WE'RE GROWING ON HER DOORFRAME
DAVID
PLAYING HIDE-AND-SEEK IN HER FANCY GARDEN
BOOO!
WAAAH!
SCARING HER SISTER, MELANIE (BUT WE CALL HER "MELON HEAD"), WHEN I SLEEP OVER
PLAYING SCHOOL IN HER ENORMOUS OLD ATTIC
WEARING THE MATCHING OUTFITS HER MOM GOT US

41

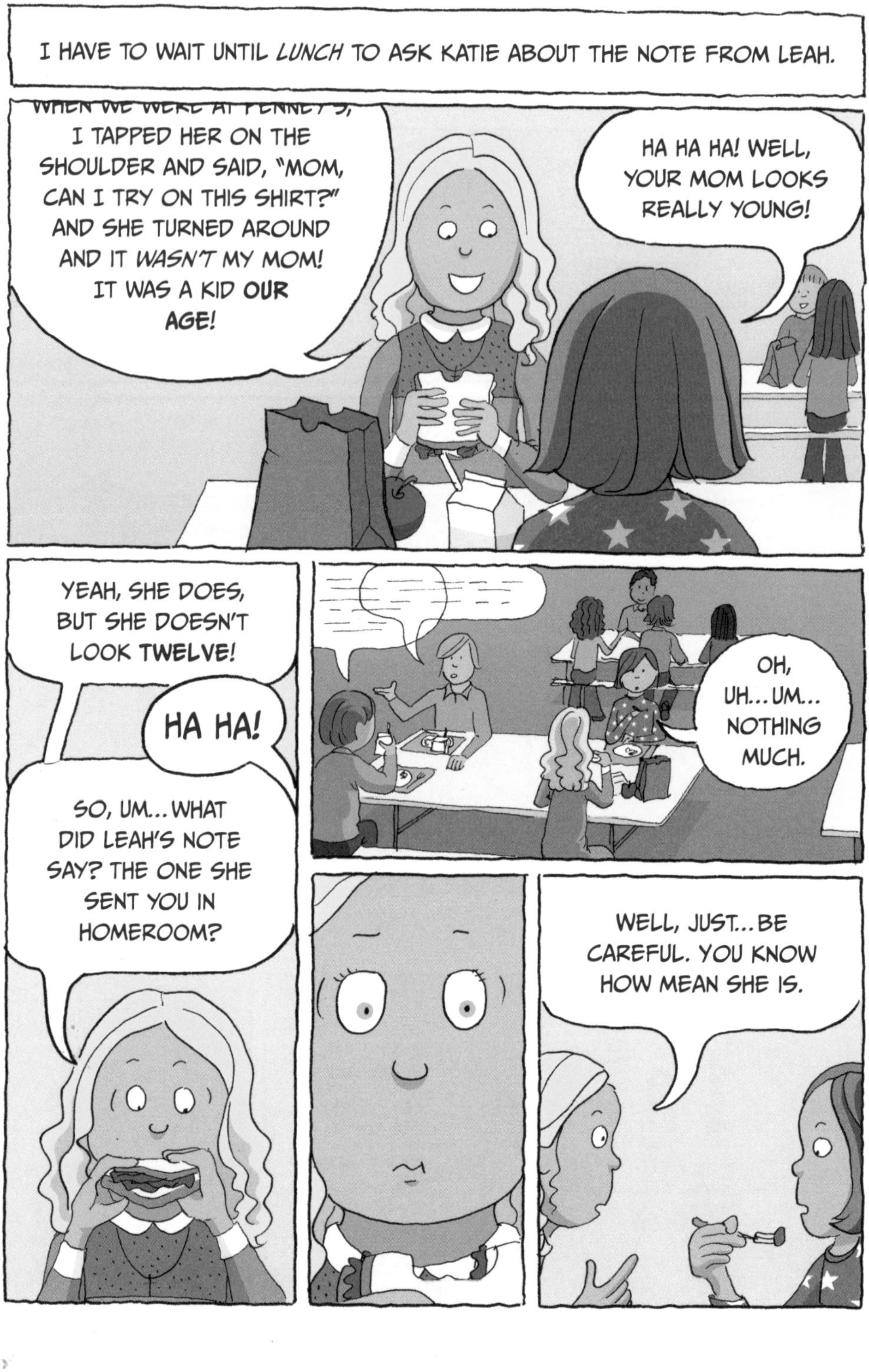
I HAVE TO WAIT UNTIL *LUNCH* TO ASK KATIE ABOUT THE NOTE FROM LEAH.
I TAPPED HER ON THE SHOULDER AND SAID, "MOM, CAN I TRY ON THIS SHIRT?" AND SHE TURNED AROUND AND IT *WASN'T* MY MOM! IT WAS A KID **OUR AGE!**
HA HA HA! WELL, YOUR MOM LOOKS REALLY YOUNG!
YEAH, SHE DOES, BUT SHE DOESN'T LOOK **TWELVE!**
HA HA!
SO, UM...WHAT DID LEAH'S NOTE SAY? THE ONE SHE SENT YOU IN HOMEROOM?
OH, UH...UM... NOTHING MUCH.
WELL, JUST...BE CAREFUL. YOU KNOW HOW MEAN SHE IS.

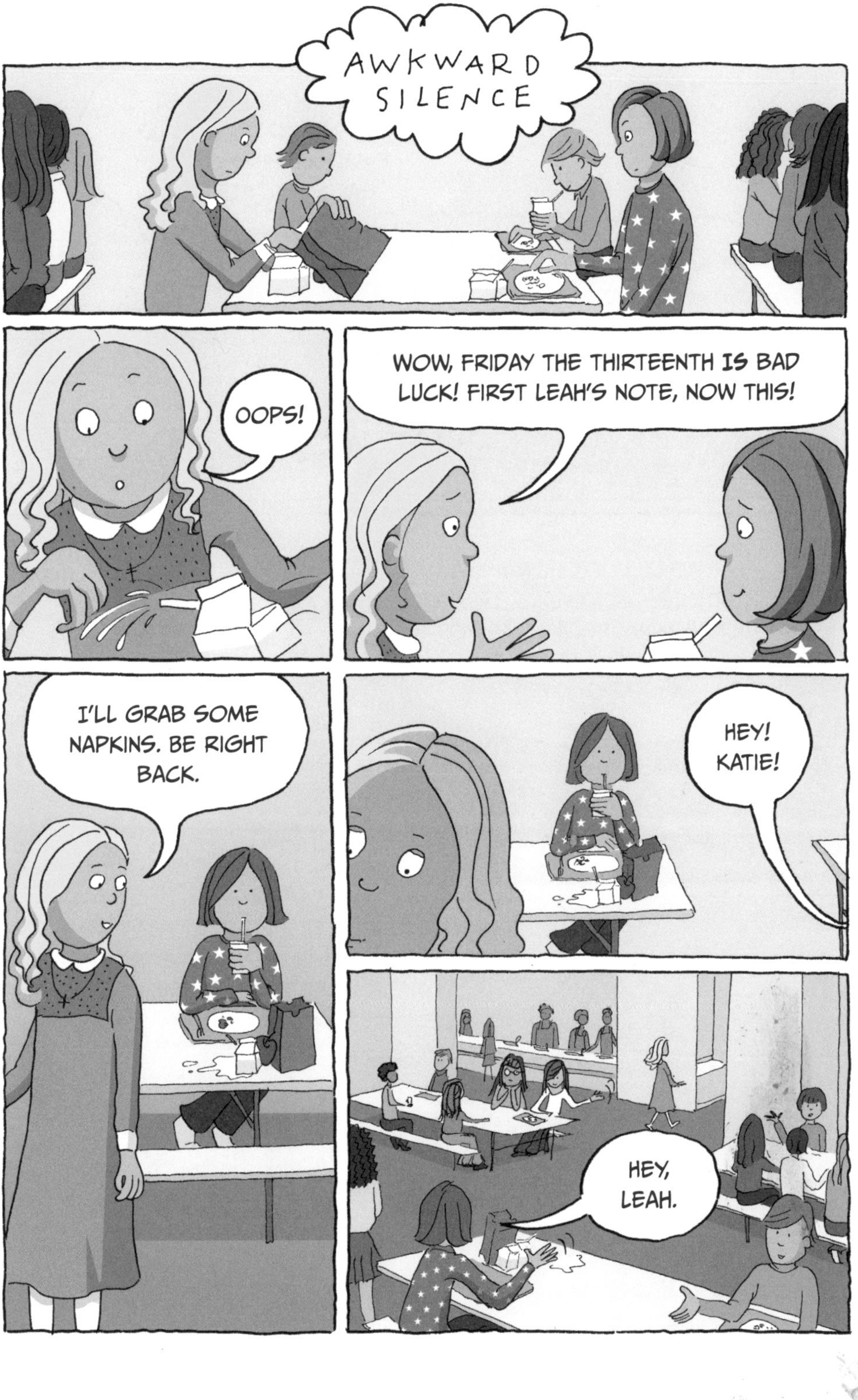
AWKWARD SILENCE
OOPS!
WOW, FRIDAY THE THIRTEENTH IS BAD LUCK! FIRST LEAH'S NOTE, NOW THIS!
I'LL GRAB SOME NAPKINS. BE RIGHT BACK.
HEY! KATIE!
HEY, LEAH.

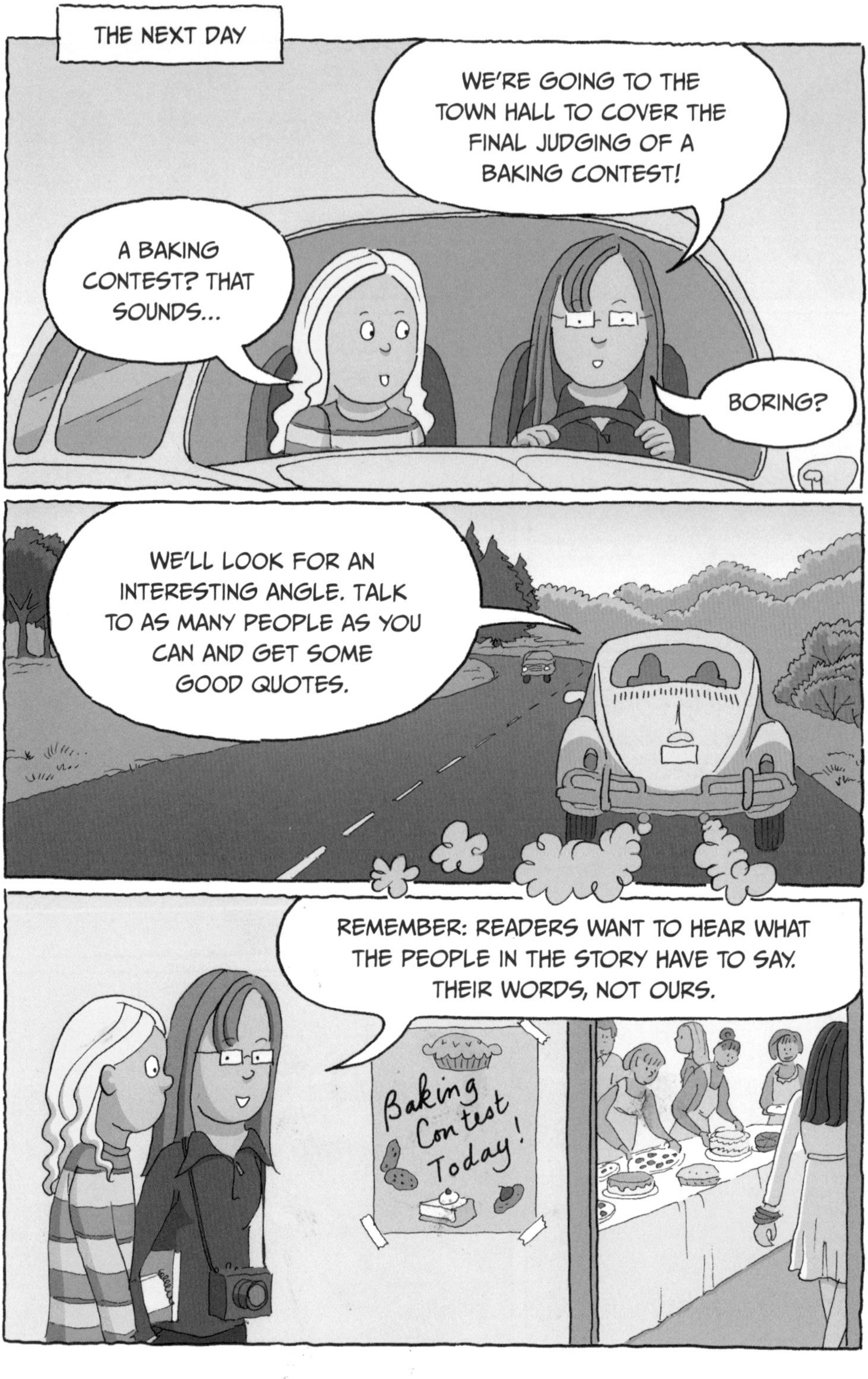
THE NEXT DAY
WE'RE GOING TO THE TOWN HALL TO COVER THE FINAL JUDGING OF A BAKING CONTEST!
A BAKING CONTEST? THAT SOUNDS...
BORING?
WE'LL LOOK FOR AN INTERESTING ANGLE. TALK TO AS MANY PEOPLE AS YOU CAN AND GET SOME GOOD QUOTES.
REMEMBER: READERS WANT TO HEAR WHAT THE PEOPLE IN THE STORY HAVE TO SAY. THEIR WORDS, NOT OURS.
Baking Contest Today!

BAKING CONTEST WINNER ANNOUNCED

By Cindy Copeland

The Litchfield County Extension Service held a cake baking contest. Miss Nancy Brown and Mrs. Sally Worthington were the lucky judges. The first prize was won by Greg Bennett, a senior at Litchfield High School. Greg is the son of Mr. and Mrs. Samuel Bennett of School Street.

Miss Brown and Mrs. Worthington were surprised to learn that a boy was the one who baked the winning cake! "We didn't say that the contest was limited to girls," Miss Brown commented, "but that's because we never expected any guys to enter!" She said that they had no idea who baked each cake because the names were hidden underneath the cake pans. Miss Brown added that Greg's Midnight Madness chocolate cake was the clear winner. Who wouldn't love a chocolate cake with fudge frosting and pudding in the middle?

As for Greg, he said that the hardest part was not choosing a recipe or baking a cake, but taking all of the teasing from the basketball team. "I had to miss practice on Thursday to bake my cake," he said, "and the other guys gave me a really hard time about it!"

The editor will write the headline.

TAP TAP TAP

Where? When?

No! The lede needs to catch a reader's attention! Start with: A boy won a baking contest!

Use active voice, not passive voice.

What was the prize? Fill in the holes!

Unnecessary!

Opinion, not fact!

Strong ending!

45

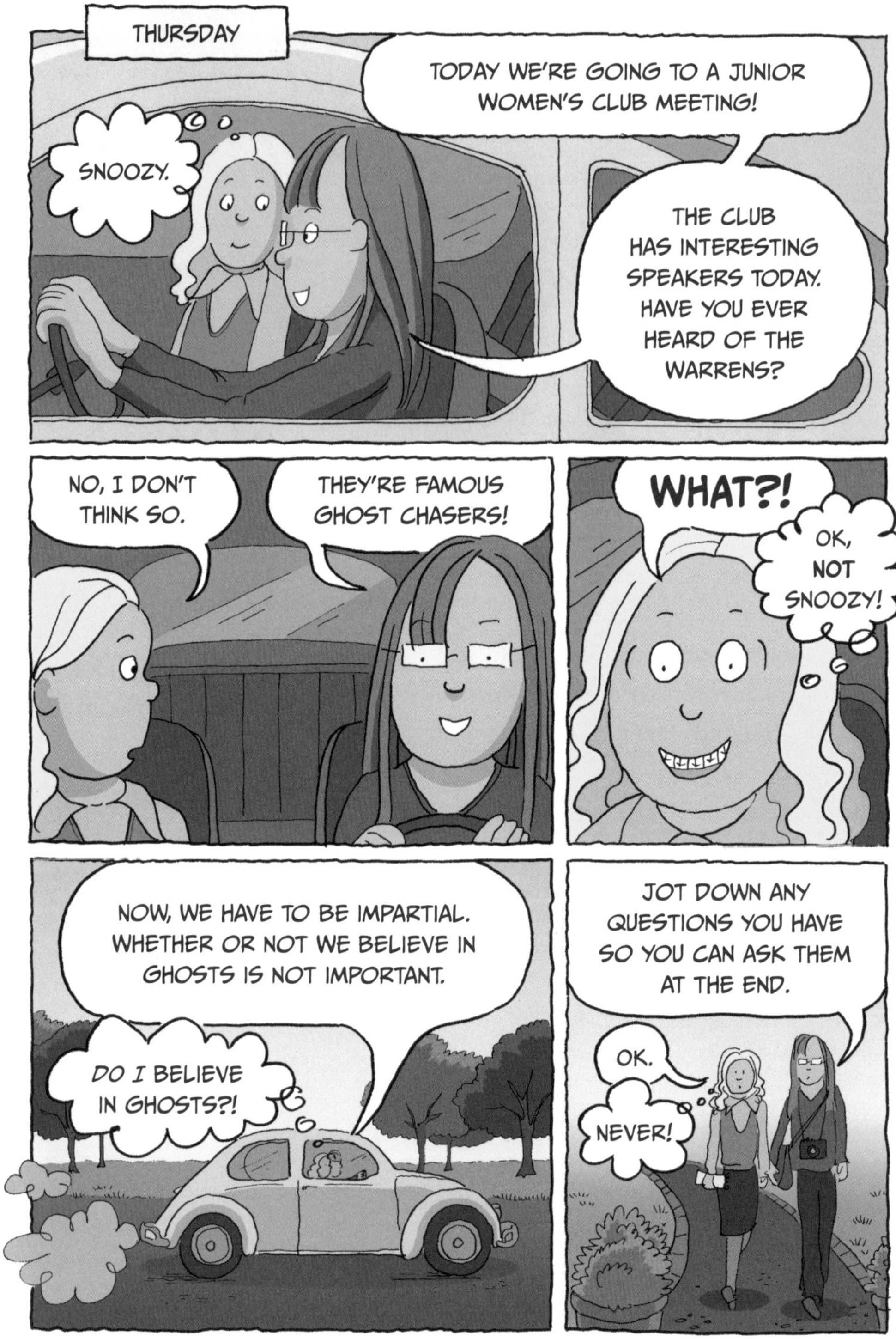
THURSDAY
TODAY WE'RE GOING TO A JUNIOR WOMEN'S CLUB MEETING!
SNOOZY.
THE CLUB HAS INTERESTING SPEAKERS TODAY. HAVE YOU EVER HEARD OF THE WARRENS?
NO, I DON'T THINK SO.
THEY'RE FAMOUS GHOST CHASERS!
WHAT?!
OK, NOT SNOOZY!
NOW, WE HAVE TO BE IMPARTIAL. WHETHER OR NOT WE BELIEVE IN GHOSTS IS NOT IMPORTANT.
DO I BELIEVE IN GHOSTS?!
JOT DOWN ANY QUESTIONS YOU HAVE SO YOU CAN ASK THEM AT THE END.
OK.
NEVER!

Never say "I"— Always use third person!

Good lede!

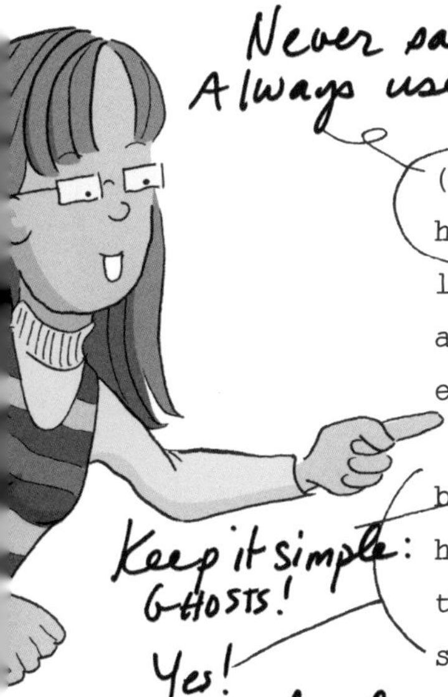

Ed and Lorraine Warren believe in ghosts! (I didn't think I believed in them until I heard the Warrens speak!) The Warrens, who live in nearby Monroe, explained why before a large crowd at a JWC meeting on Saturday evening.

Say "Junior Women's Club"

For almost 30 years, the Warrens have been investigating claims of apparitions and haunted houses. They presented a slide show that featured some of the 300 cases they have studied, many of them in Connecticut.

Keep it simple: GHOSTS!

Yes! You answered who, what, when, where and why!

cut unimportant details

Dressed in a brightly colored shirt, Mr. Warren said that the recent bestseller, The Exorcist, is based on a true story of a boy who became possessed because he used a Ouija board. He warned of potential dangers that amateurs face if they try to contact non-human spirits through witchcraft and black magic. He said that it's very dangerous for people who do not know what they are doing to experiment with such things. Once you have contacted negative beings, he said, "it's not very easy to get rid of them."

Don't repeat yourself! Newspapers don't have extra space!

After the first mention of his name, use "Warren."

Mr. Warren said that he first became interested in supernatural things when he was a child and his family moved into a haunted house.

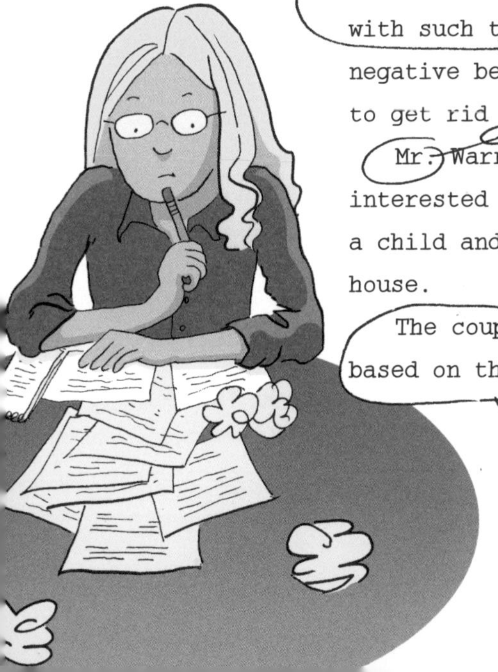

The couple will be appearing in a TV show based on their research in the coming months.

Good. This can be cut if it won't fit on the page.

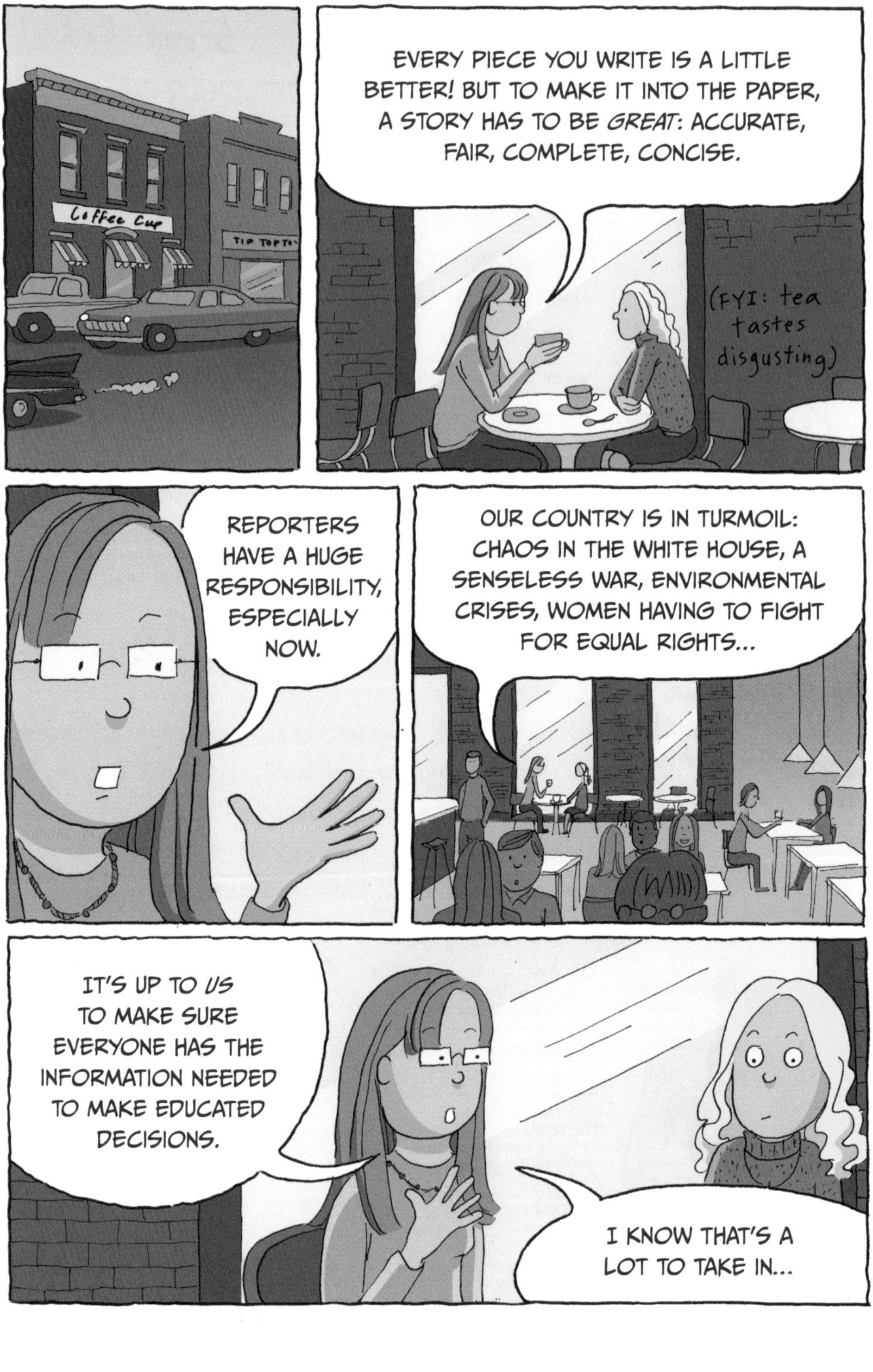

Coffee Cup
TIP TOP TO
EVERY PIECE YOU WRITE IS A LITTLE BETTER! BUT TO MAKE IT INTO THE PAPER, A STORY HAS TO BE *GREAT*: ACCURATE, FAIR, COMPLETE, CONCISE.
(FYI: tea tastes disgusting.)
REPORTERS HAVE A HUGE RESPONSIBILITY, ESPECIALLY NOW.
OUR COUNTRY IS IN TURMOIL: CHAOS IN THE WHITE HOUSE, A SENSELESS WAR, ENVIRONMENTAL CRISES, WOMEN HAVING TO FIGHT FOR EQUAL RIGHTS...
IT'S UP TO *US* TO MAKE SURE EVERYONE HAS THE INFORMATION NEEDED TO MAKE EDUCATED DECISIONS.
I KNOW THAT'S A LOT TO TAKE IN...

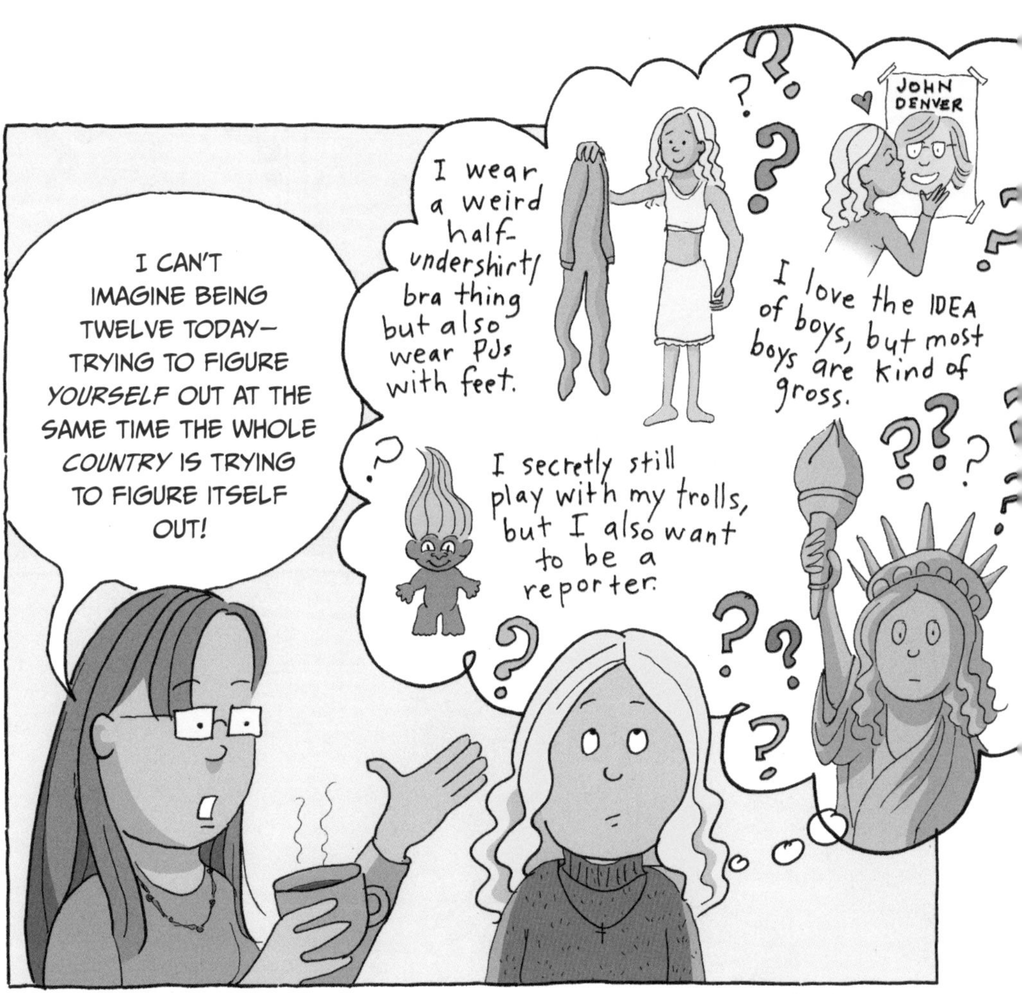
I CAN'T IMAGINE BEING TWELVE TODAY—TRYING TO FIGURE *YOURSELF* OUT AT THE SAME TIME THE WHOLE *COUNTRY* IS TRYING TO FIGURE ITSELF OUT!
I wear a weird half-undershirt/bra thing but also wear PJs with feet.
JOHN DENVER
I love the IDEA of boys, but most boys are kind of gross.
I secretly still play with my trolls, but I also want to be a reporter.

LESLIE'S RIGHT. BEING TWELVE *IS* SUPER WEIRD AND CONFUSING.

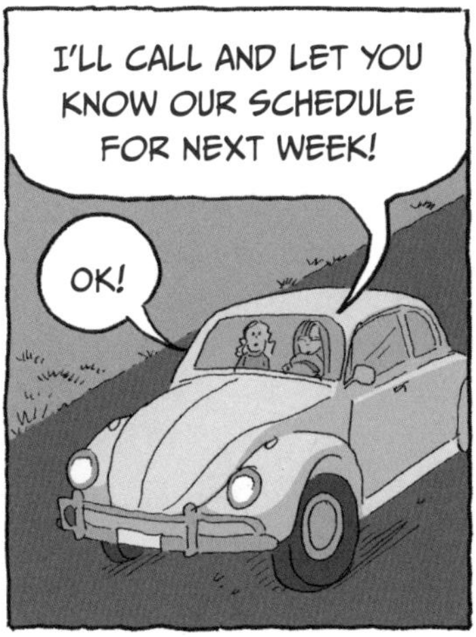
I'LL CALL AND LET YOU KNOW OUR SCHEDULE FOR NEXT WEEK!
OK!

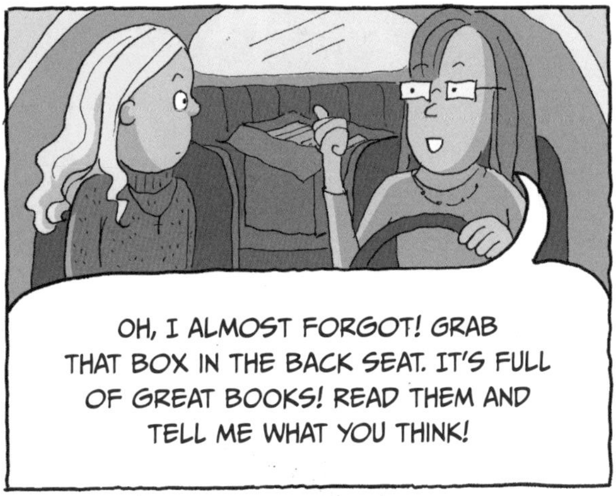
OH, I ALMOST FORGOT! GRAB THAT BOX IN THE BACK SEAT. IT'S FULL OF GREAT BOOKS! READ THEM AND TELL ME WHAT YOU THINK!

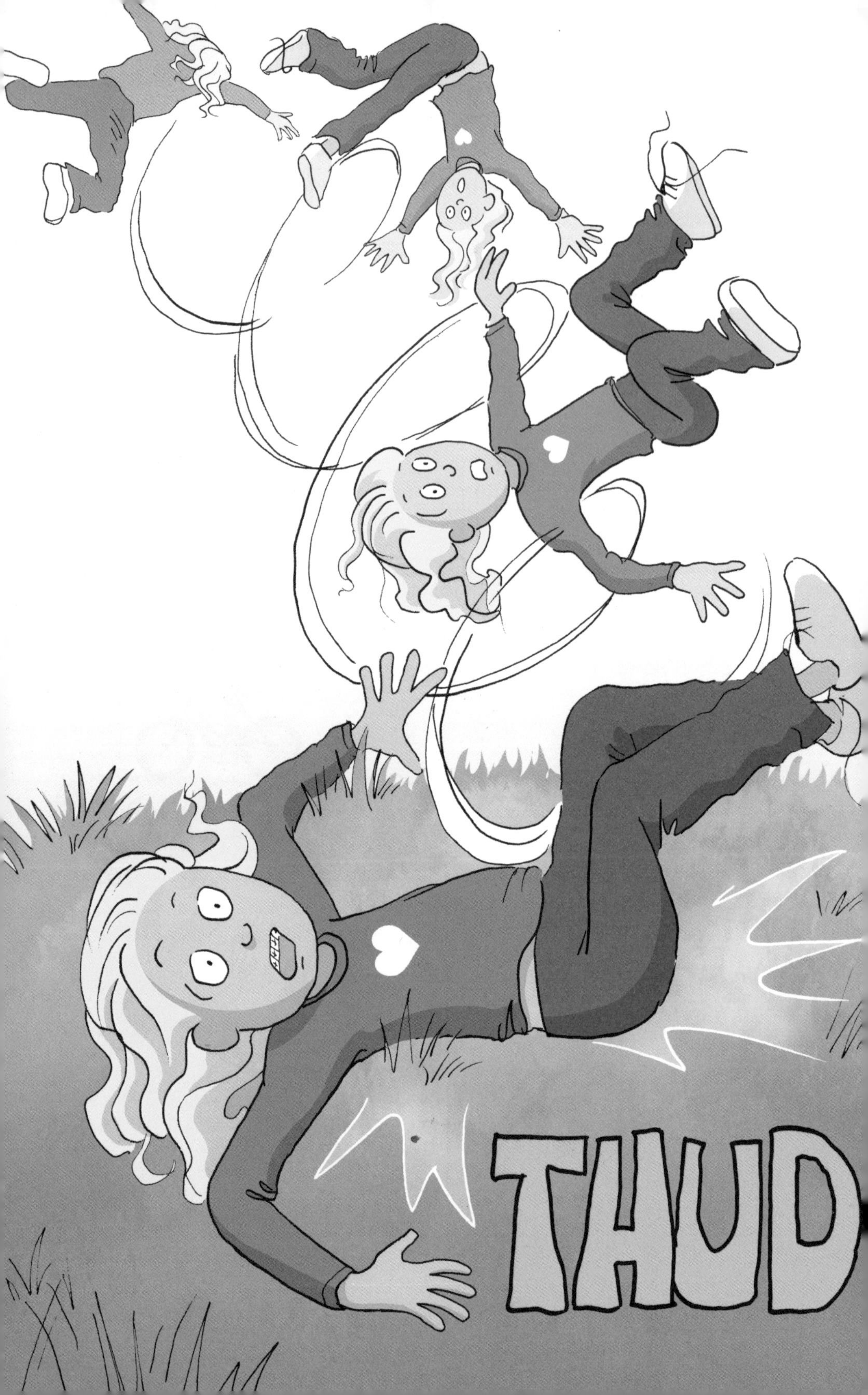
THUD

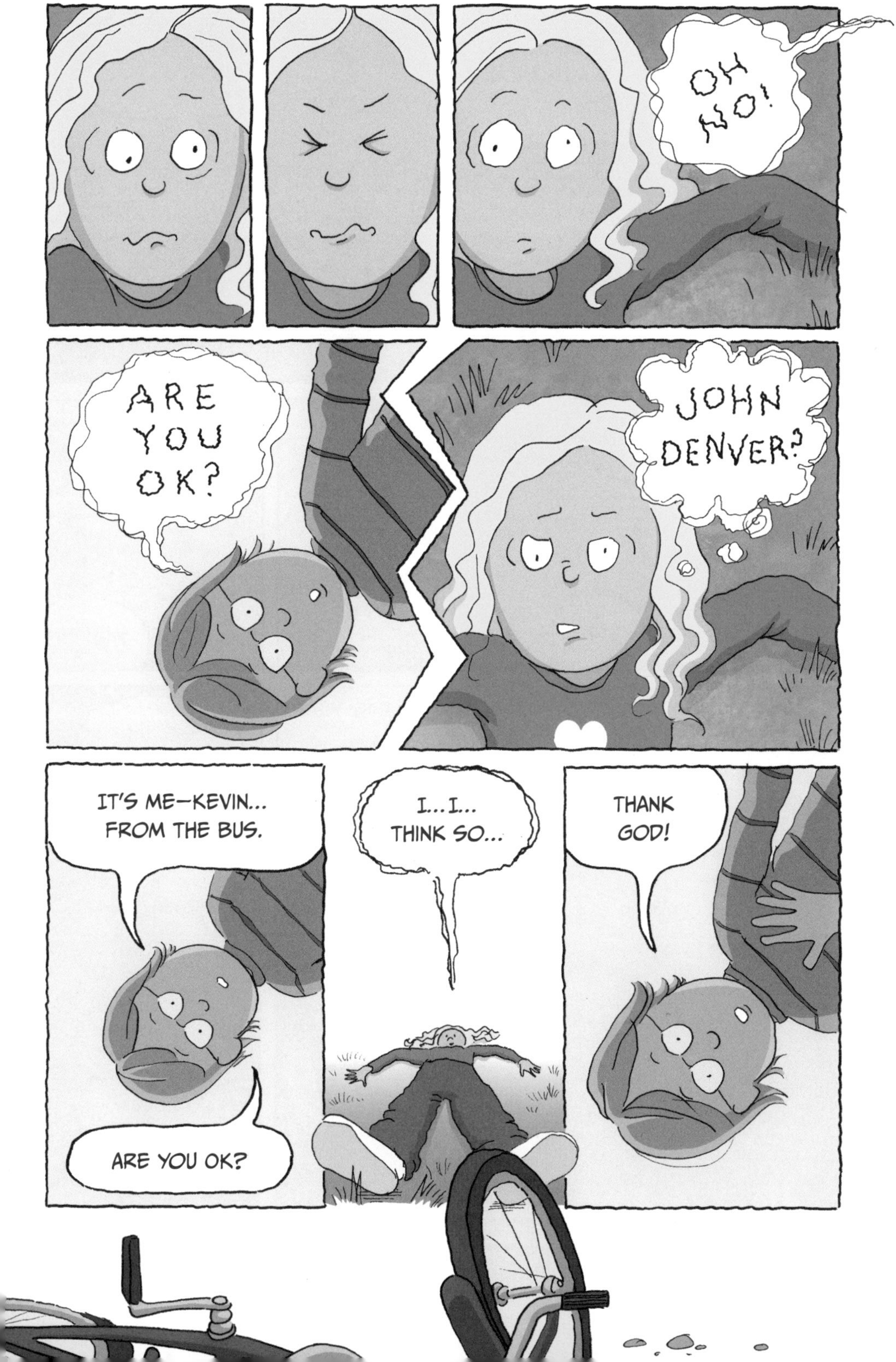
OH NO!
ARE YOU OK?
JOHN DENVER?
IT'S ME—KEVIN... FROM THE BUS.
ARE YOU OK?
I... I... THINK SO...
THANK GOD!

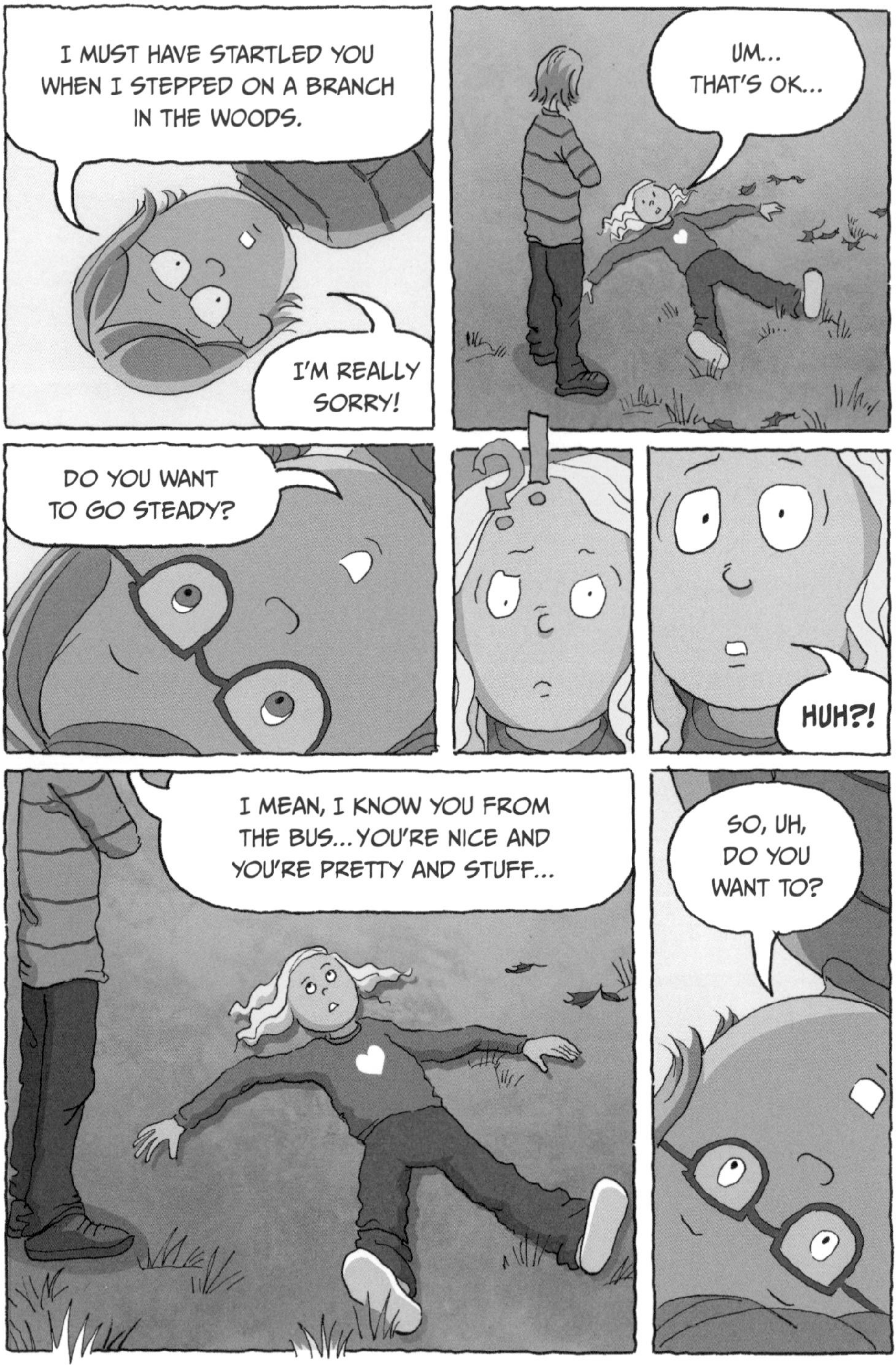
I MUST HAVE STARTLED YOU WHEN I STEPPED ON A BRANCH IN THE WOODS.
I'M REALLY SORRY!
UM... THAT'S OK...
DO YOU WANT TO GO STEADY?
HUH?!
I MEAN, I KNOW YOU FROM THE BUS...YOU'RE NICE AND YOU'RE PRETTY AND STUFF...
SO, UH, DO YOU WANT TO?

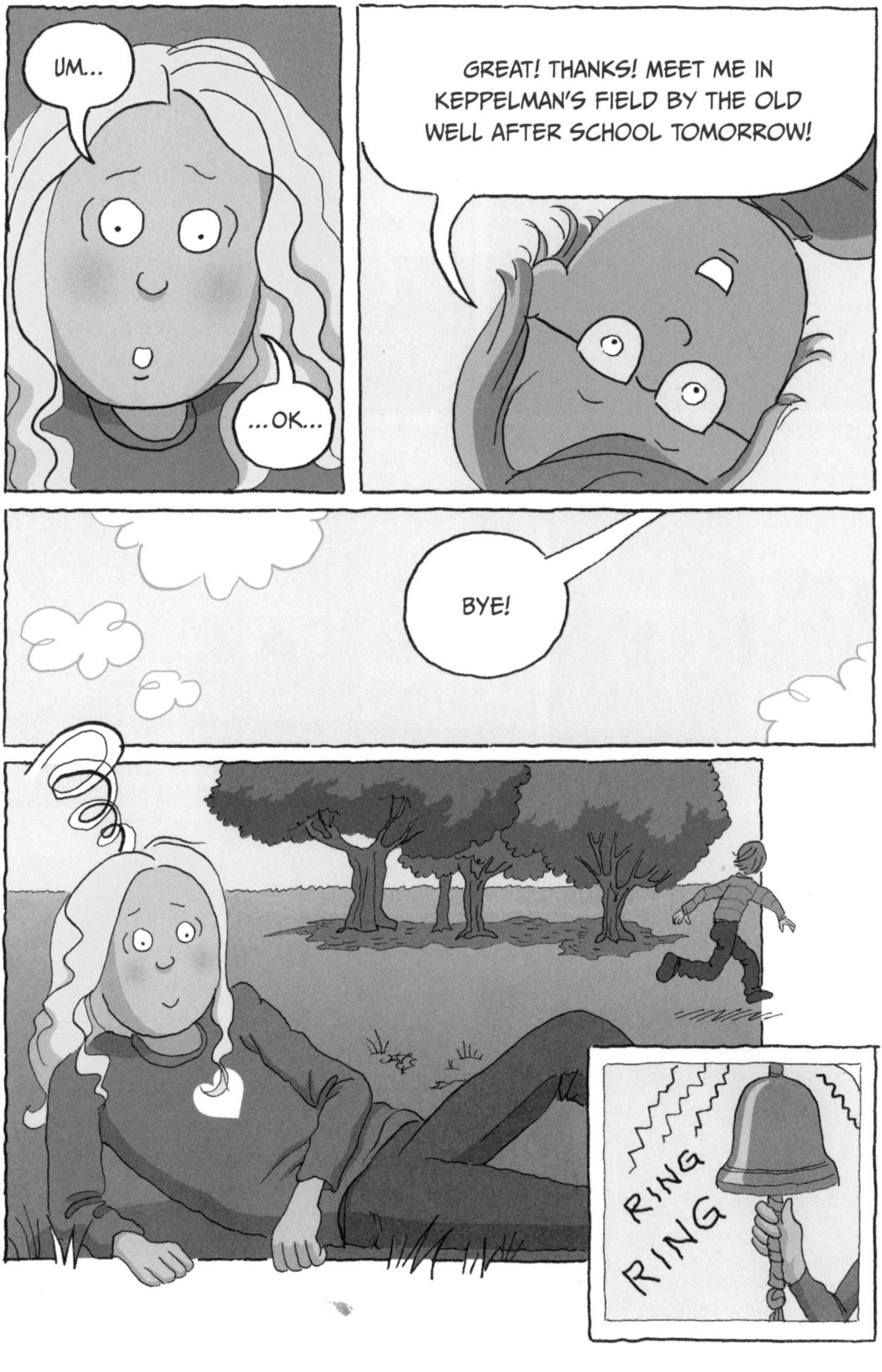
UM...
...OK...
GREAT! THANKS! MEET ME IN KEPPELMAN'S FIELD BY THE OLD WELL AFTER SCHOOL TOMORROW!
BYE!
RING
RING

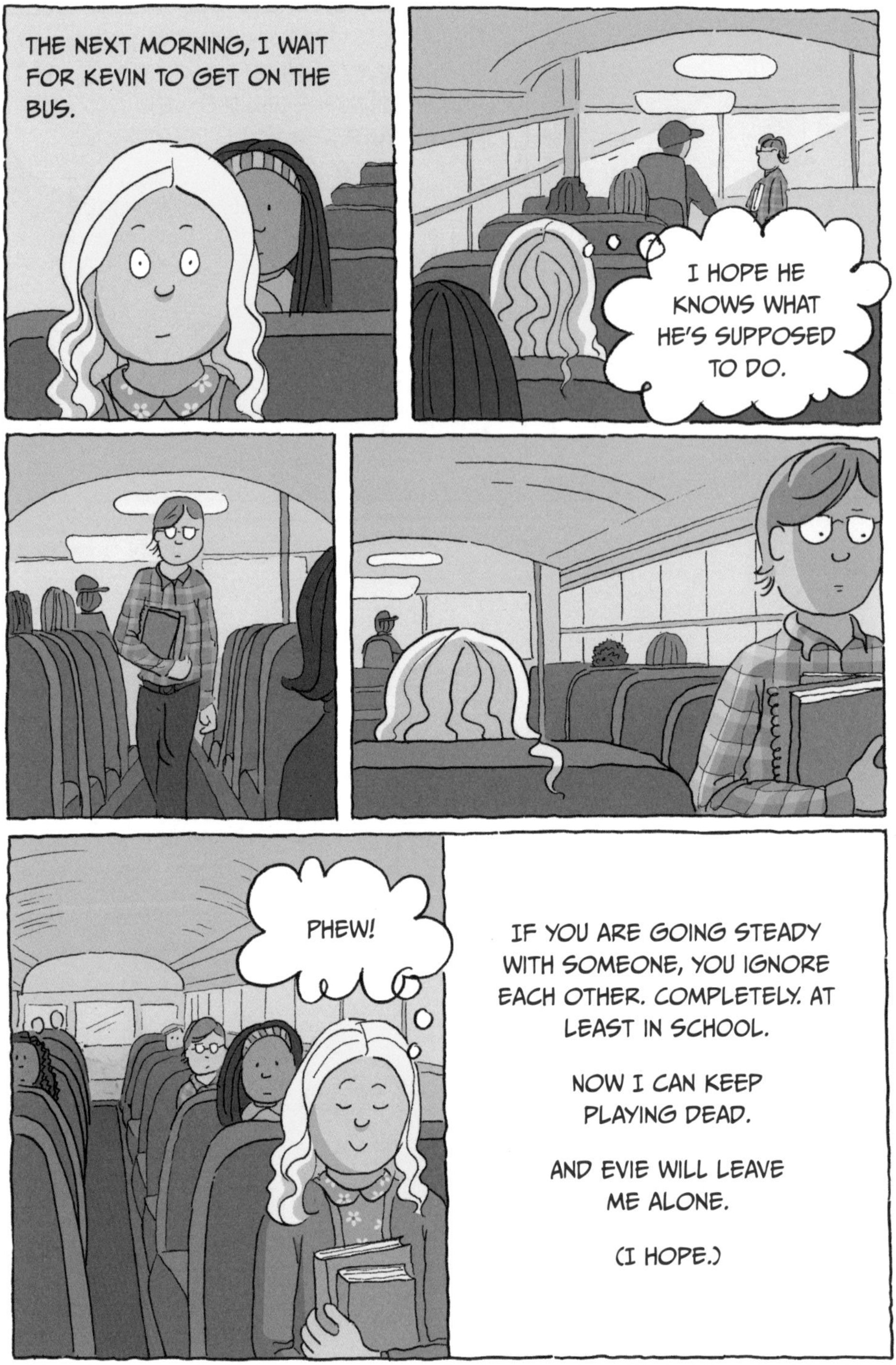
THE NEXT MORNING, I WAIT FOR KEVIN TO GET ON THE BUS.
I HOPE HE KNOWS WHAT HE'S SUPPOSED TO DO.
PHEW!
IF YOU ARE GOING STEADY WITH SOMEONE, YOU IGNORE EACH OTHER. COMPLETELY. AT LEAST IN SCHOOL.
NOW I CAN KEEP PLAYING DEAD.
AND EVIE WILL LEAVE ME ALONE.
(I HOPE.)

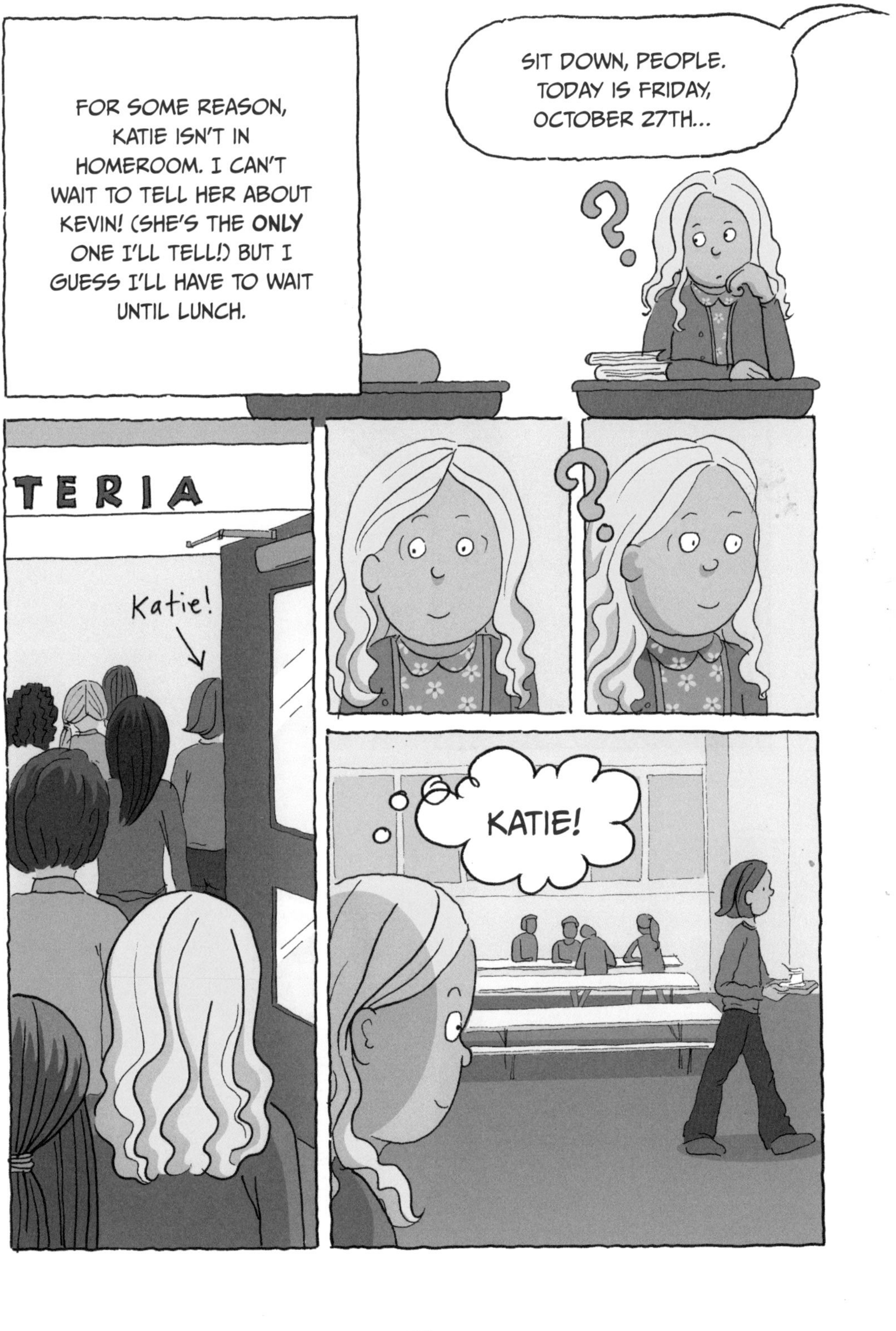
FOR SOME REASON, KATIE ISN'T IN HOMEROOM. I CAN'T WAIT TO TELL HER ABOUT KEVIN! (SHE'S THE **ONLY** ONE I'LL TELL!) BUT I GUESS I'LL HAVE TO WAIT UNTIL LUNCH.
SIT DOWN, PEOPLE. TODAY IS FRIDAY, OCTOBER 27TH...
TERIA
Katie!
KATIE!

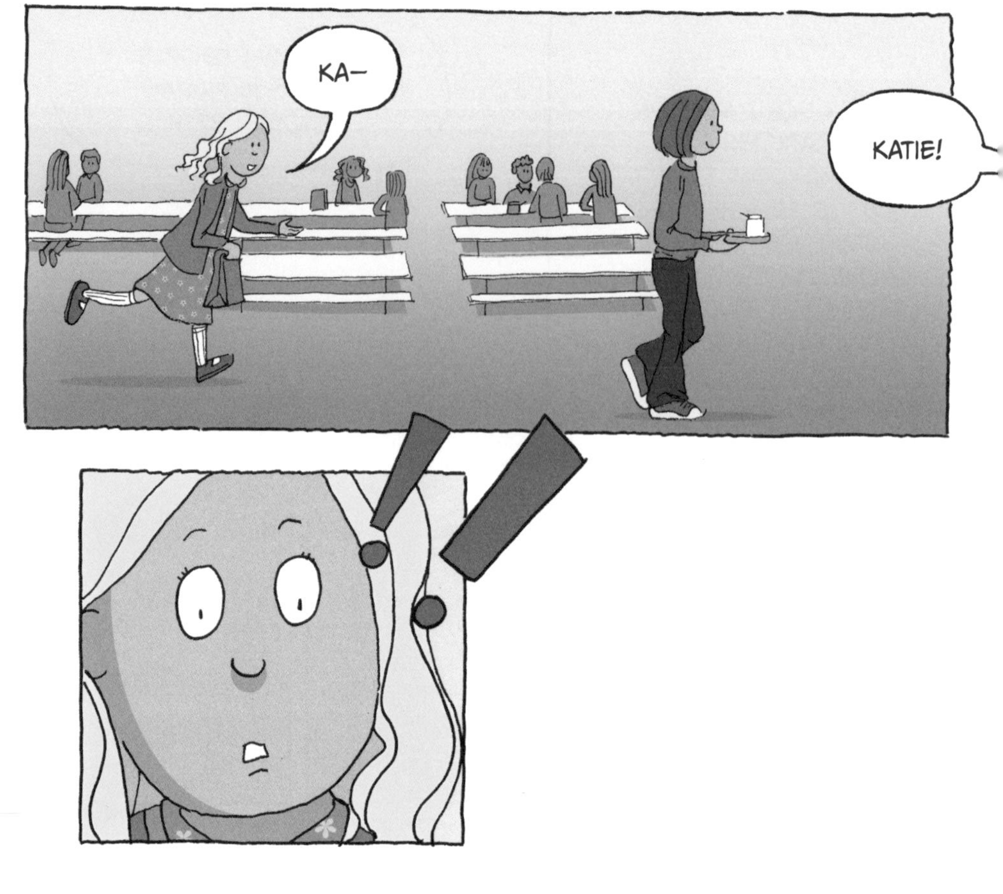
KA–
KATIE!

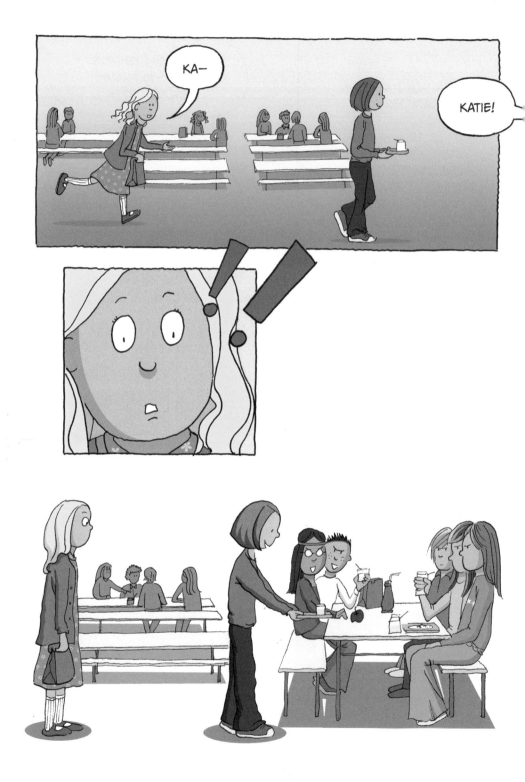

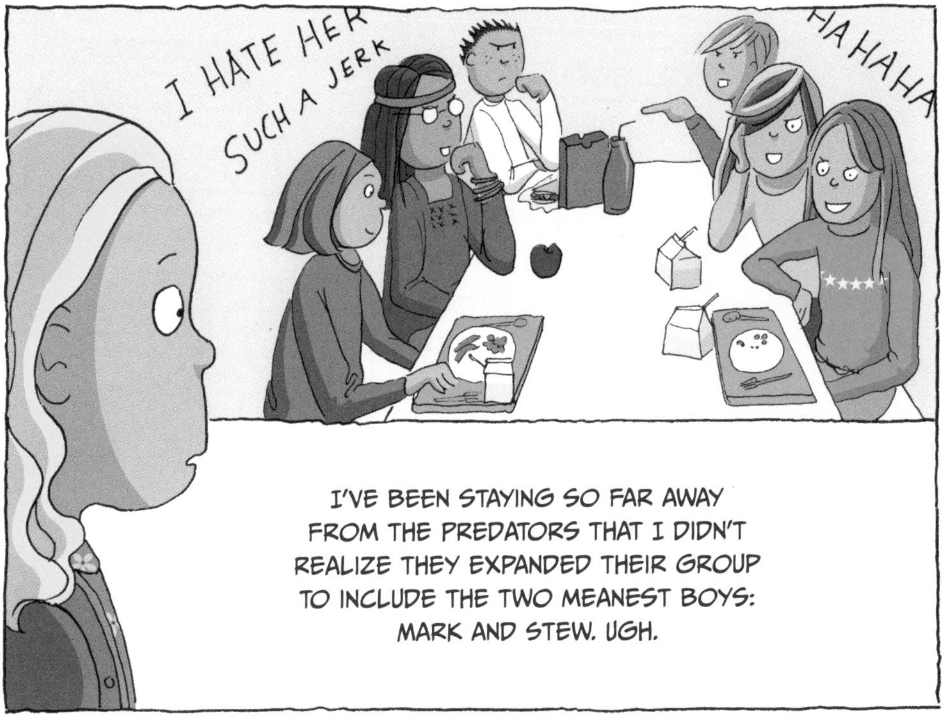
I HATE HER
SUCH A JERK
HAHAHAHA
I'VE BEEN STAYING SO FAR AWAY FROM THE PREDATORS THAT I DIDN'T REALIZE THEY EXPANDED THEIR GROUP TO INCLUDE THE TWO MEANEST BOYS: MARK AND STEW. UGH.

NOW WHAT?!

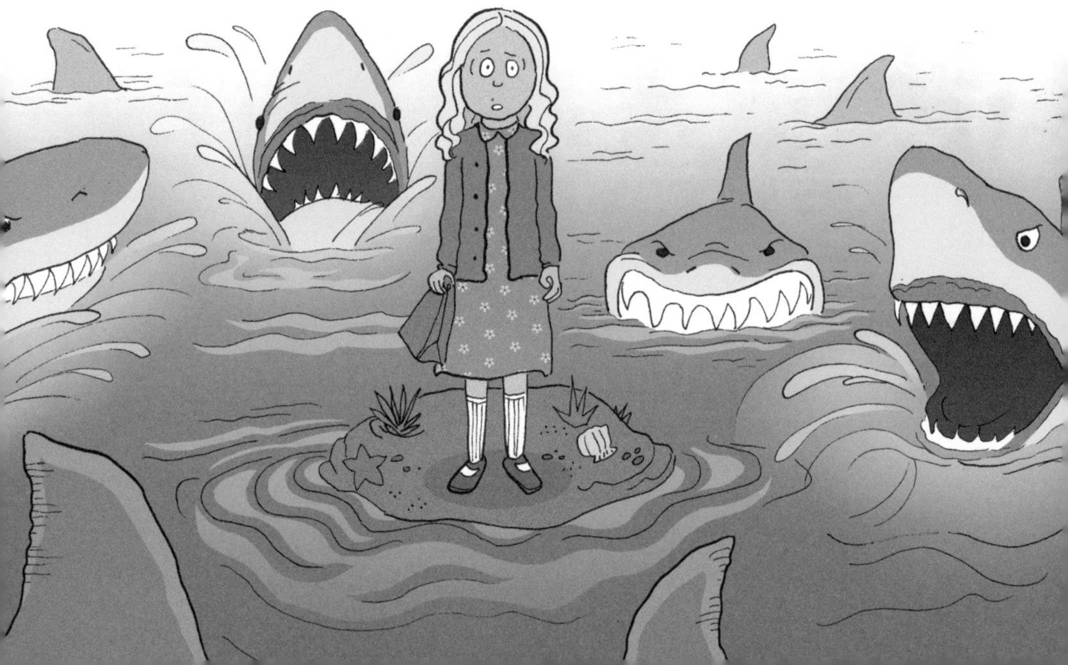

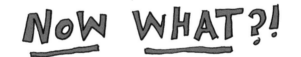

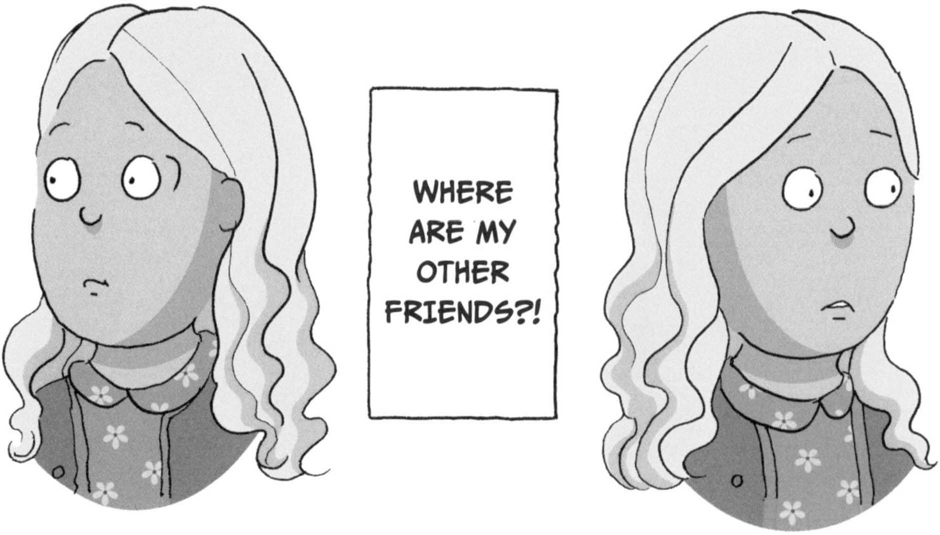
WHERE ARE MY OTHER FRIENDS?!

MOLLY MUST HAVE GONE TO SEÑORITA BERKOWITZ'S ROOM FOR EXTRA HELP IN SPANISH...IS BARB SELLING DONUTS FOR STUDENT COUNCIL? OR DOES SHE ONLY DO THAT *BEFORE* SCHOOL? I DON'T SEE PENNY, MY FRIEND FROM NATURE CAMP AND GIRL SCOUTS...

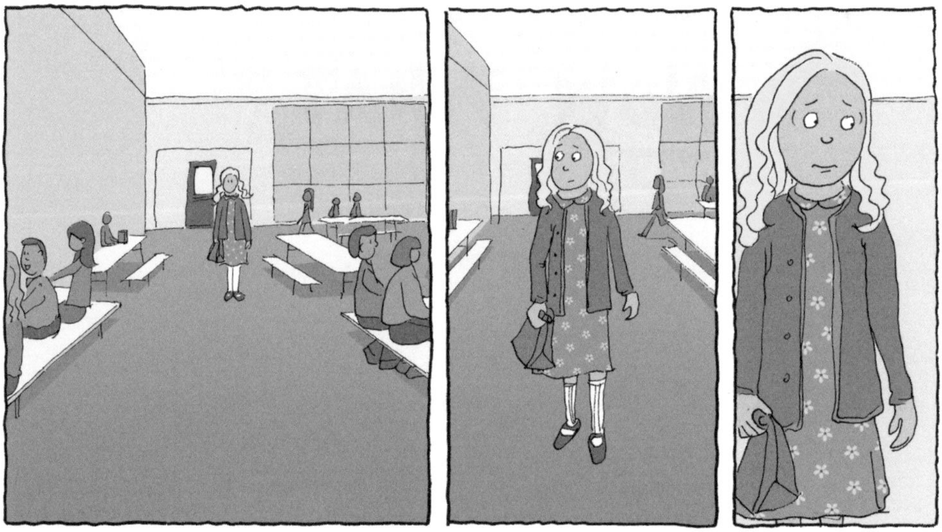

I DON'T SEE ANYONE I CAN SIT WITH...
I'M RUNNING OUT OF OPTIONS...

AND STARTING TO PANIC...

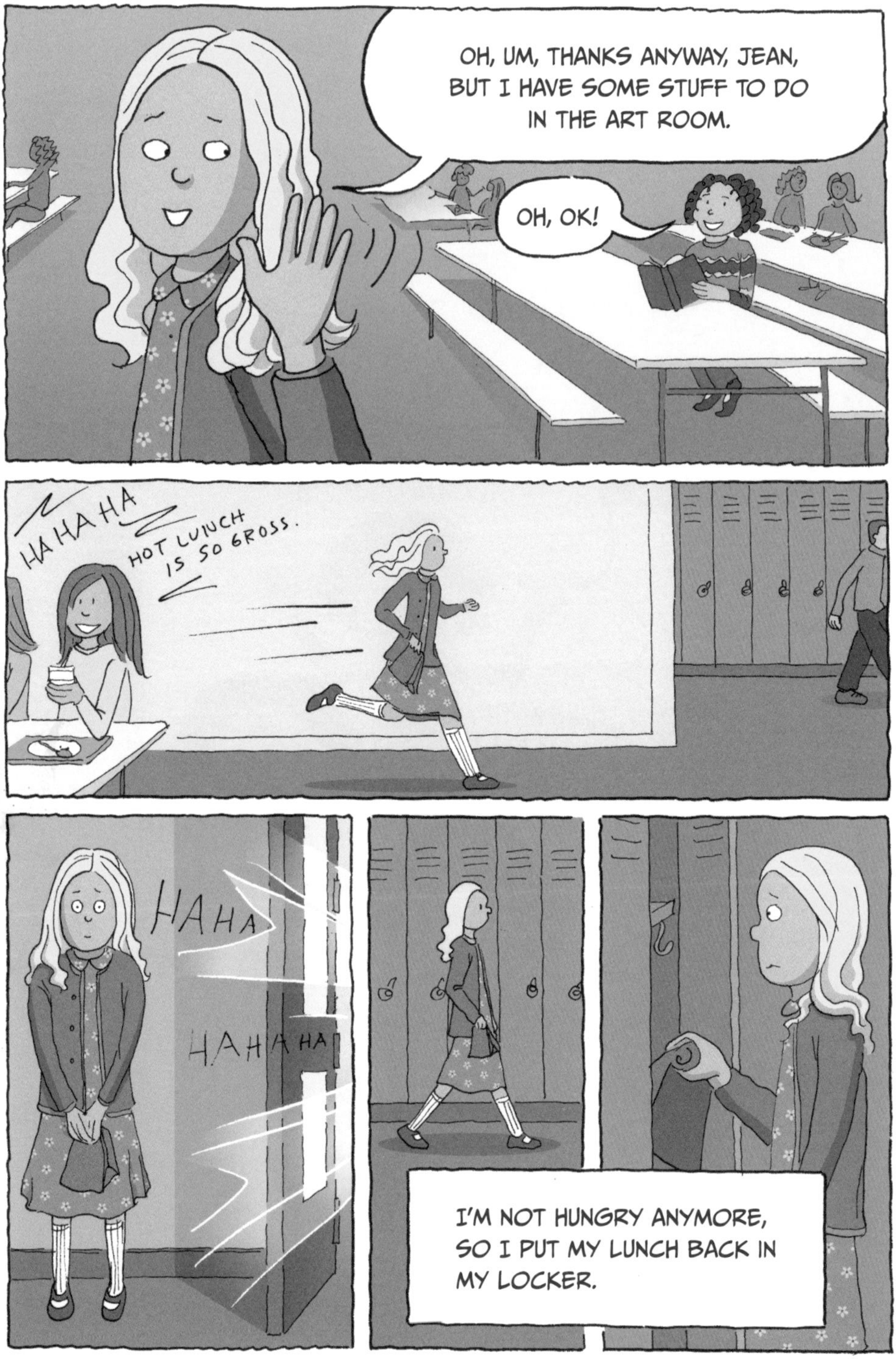
OH, UM, THANKS ANYWAY, JEAN, BUT I HAVE SOME STUFF TO DO IN THE ART ROOM.
OH, OK!
HAHAHA
HOT LUNCH IS SO GROSS.
HAHA
HAHAHA
I'M NOT HUNGRY ANYMORE, SO I PUT MY LUNCH BACK IN MY LOCKER.

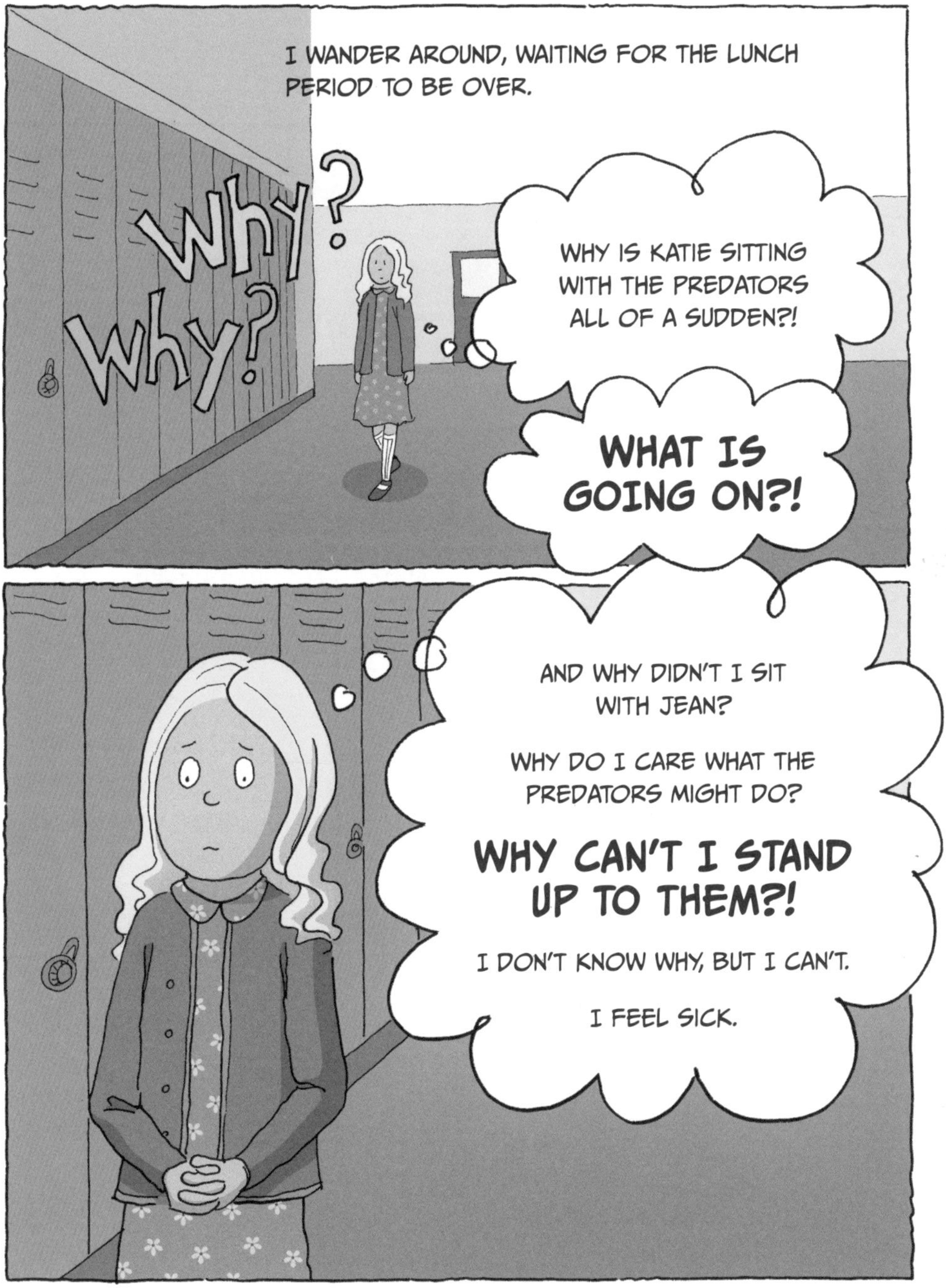
I WANDER AROUND, WAITING FOR THE LUNCH PERIOD TO BE OVER.
WHY? WHY?
WHY IS KATIE SITTING WITH THE PREDATORS ALL OF A SUDDEN?!
WHAT IS GOING ON?!
AND WHY DIDN'T I SIT WITH JEAN?
WHY DO I CARE WHAT THE PREDATORS MIGHT DO?
WHY CAN'T I STAND UP TO THEM?!
I DON'T KNOW WHY, BUT I CAN'T.
I FEEL SICK.

SEVENTEEN MINUTES FEELS SHORT WHEN I'M EATING LUNCH WITH KATIE BUT **VERY LONG** WHEN I'M PACING AND WORRYING.

I HAVE TO WAIT *TWO WHOLE PERIODS* BEFORE I CAN TALK TO KATIE IN ART CLASS.

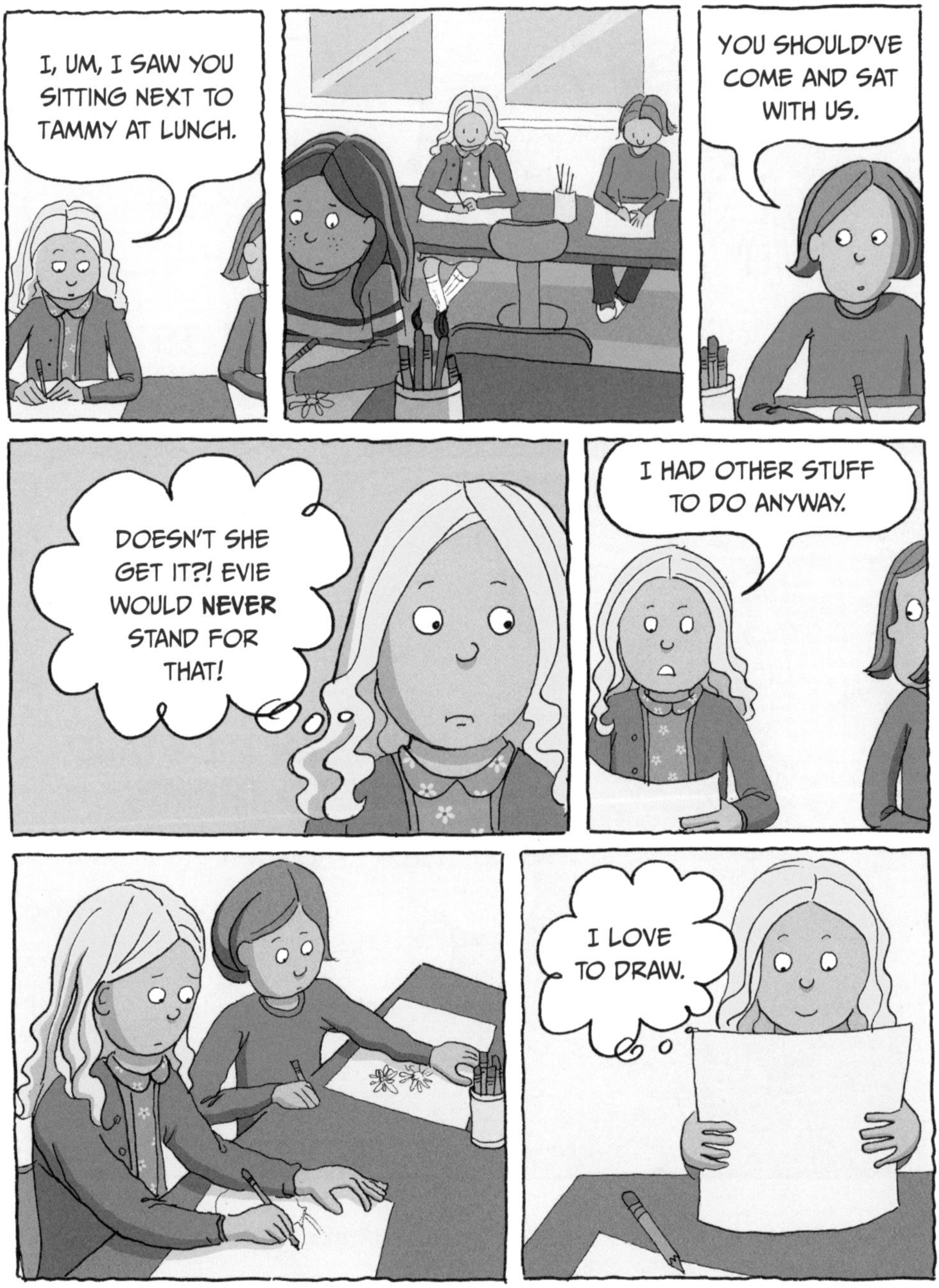
I, UM, I SAW YOU SITTING NEXT TO TAMMY AT LUNCH.
YOU SHOULD'VE COME AND SAT WITH US.
DOESN'T SHE GET IT?! EVIE WOULD **NEVER** STAND FOR THAT!
I HAD OTHER STUFF TO DO ANYWAY.
I LOVE TO DRAW.

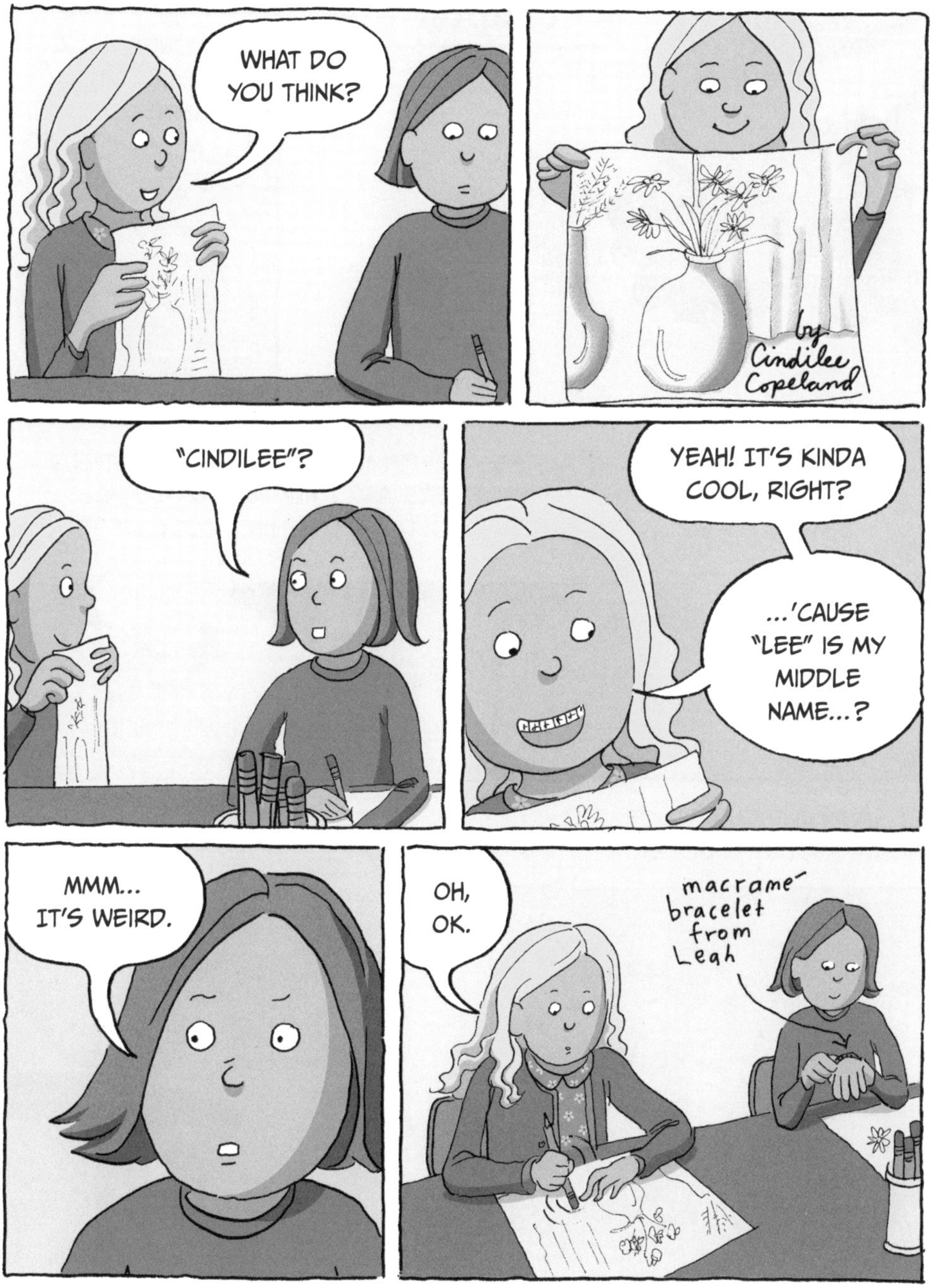
WHAT DO YOU THINK?
by Cindilee Copeland
"CINDILEE"?
YEAH! IT'S KINDA COOL, RIGHT?
...'CAUSE "LEE" IS MY MIDDLE NAME...?
MMM... IT'S WEIRD.
OH, OK.
macrame bracelet from Leah

I FORGET TO TELL HER ABOUT KEVIN.

Chapter 6

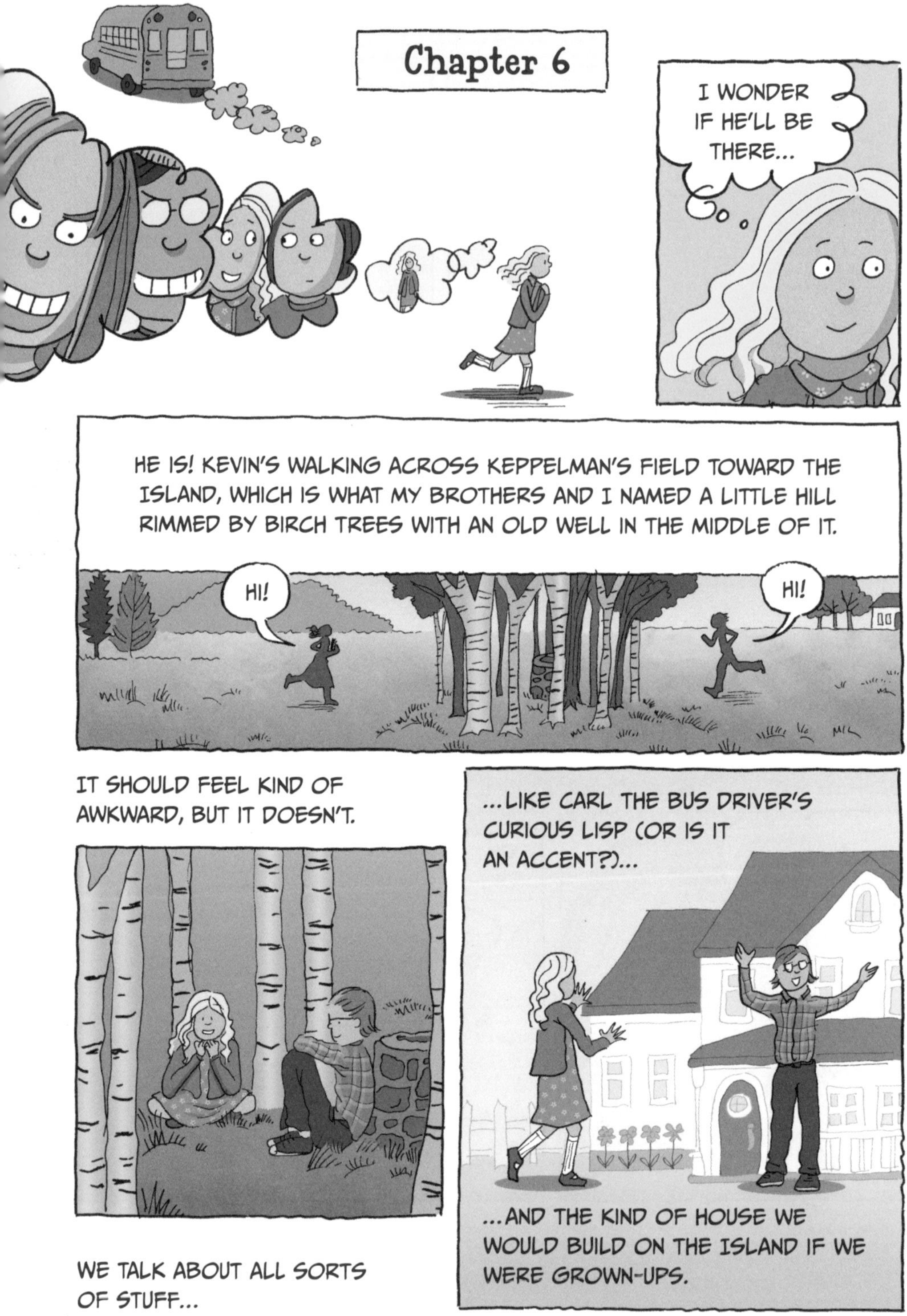

I WONDER IF HE'LL BE THERE...
HE IS! KEVIN'S WALKING ACROSS KEPPELMAN'S FIELD TOWARD THE ISLAND, WHICH IS WHAT MY BROTHERS AND I NAMED A LITTLE HILL RIMMED BY BIRCH TREES WITH AN OLD WELL IN THE MIDDLE OF IT.
HI!
HI!
IT SHOULD FEEL KIND OF AWKWARD, BUT IT DOESN'T.
WE TALK ABOUT ALL SORTS OF STUFF...
...LIKE CARL THE BUS DRIVER'S CURIOUS LISP (OR IS IT AN ACCENT?)...
...AND THE KIND OF HOUSE WE WOULD BUILD ON THE ISLAND IF WE WERE GROWN-UPS.

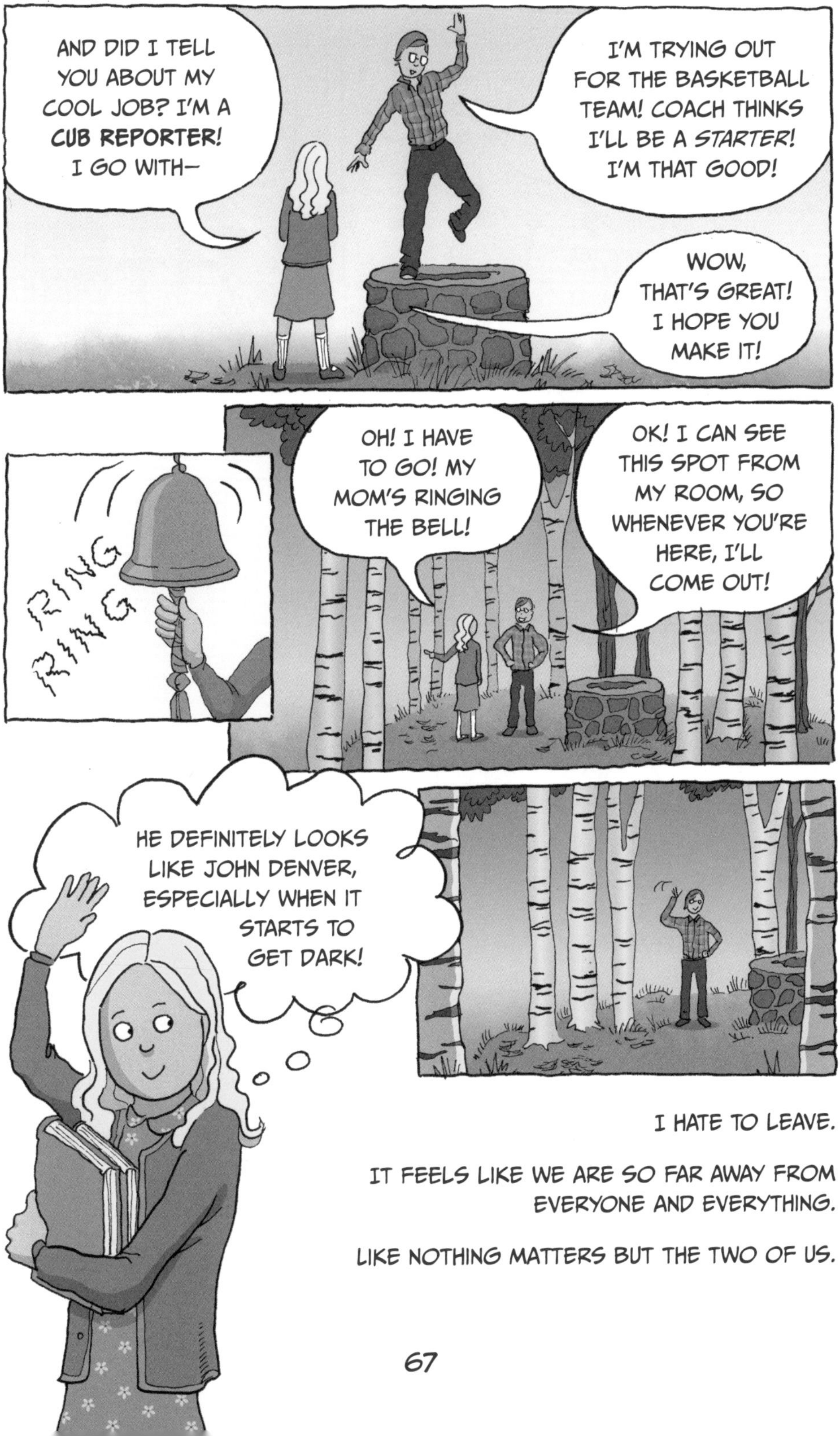
AND DID I TELL YOU ABOUT MY COOL JOB? I'M A **CUB REPORTER!** I GO WITH—
I'M TRYING OUT FOR THE BASKETBALL TEAM! COACH THINKS I'LL BE A *STARTER!* I'M THAT GOOD!
WOW, THAT'S GREAT! I HOPE YOU MAKE IT!
RING RING
OH! I HAVE TO GO! MY MOM'S RINGING THE BELL!
OK! I CAN SEE THIS SPOT FROM MY ROOM, SO WHENEVER YOU'RE HERE, I'LL COME OUT!
HE DEFINITELY LOOKS LIKE JOHN DENVER, ESPECIALLY WHEN IT STARTS TO GET DARK!
I HATE TO LEAVE.
IT FEELS LIKE WE ARE SO FAR AWAY FROM EVERYONE AND EVERYTHING.
LIKE NOTHING MATTERS BUT THE TWO OF US.

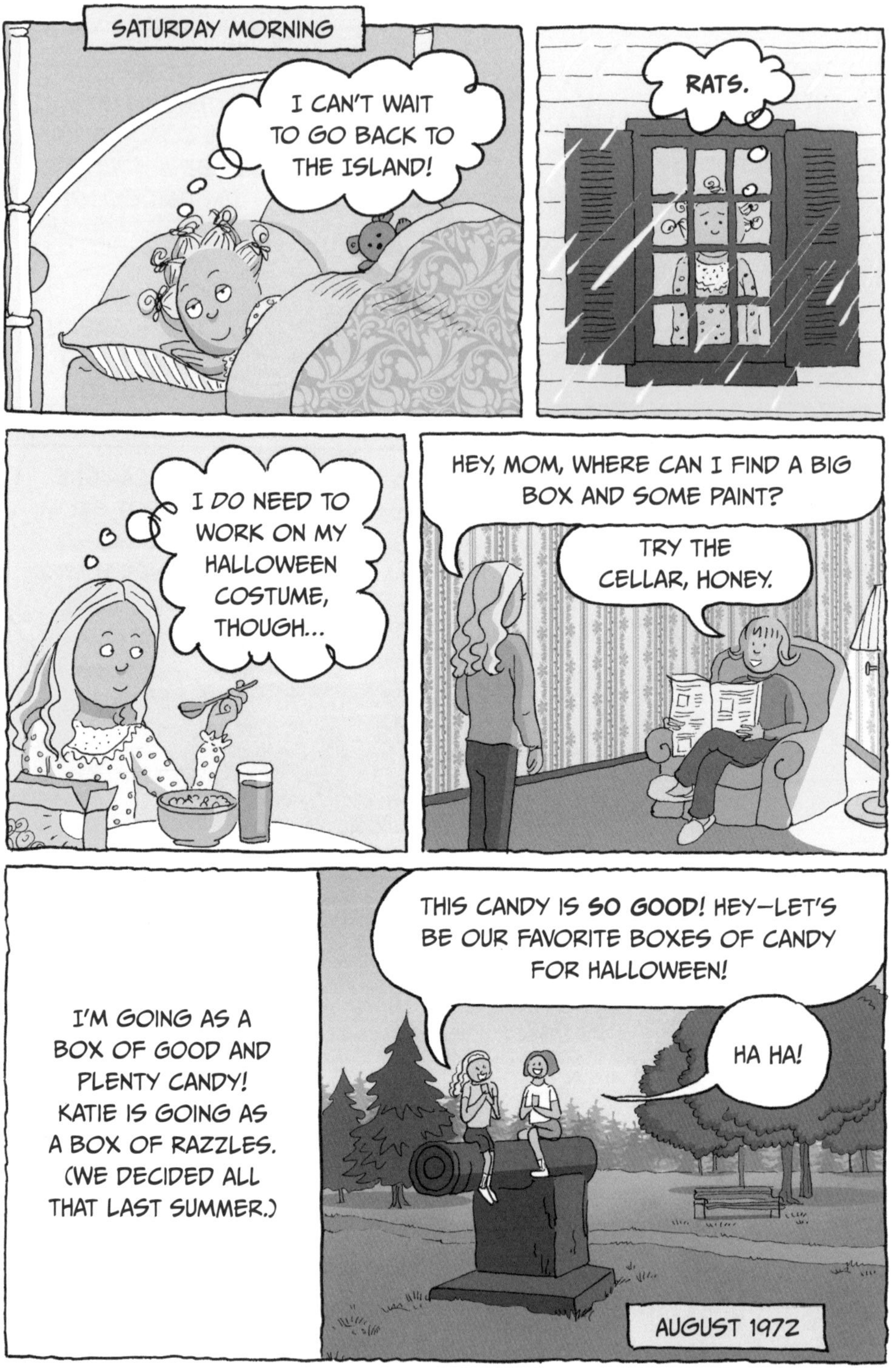
SATURDAY MORNING
I CAN'T WAIT TO GO BACK TO THE ISLAND!
RATS.
I *DO* NEED TO WORK ON MY HALLOWEEN COSTUME, THOUGH...
HEY, MOM, WHERE CAN I FIND A BIG BOX AND SOME PAINT?
TRY THE CELLAR, HONEY.
I'M GOING AS A BOX OF GOOD AND PLENTY CANDY! KATIE IS GOING AS A BOX OF RAZZLES. (WE DECIDED ALL THAT LAST SUMMER.)
THIS CANDY IS **SO GOOD!** HEY—LET'S BE OUR FAVORITE BOXES OF CANDY FOR HALLOWEEN!
HA HA!
AUGUST 1972

WE ALWAYS GO TRICK-OR-TREATING IN COSTUMES THAT GO TOGETHER.

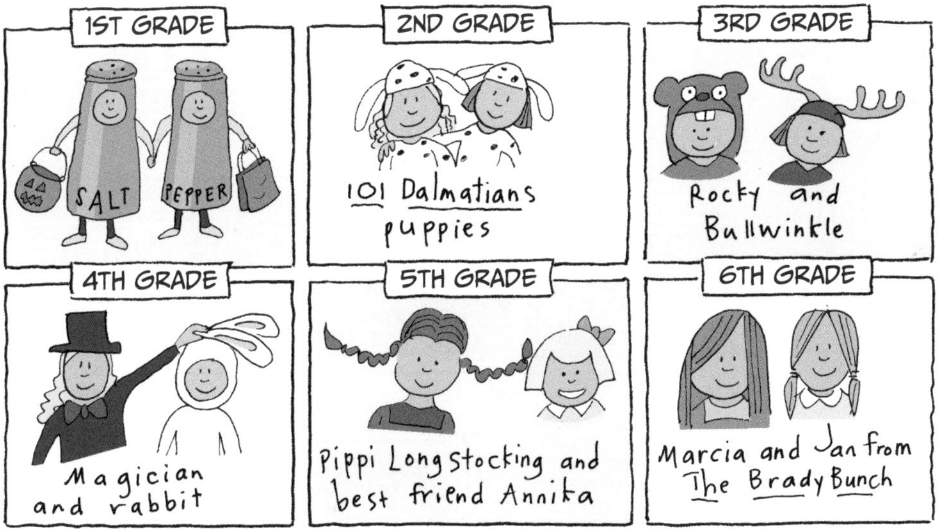
1ST GRADE
SALT
PEPPER
2ND GRADE
101 Dalmatians puppies
3RD GRADE
Rocky and Bullwinkle
4TH GRADE
Magician and rabbit
5TH GRADE
Pippi Longstocking and best friend Annika
6TH GRADE
Marcia and Jan from The Brady Bunch

AND NOW... **SEVENTH GRADE!**

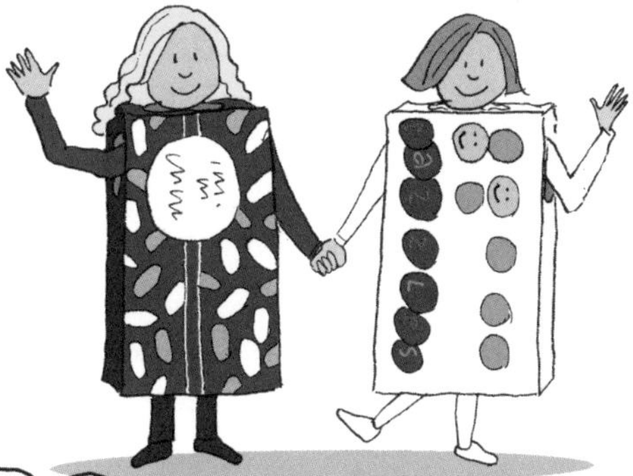

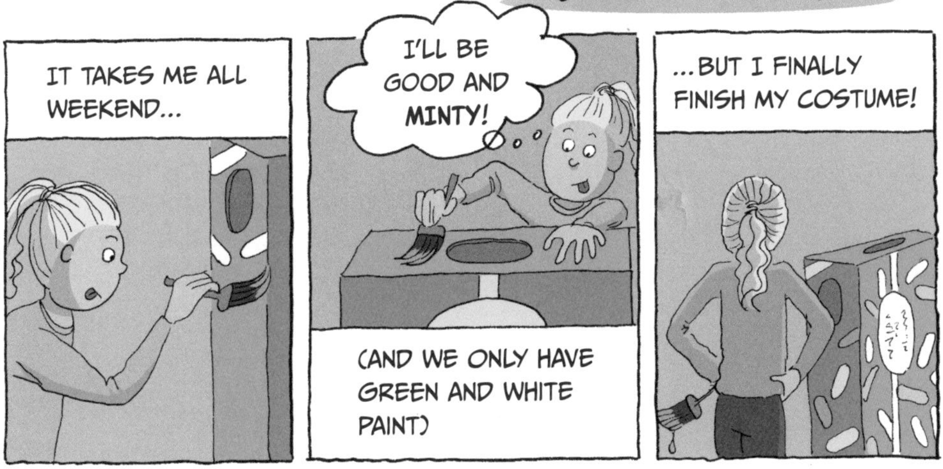
IT TAKES ME ALL WEEKEND...
I'LL BE GOOD AND **MINTY!**
(AND WE ONLY HAVE GREEN AND WHITE PAINT)
...BUT I FINALLY FINISH MY COSTUME!

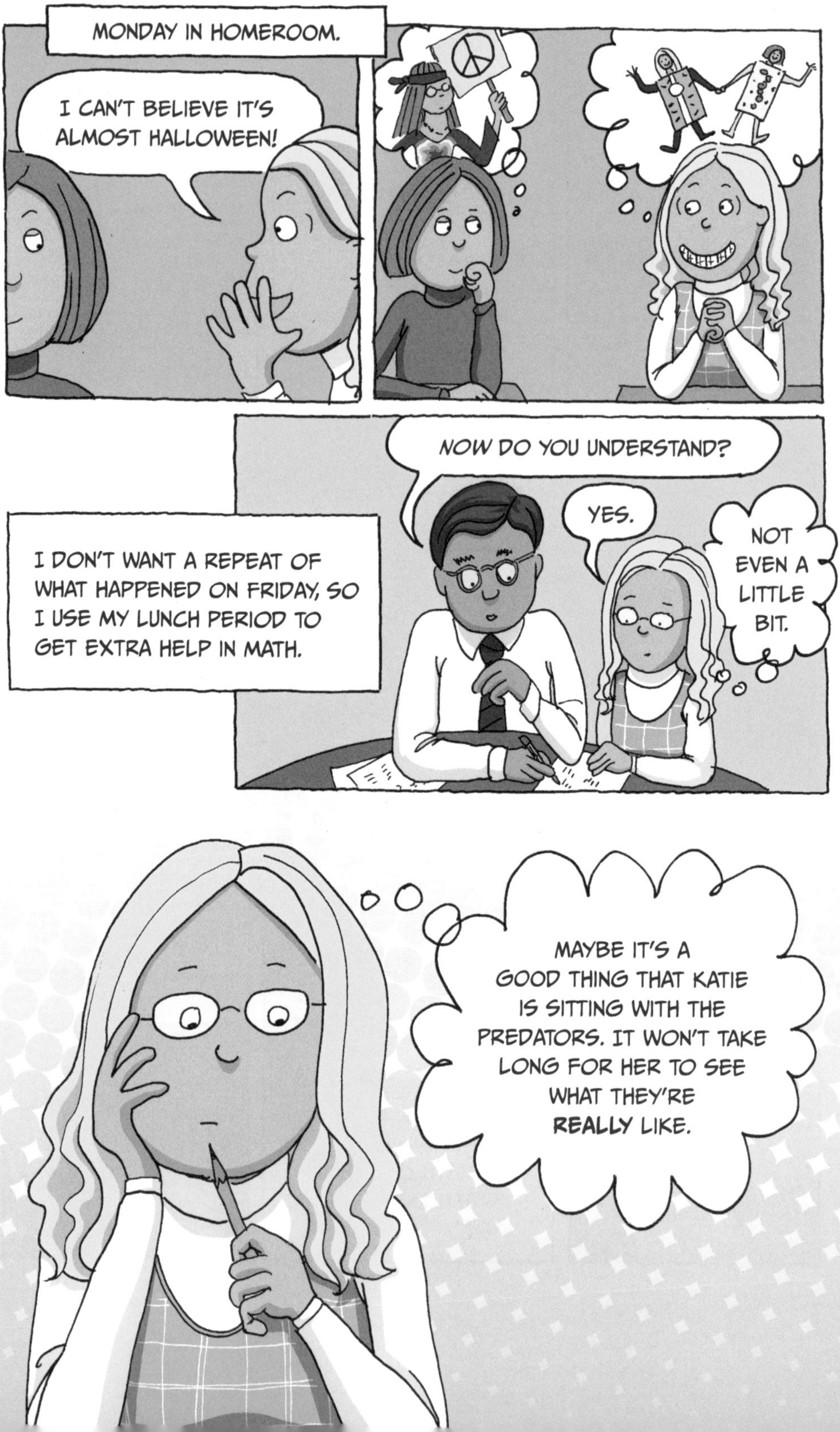
MONDAY IN HOMEROOM.
I CAN'T BELIEVE IT'S ALMOST HALLOWEEN!
NOW DO YOU UNDERSTAND?
I DON'T WANT A REPEAT OF WHAT HAPPENED ON FRIDAY, SO I USE MY LUNCH PERIOD TO GET EXTRA HELP IN MATH.
YES.
NOT EVEN A LITTLE BIT.
MAYBE IT'S A GOOD THING THAT KATIE IS SITTING WITH THE PREDATORS. IT WON'T TAKE LONG FOR HER TO SEE WHAT THEY'RE **REALLY** LIKE.

71

73

75

ON OUR WAY TO TOWN HALL, LESLIE ONLY WANTS TO TALK ABOUT THE ELECTION. I HAVE MORE IMPORTANT THINGS ON MY MIND. AT LEAST AT FIRST.

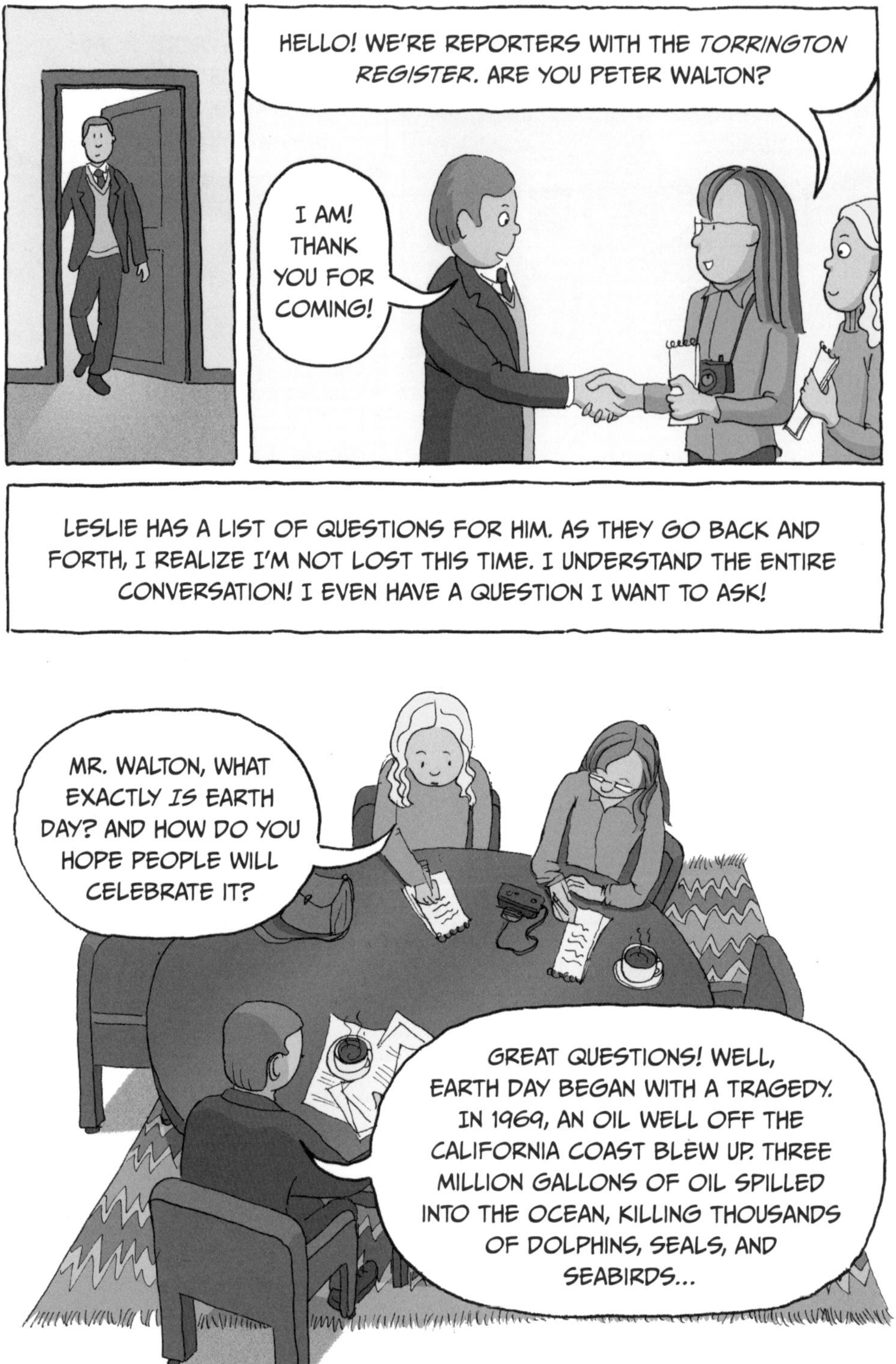
HELLO! WE'RE REPORTERS WITH THE *TORRINGTON REGISTER*. ARE YOU PETER WALTON?
I AM! THANK YOU FOR COMING!
LESLIE HAS A LIST OF QUESTIONS FOR HIM. AS THEY GO BACK AND FORTH, I REALIZE I'M NOT LOST THIS TIME. I UNDERSTAND THE ENTIRE CONVERSATION! I EVEN HAVE A QUESTION I WANT TO ASK!
MR. WALTON, WHAT EXACTLY *IS* EARTH DAY? AND HOW DO YOU HOPE PEOPLE WILL CELEBRATE IT?
GREAT QUESTIONS! WELL, EARTH DAY BEGAN WITH A TRAGEDY. IN 1969, AN OIL WELL OFF THE CALIFORNIA COAST BLEW UP. THREE MILLION GALLONS OF OIL SPILLED INTO THE OCEAN, KILLING THOUSANDS OF DOLPHINS, SEALS, AND SEABIRDS...

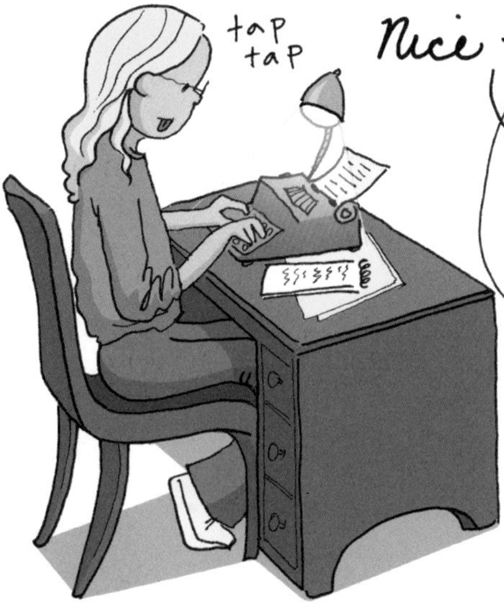
tap
tap
Nice lede!

The dedicated volunteers who have been operating a make-shift recycling center on Goshen Road want town selectmen to pass a law forcing people to recycle glass and paper.

According to Peter Walton, the chairman of Eco-Action, which runs the center, the volunteer effort proves that there is local interest in recycling. The center is open 24 hours a day, with signs directing people to drop off glass (sorted by color) at a large barn and clean waste paper at a small shed. About 5,000 pounds of glass are crushed at the center every week, he reported.

"The state has said that the dump will be full within two years," Walton said. "I would like to see a government organization handle recycling, but in the meantime, there are many volunteers willing to take on the job."

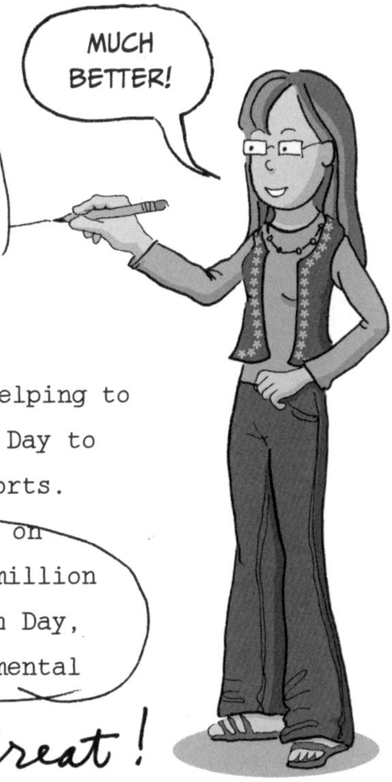
MUCH
BETTER!
Great!

Walton said that Eco-Action will be helping to organize a parade in the spring on Earth Day to help publicize the group's recycling efforts.

Earth Day is a national event focused on protecting the environment. In 1970, 20 million Americans demonstrated on the first Earth Day, which led to the creation of the Environmental Protection Agency.

THANK GOODNESS THINGS ARE GOING WELL *OUTSIDE* OF SCHOOL. BECAUSE RIGHT NOW, BEING *IN* SCHOOL GIVES ME A STOMACHACHE.

TOO MUCH STUFF IS CHANGING.
IT'S JUST... CONFUSING.

NOW KATIE HANGS OUT WITH THE PREDATORS EVERY MORNING IN THE
ELEVATOR ALCOVE. AND SHE ALWAYS SITS WITH THEM AT LUNCH, TOO.

BUT THEN SOMETIMES IT'S LIKE IT ALWAYS WAS. LIKE *NOTHING* HAS CHANGED.

AND *THAT'S* CONFUSING, TOO.

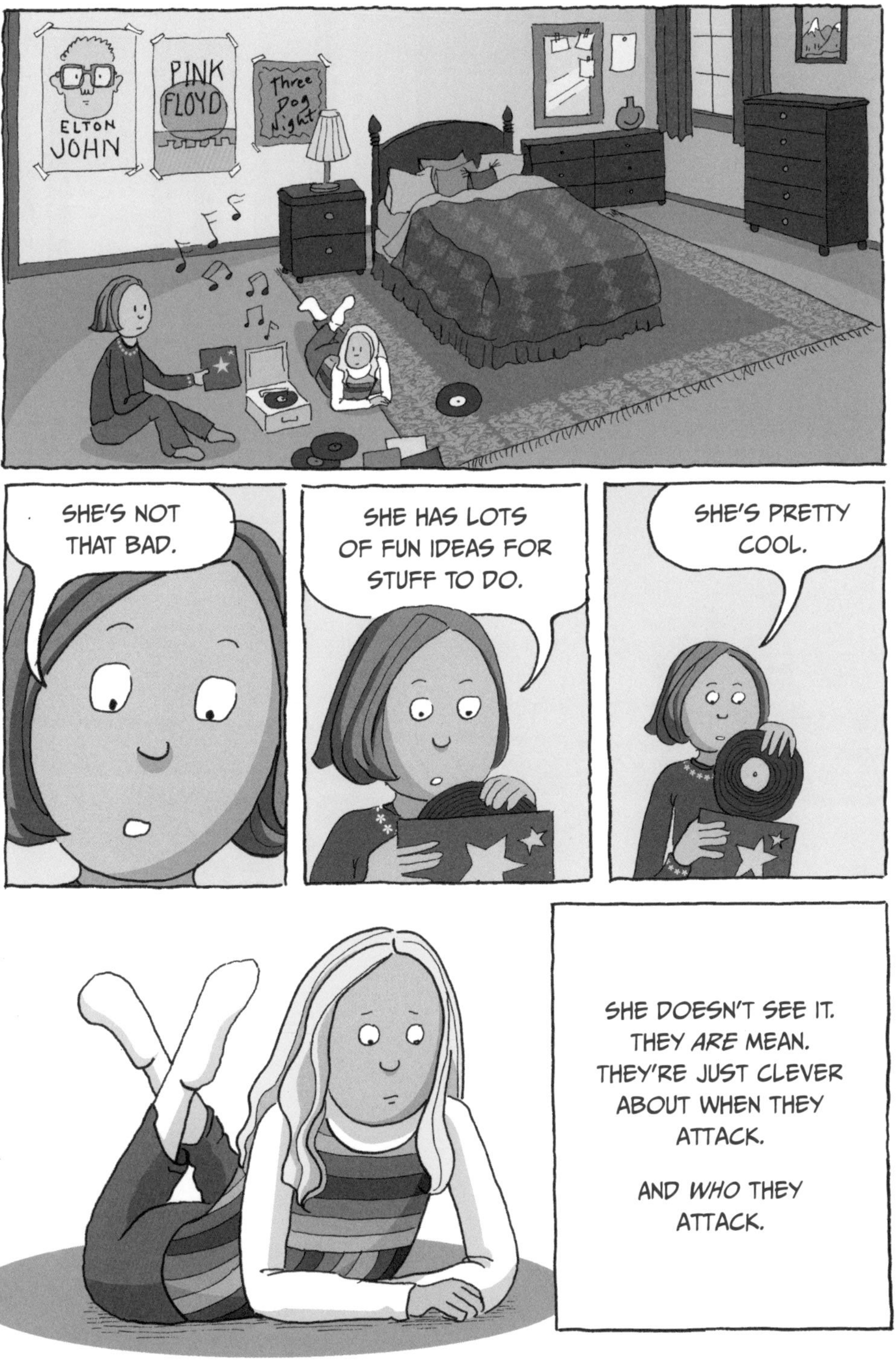
ELTON JOHN
PINK FLOYD
Three Dog Night
SHE'S NOT THAT BAD.
SHE HAS LOTS OF FUN IDEAS FOR STUFF TO DO.
SHE'S PRETTY COOL.
SHE DOESN'T SEE IT. THEY *ARE* MEAN. THEY'RE JUST CLEVER ABOUT WHEN THEY ATTACK.
AND *WHO* THEY ATTACK.

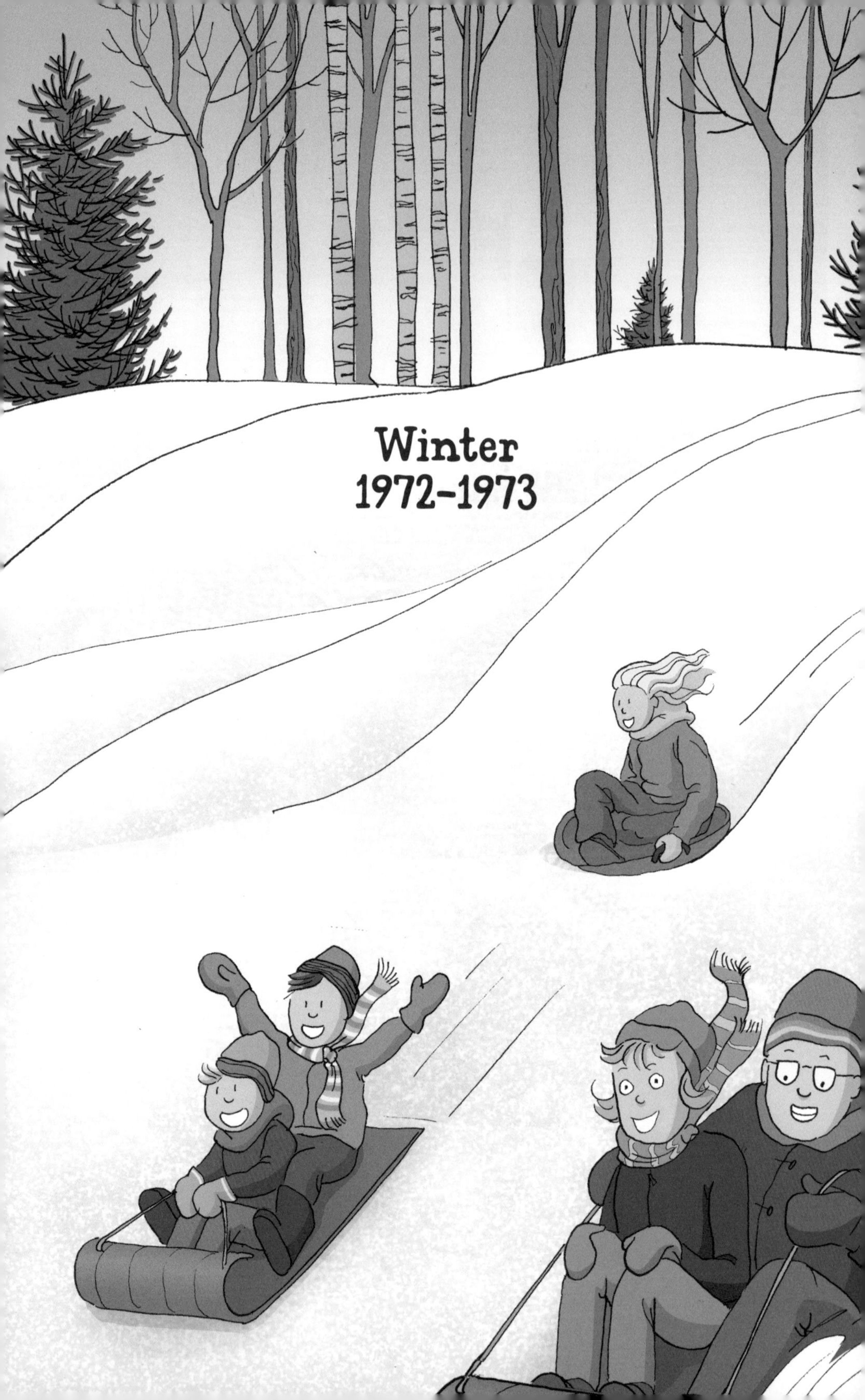
Winter
1972–1973

93

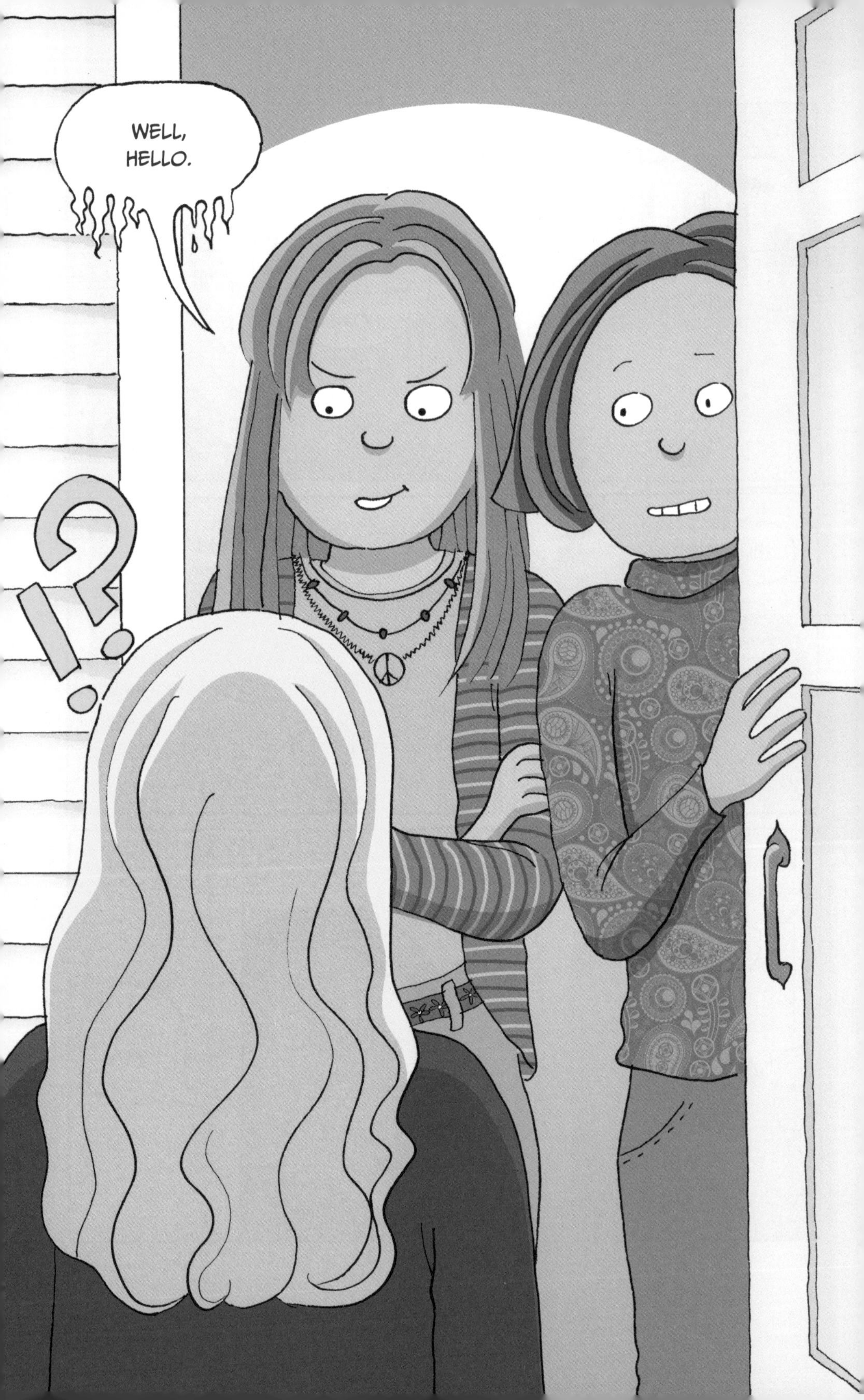
WELL, HELLO.
?!

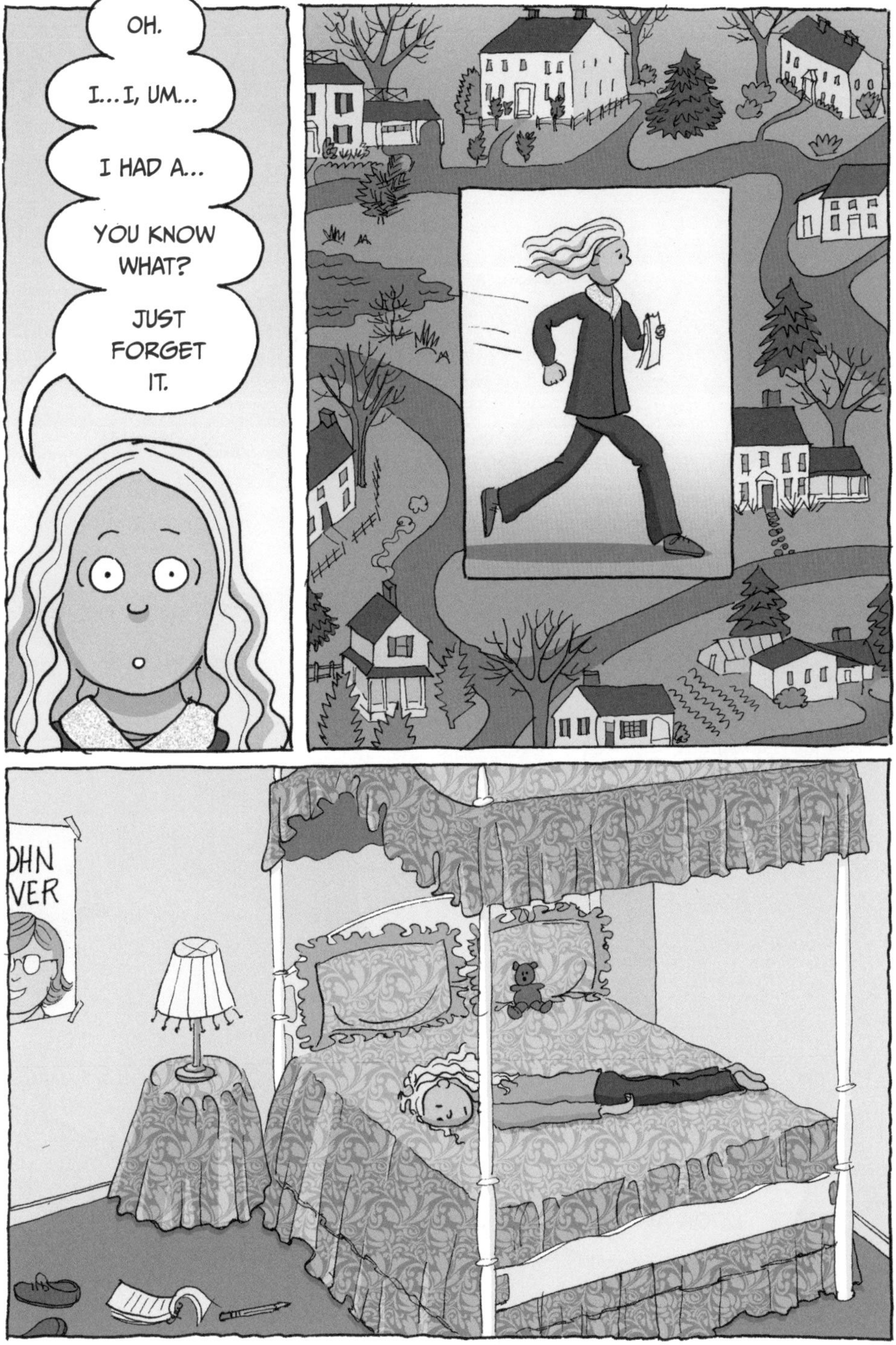
OH.
I... I, UM...
I HAD A...
YOU KNOW WHAT?
JUST FORGET IT.

WHEN YOU SEE EACH OTHER ONLY A COUPLE OF TIMES A YEAR, THERE'S A LOT OF SHOWING OFF THAT HAPPENS.

Chapter 9

BECAUSE IT'S THE HOLIDAY SEASON, LESLIE AND I HAVE LOTS OF CHRISTMAS AND HANUKKAH EVENTS TO COVER.

101

PHOTOGRAPHY FOR BEGINNERS

Tips for beginners

Interesting light can make a good photograph *great.* Try taking photos one hour *before* sunset or *after* sunrise: photography's "golden hour."

EXPERIMENT WITH DIFFERENT ANGLES! **Don't take every shot at eye level.** Try crouching or standing on a chair or climbing a staircase! Remember to rotate your camera so that some of your shots are vertical. See the world in a different way in order to create exciting images!

Learn the rules of photography so that you can break them intentionally as you become a better photographer!

Strong composition is the **most important** element of a great photo. You want your image to be eye-catching and you don't want viewers to be confused about what they should look at. Imagine your shot as a tic-tac-toe grid and place your subject on one of the spots where the lines intersect.

FOCUS ON YOUR SUBJECT'S EYES We are naturally drawn to a person's—or animal's—eyes in a photograph, so be sure that they are in focus.

Learn how to hold your camera to avoid blurry images: One hand should support the body of the camera; the other should hold the lens. Your elbows should be tight against your body. Just as you press the shutter-release button, hold your breath!

Look at great photographs for inspiration!
Visit an art gallery or look through books of photography. Think about what makes each photograph appealing, and imagine what techniques you can use yourself.

Zoom in and fill the frame! Your subject is important!

Keep both eyes open as you prepare to take a photo! You want to connect with your subject and also see what's happening outside of the frame: you may want to capture a dog that's just about to leap into view!

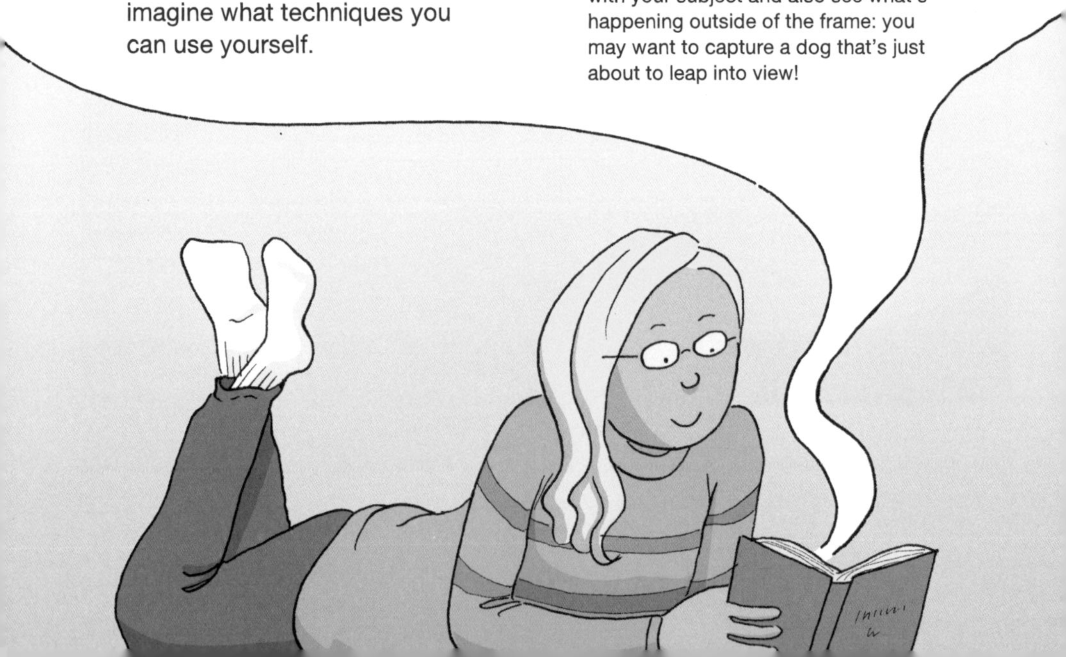

EVEN THOUGH THE BEST PRESENTS ARE ALWAYS THE ONES YOU DON'T EXPECT...

...I DO HOPE I'VE DROPPED ENOUGH HINTS ABOUT A CAMERA. I *NEED* ONE FOR MY *JOB!*

THE NEXT MORNING, SANTA DOES A PRETTY GOOD JOB WITH THE REST OF OUR PRESENTS.

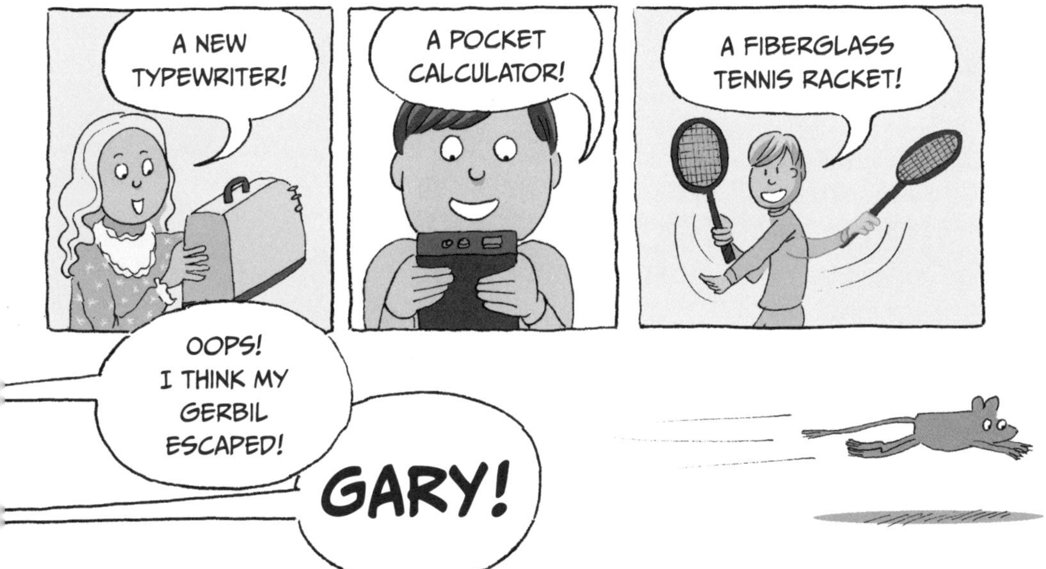
A NEW TYPEWRITER!
A POCKET CALCULATOR!
A FIBERGLASS TENNIS RACKET!
OOPS! I THINK MY GERBIL ESCAPED!
GARY!

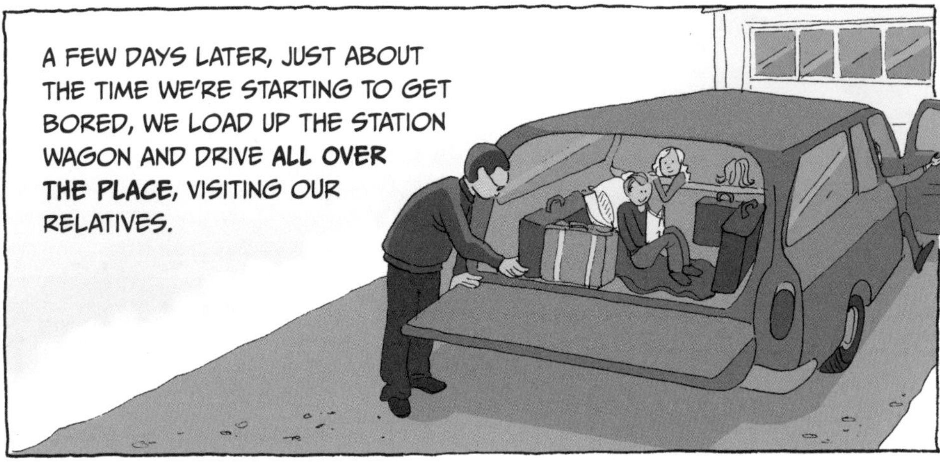
A FEW DAYS LATER, JUST ABOUT THE TIME WE'RE STARTING TO GET BORED, WE LOAD UP THE STATION WAGON AND DRIVE **ALL OVER THE PLACE**, VISITING OUR RELATIVES.

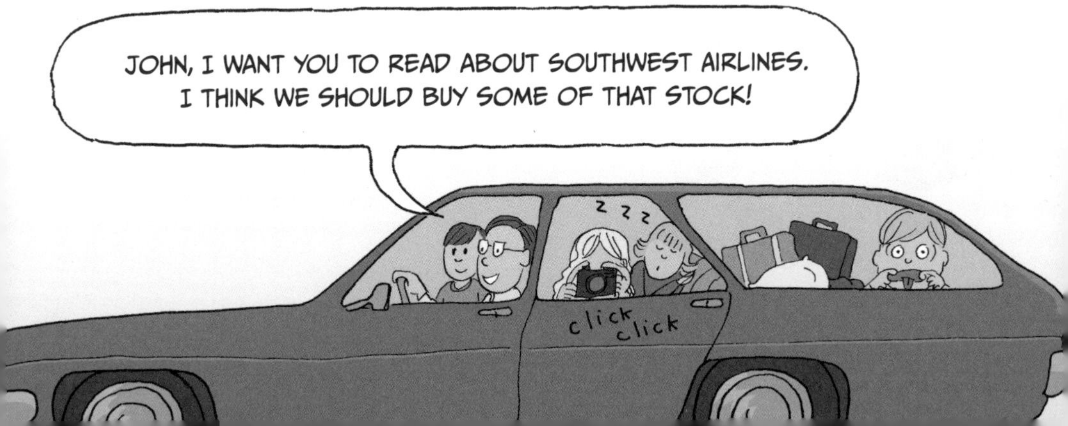
JOHN, I WANT YOU TO READ ABOUT SOUTHWEST AIRLINES. I THINK WE SHOULD BUY SOME OF THAT STOCK!
Z Z Z
click click

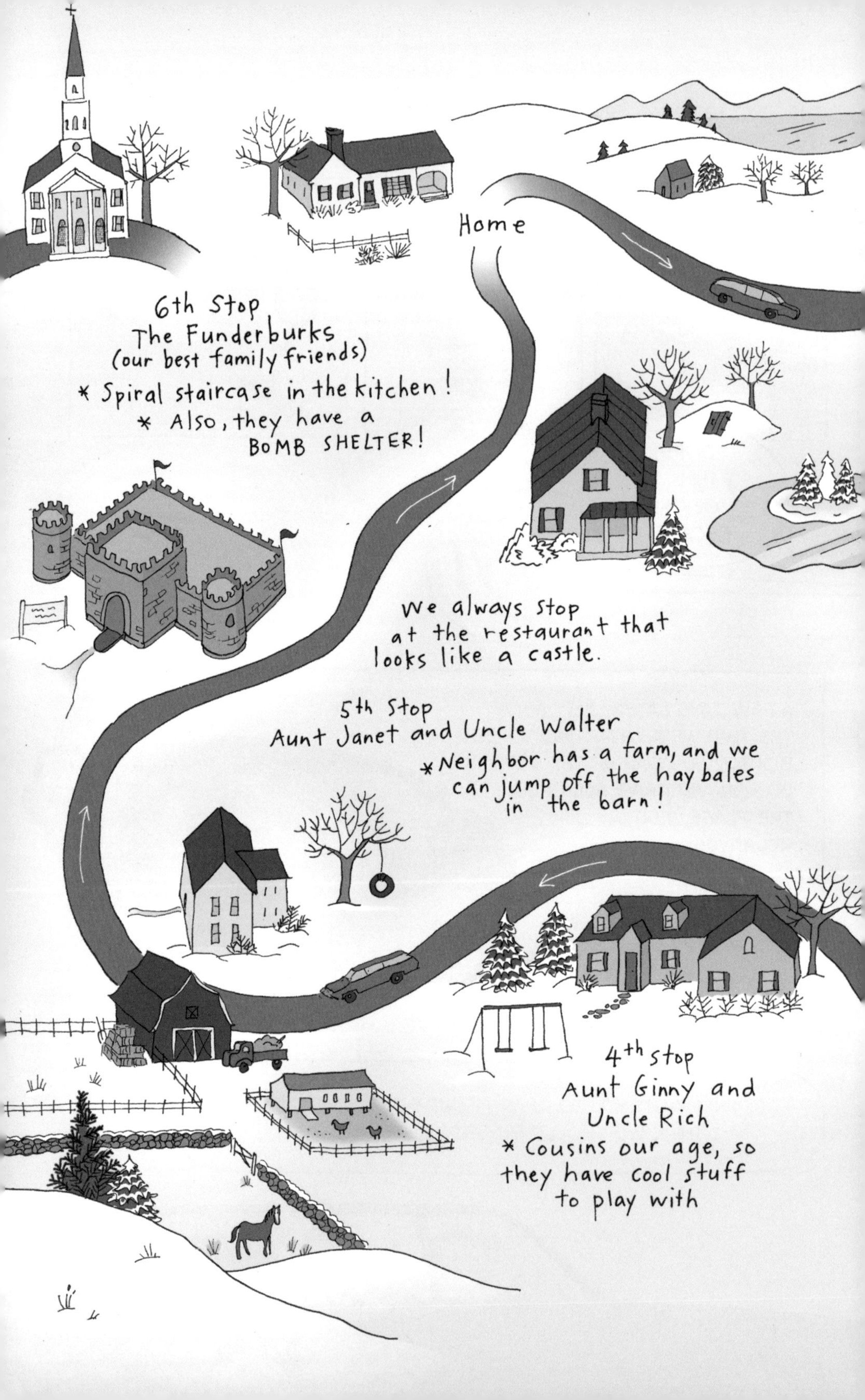
Home
6th Stop
The Funderburks
(our best family friends)
* Spiral staircase in the kitchen!
* Also, they have a BOMB SHELTER!
We always stop at the restaurant that looks like a castle.
5th Stop
Aunt Janet and Uncle Walter
* Neighbor has a farm, and we can jump off the hay bales in the barn!
4th Stop
Aunt Ginny and Uncle Rich
* Cousins our age, so they have cool stuff to play with

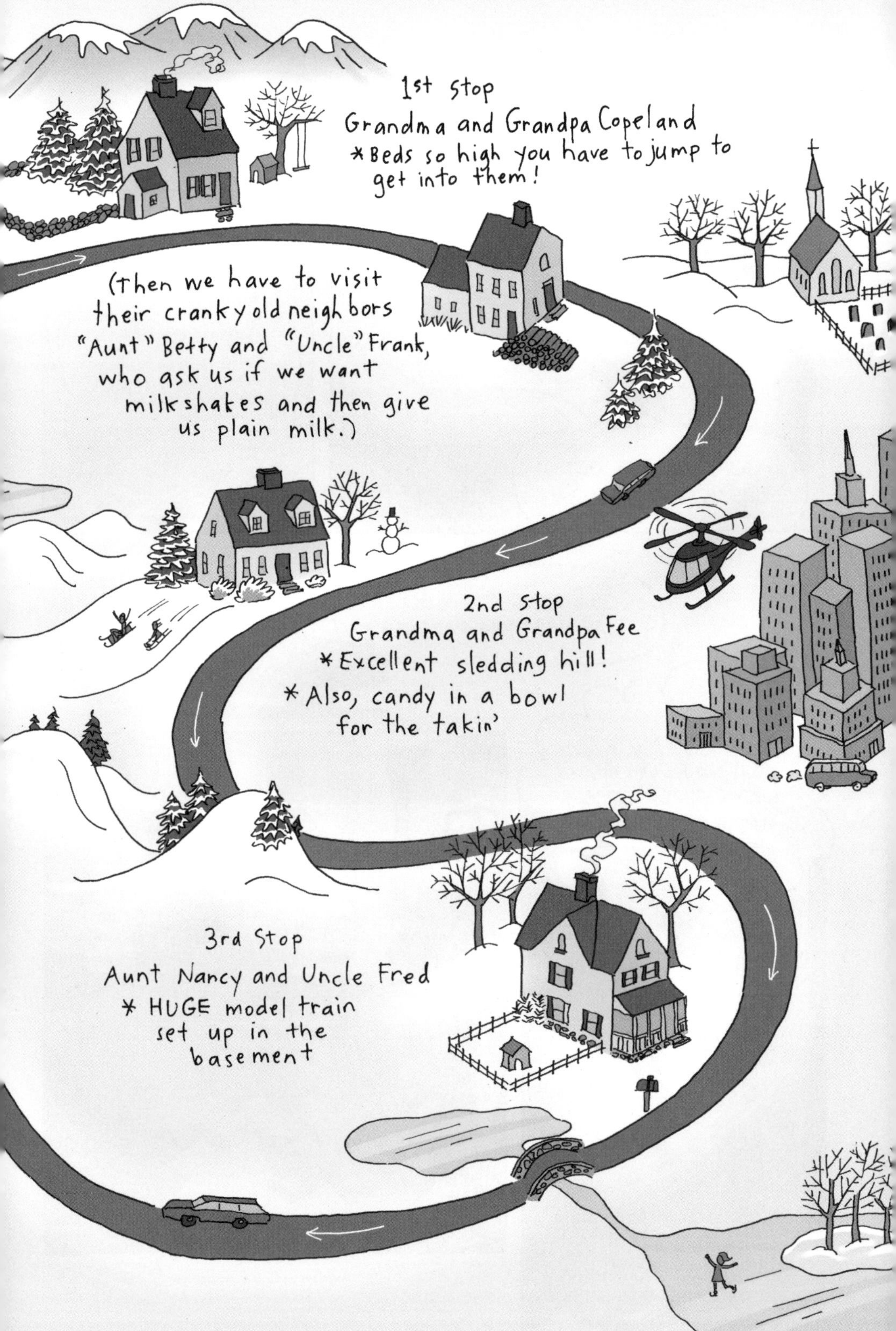
1st Stop
Grandma and Grandpa Copeland
*Beds so high you have to jump to get into them!
(Then we have to visit their cranky old neighbors "Aunt" Betty and "Uncle" Frank, who ask us if we want milkshakes and then give us plain milk.)
2nd Stop
Grandma and Grandpa Fee
*Excellent sledding hill!
*Also, candy in a bowl for the takin'
3rd Stop
Aunt Nancy and Uncle Fred
* HUGE model train set up in the basement

108

110

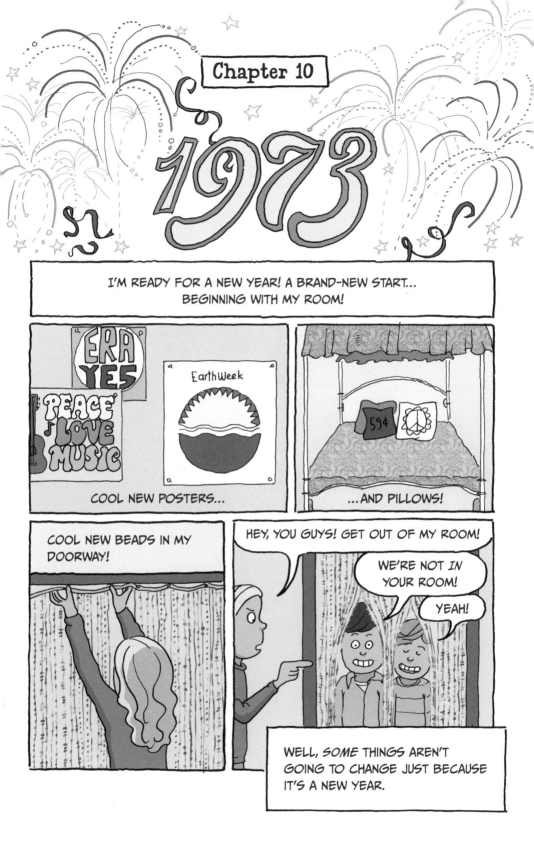

116

117

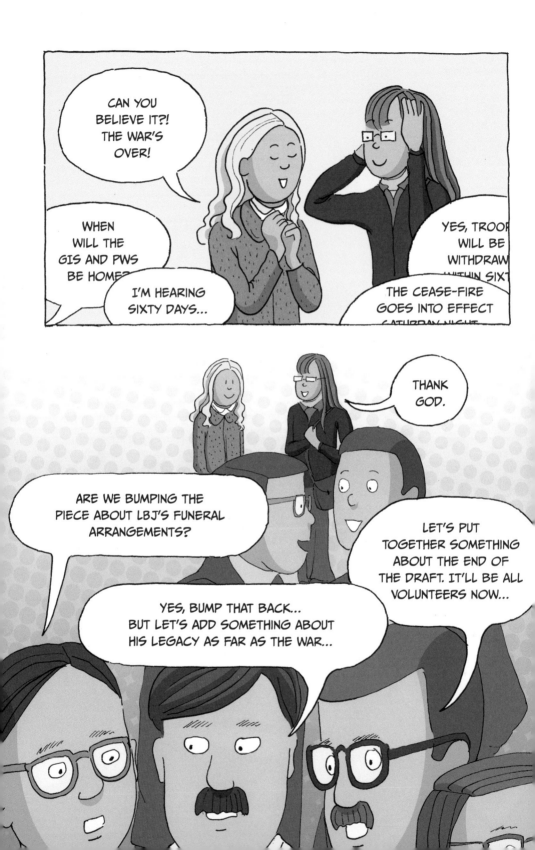

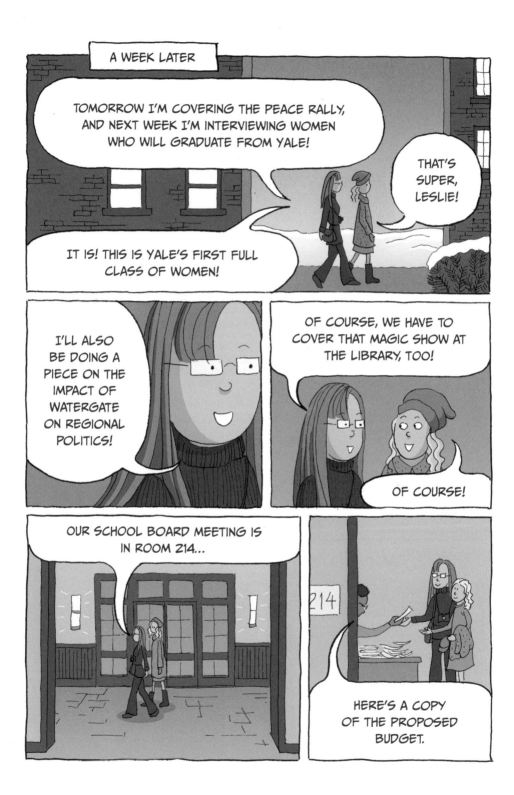

125

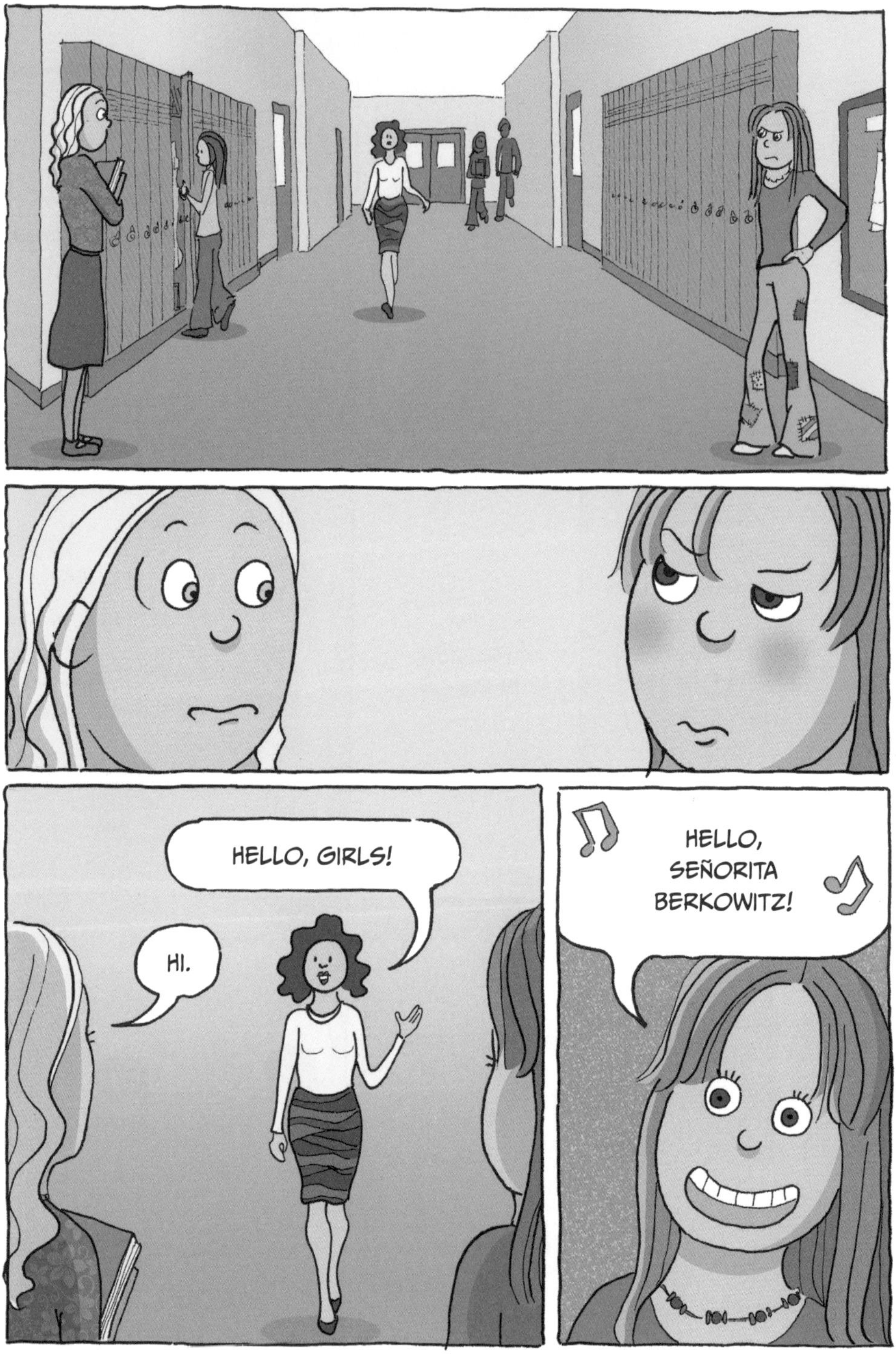
HELLO, GIRLS!
HI.
HELLO, SEÑORITA BERKOWITZ!

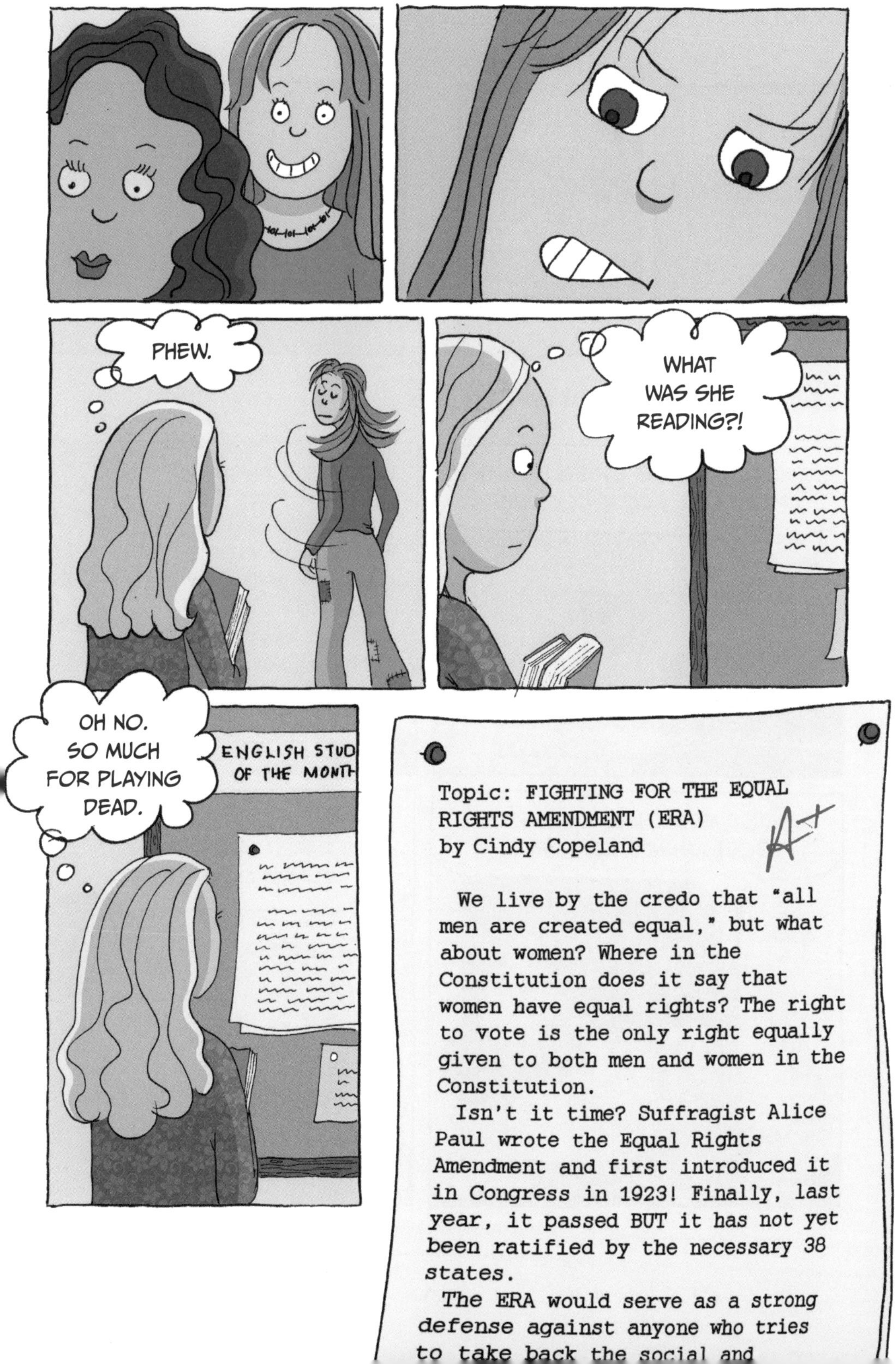
PHEW.
WHAT WAS SHE READING?!
OH NO. SO MUCH FOR PLAYING DEAD.
ENGLISH STUD
OF THE MONTH
Topic: FIGHTING FOR THE EQUAL RIGHTS AMENDMENT (ERA)
by Cindy Copeland
A+
We live by the credo that "all men are created equal," but what about women? Where in the Constitution does it say that women have equal rights? The right to vote is the only right equally given to both men and women in the Constitution.
Isn't it time? Suffragist Alice Paul wrote the Equal Rights Amendment and first introduced it in Congress in 1923! Finally, last year, it passed BUT it has not yet been ratified by the necessary 38 states.
The ERA would serve as a strong defense against anyone who tries to take back the social and

I MAKE A POINT OF LAYING LOW IN SCHOOL...

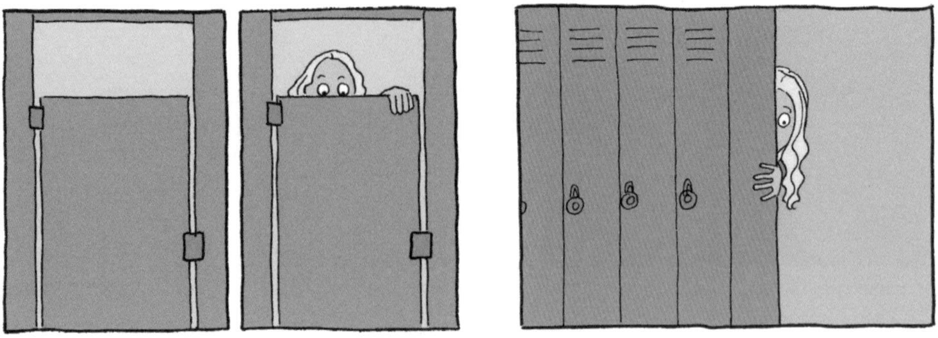

...BUT *AFTER* SCHOOL, I AM *VERY VISIBLE!*

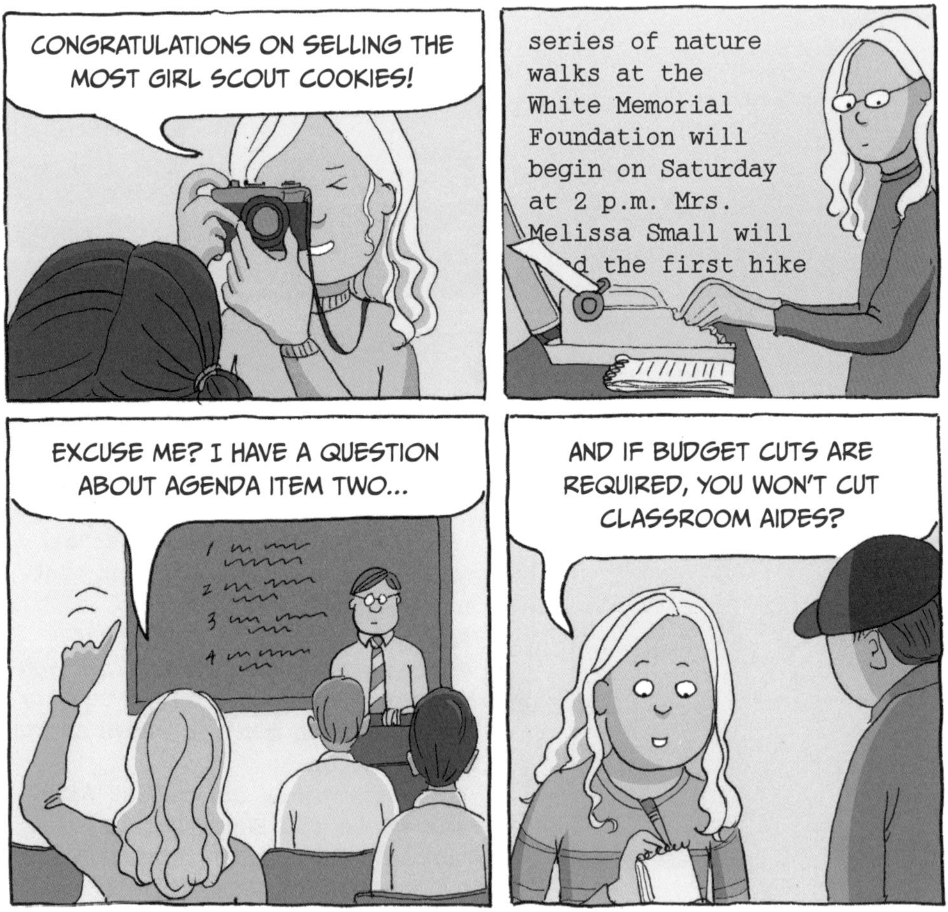
CONGRATULATIONS ON SELLING THE MOST GIRL SCOUT COOKIES!
series of nature walks at the White Memorial Foundation will begin on Saturday at 2 p.m. Mrs. Melissa Small will
d the first hike
EXCUSE ME? I HAVE A QUESTION ABOUT AGENDA ITEM TWO...
1
2
3
4
AND IF BUDGET CUTS ARE REQUIRED, YOU WON'T CUT CLASSROOM AIDES?

WHEN A WEEK GOES BY WITHOUT EVIE DOING ANYTHING MEAN, I BEGIN TO RELAX.

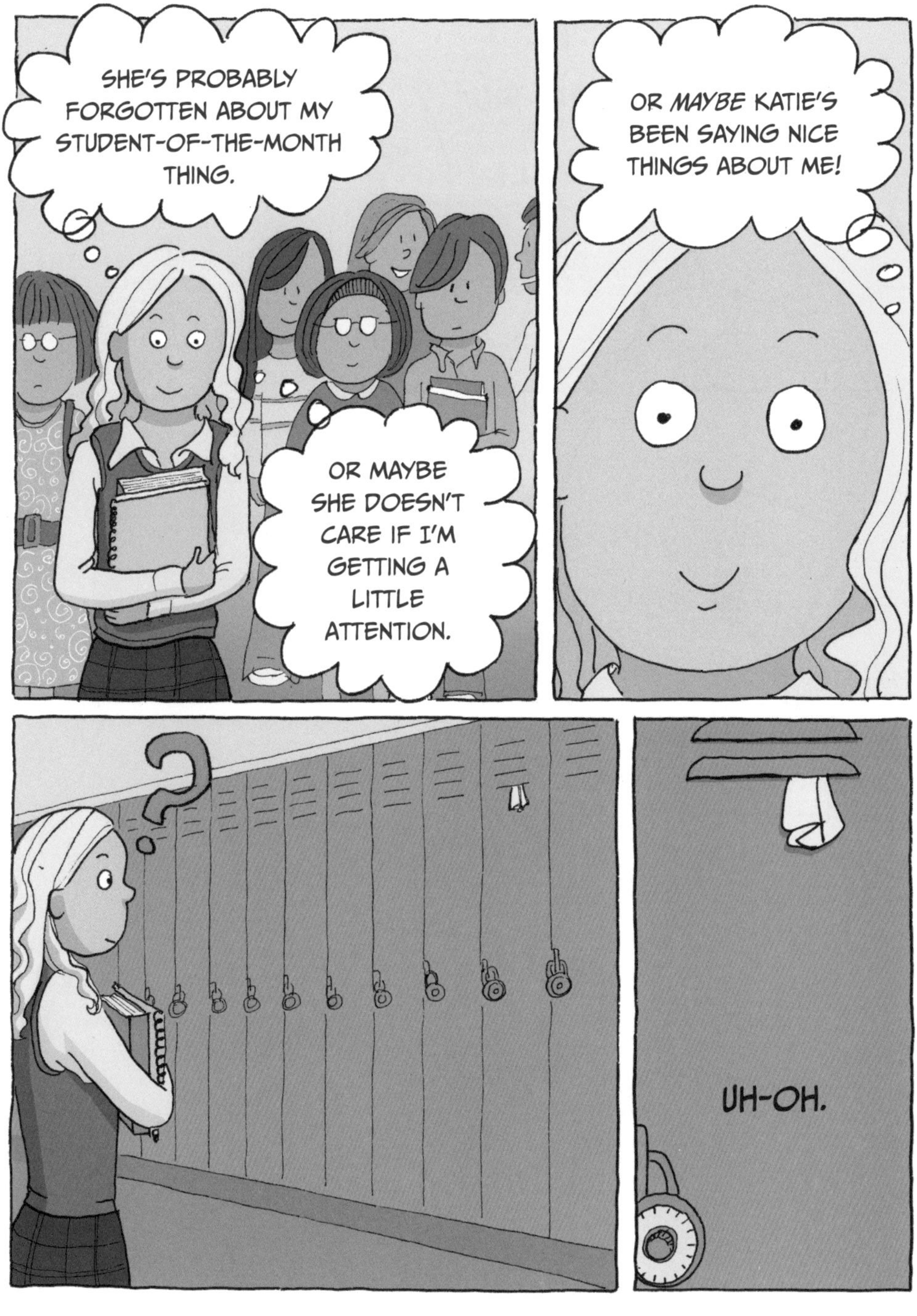

SHE'S PROBABLY FORGOTTEN ABOUT MY STUDENT-OF-THE-MONTH THING.
OR MAYBE SHE DOESN'T CARE IF I'M GETTING A LITTLE ATTENTION.
OR MAYBE KATIE'S BEEN SAYING NICE THINGS ABOUT ME!
?
UH-OH.

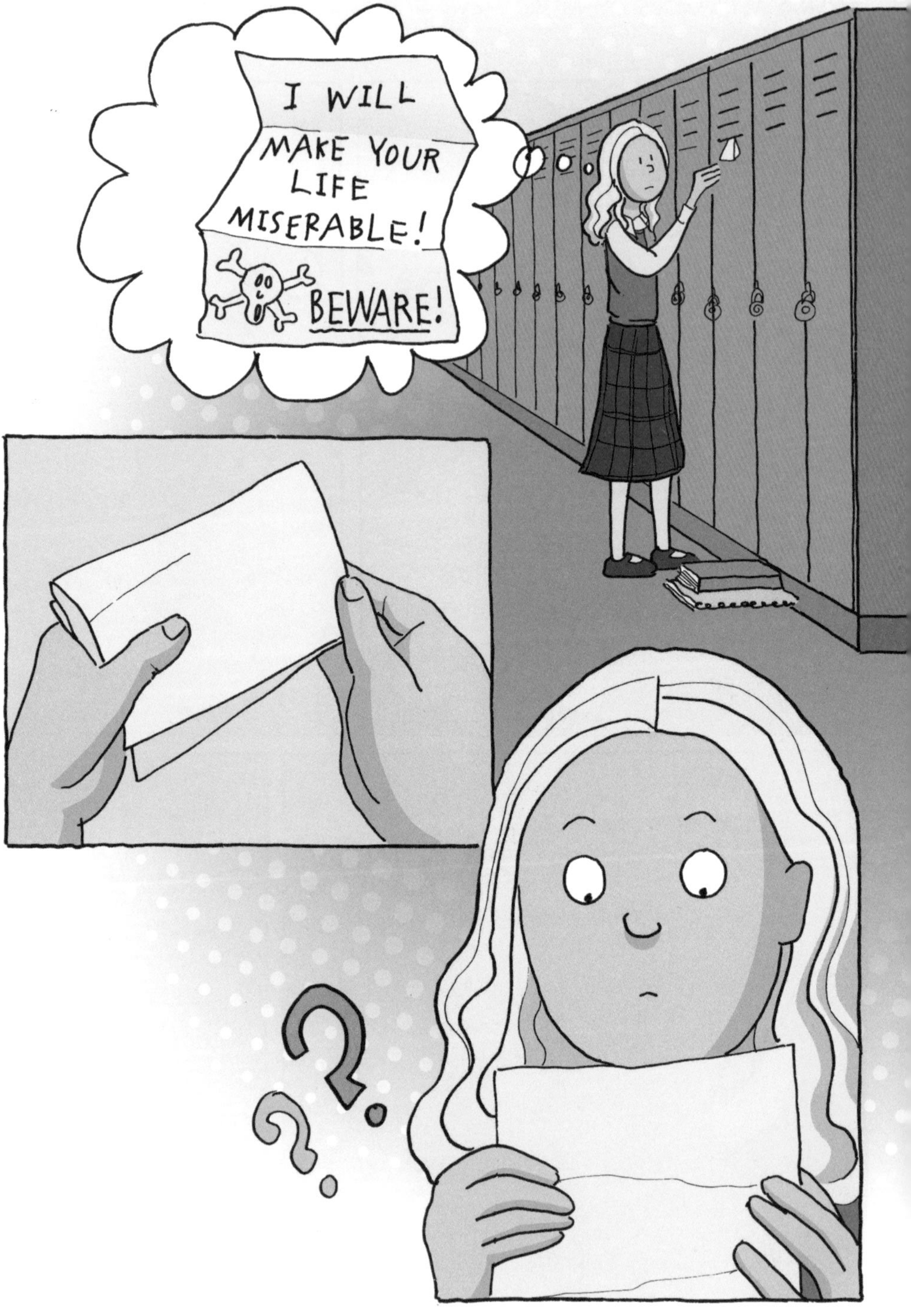
I WILL
MAKE YOUR LIFE MISERABLE!
BEWARE!

Hi Cindy,
You haven't been to The Island lately so I couldn't ask you in person.
Do you want to go to the Valentine's Day dance with me?
♡, Kevin
YES! I VERY MUCH WANT TO GO!

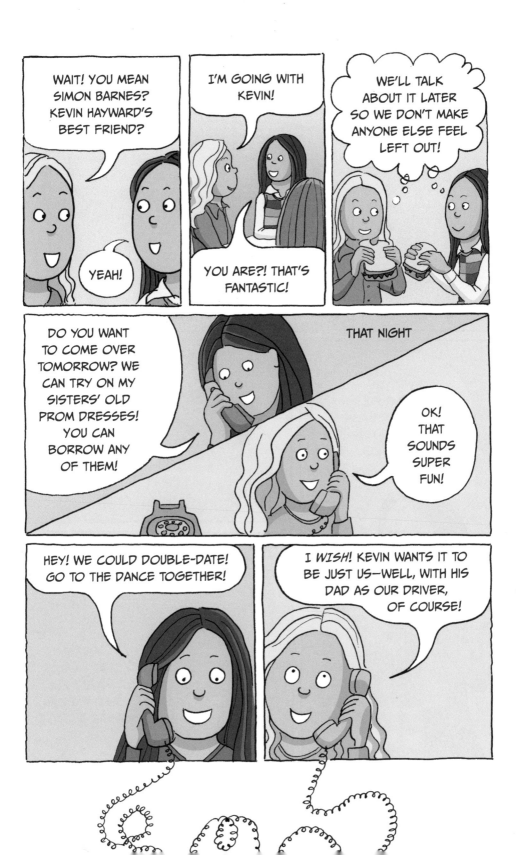

THE NEXT AFTERNOON WE RAID HER SISTERS' CLOSET.

IT WOULD HAVE BEEN FUN TO GET READY FOR THE DANCE WITH PENNY, BUT I'M KIND OF FLATTERED THAT KEVIN WANTS ME ALL TO HIMSELF. (IT'S GONNA BE AMAZING!)

140

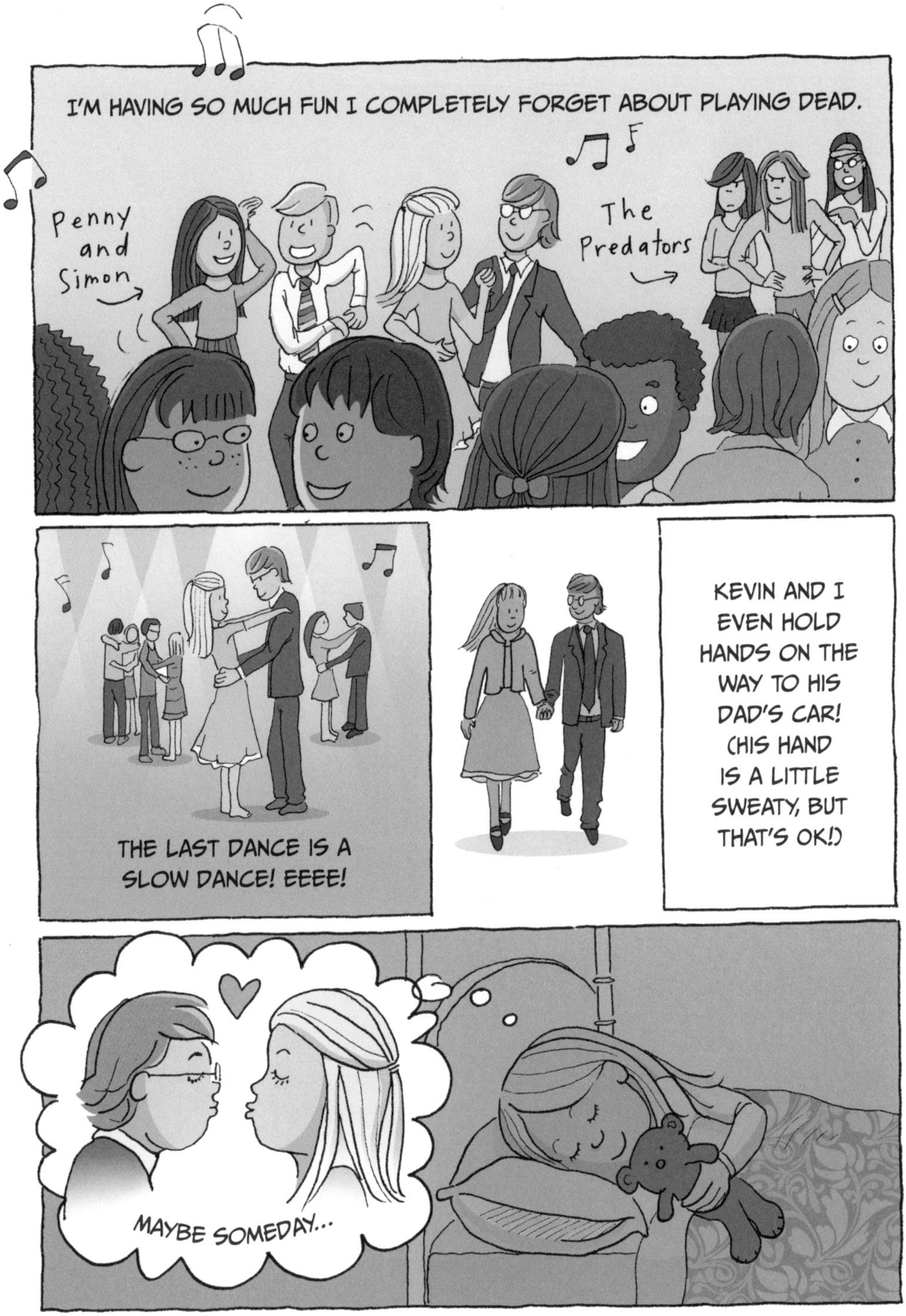
I'M HAVING SO MUCH FUN I COMPLETELY FORGET ABOUT PLAYING DEAD.
Penny and Simon
The Predators
THE LAST DANCE IS A SLOW DANCE! EEEE!
KEVIN AND I EVEN HOLD HANDS ON THE WAY TO HIS DAD'S CAR! (HIS HAND IS A LITTLE SWEATY, BUT THAT'S OK!)
MAYBE SOMEDAY...

IT'S A **PERFECT** NIGHT.

Chapter 12

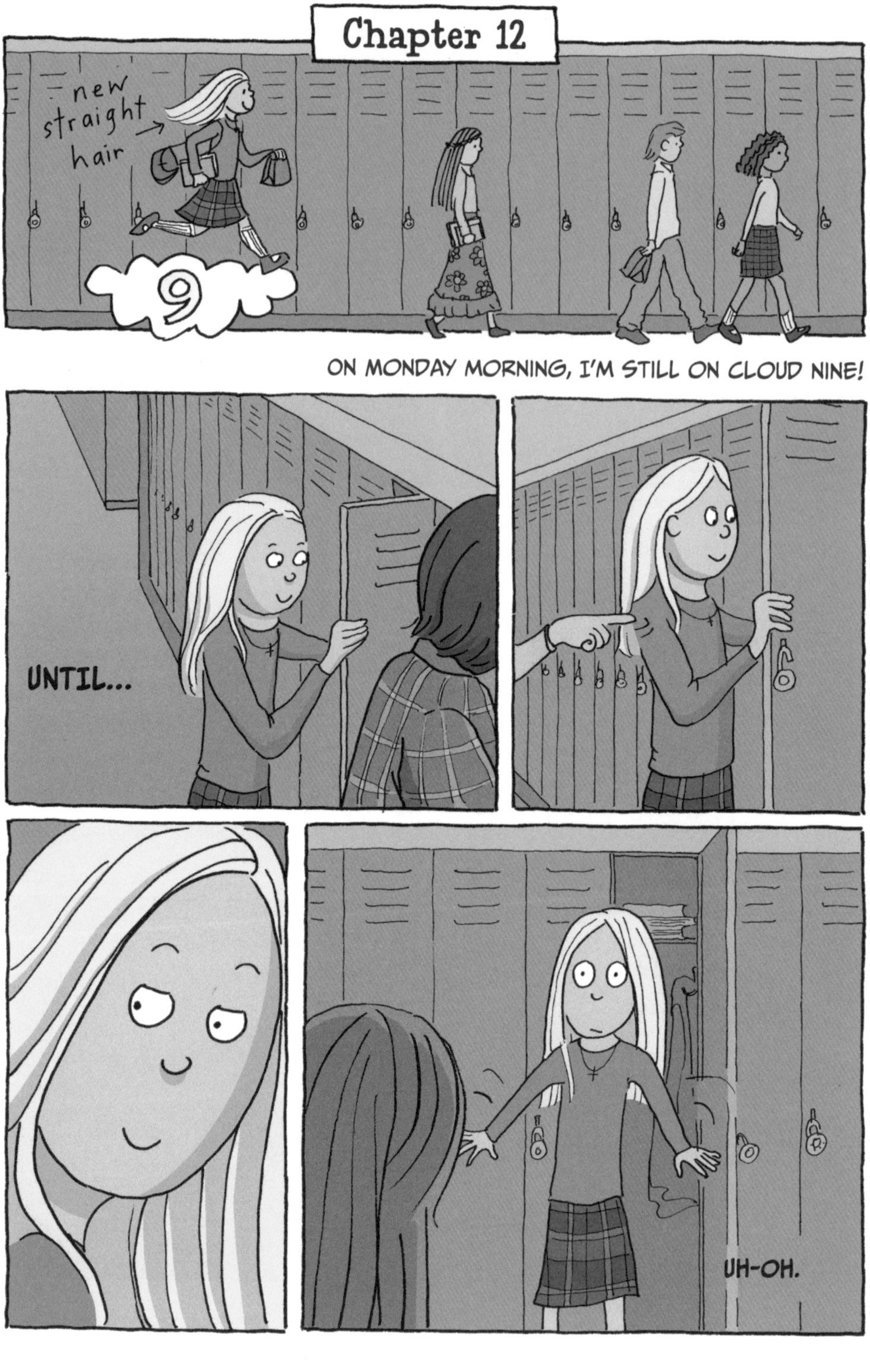
new straight hair
9
ON MONDAY MORNING, I'M STILL ON CLOUD NINE!
UNTIL...
UH-OH.

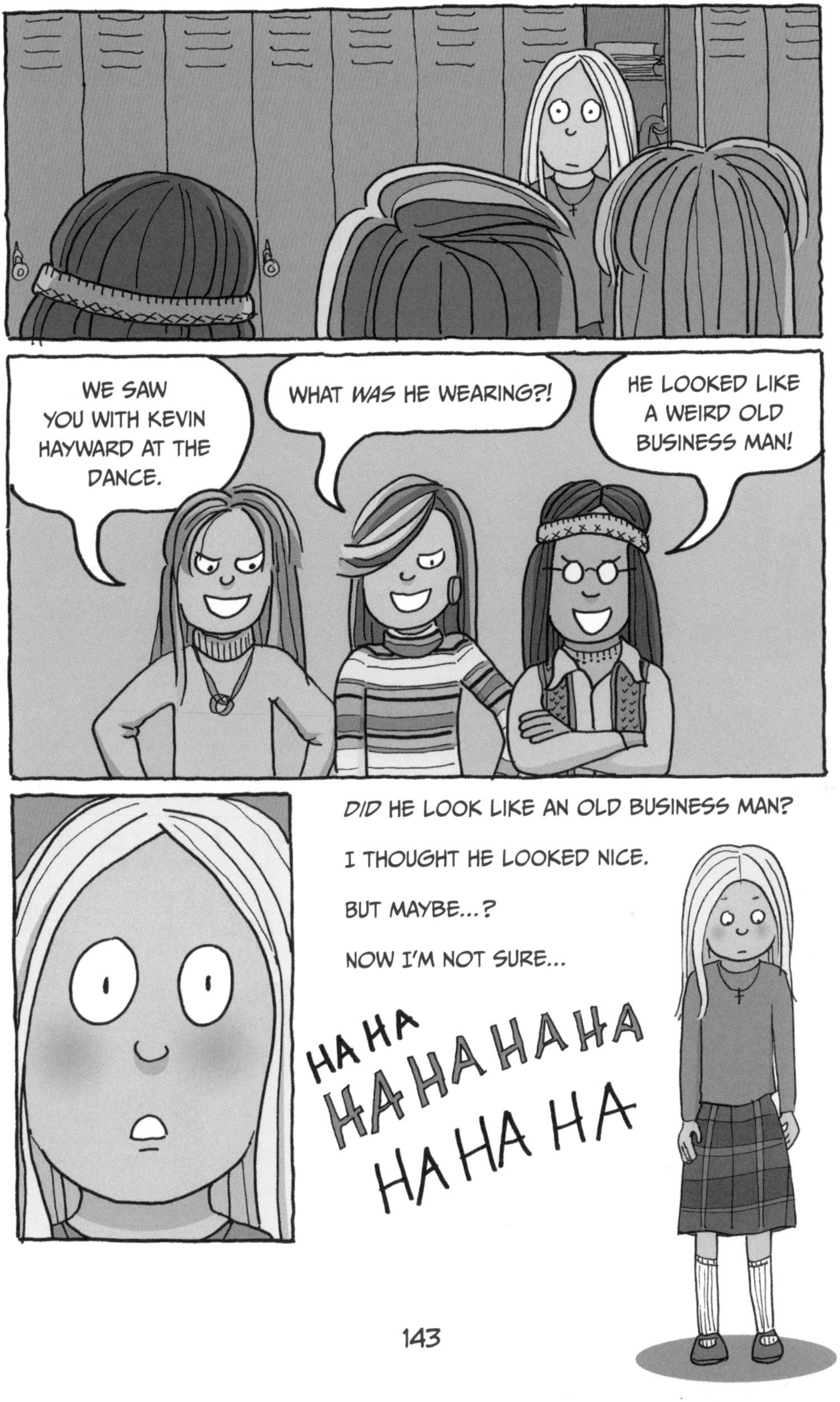

WE SAW YOU WITH KEVIN HAYWARD AT THE DANCE.
WHAT *WAS* HE WEARING?!
HE LOOKED LIKE A WEIRD OLD BUSINESS MAN!
DID HE LOOK LIKE AN OLD BUSINESS MAN?
I THOUGHT HE LOOKED NICE.
BUT MAYBE...?
NOW I'M NOT SURE...
HA HA
HA HA HA HA HA
HA HA HA

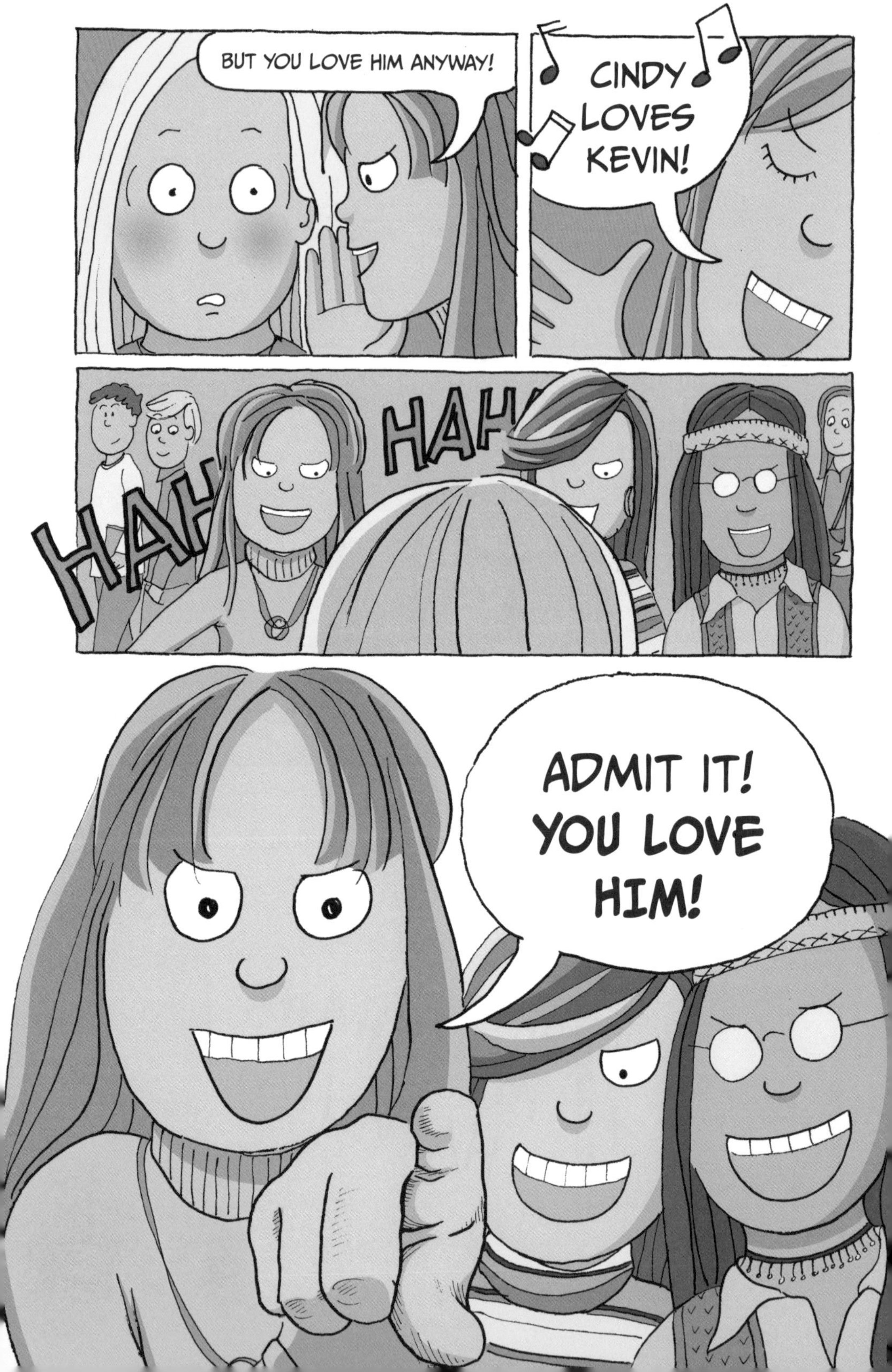
BUT YOU LOVE HIM ANYWAY!
CINDY LOVES KEVIN!
HAH HAH
ADMIT IT! YOU LOVE HIM!

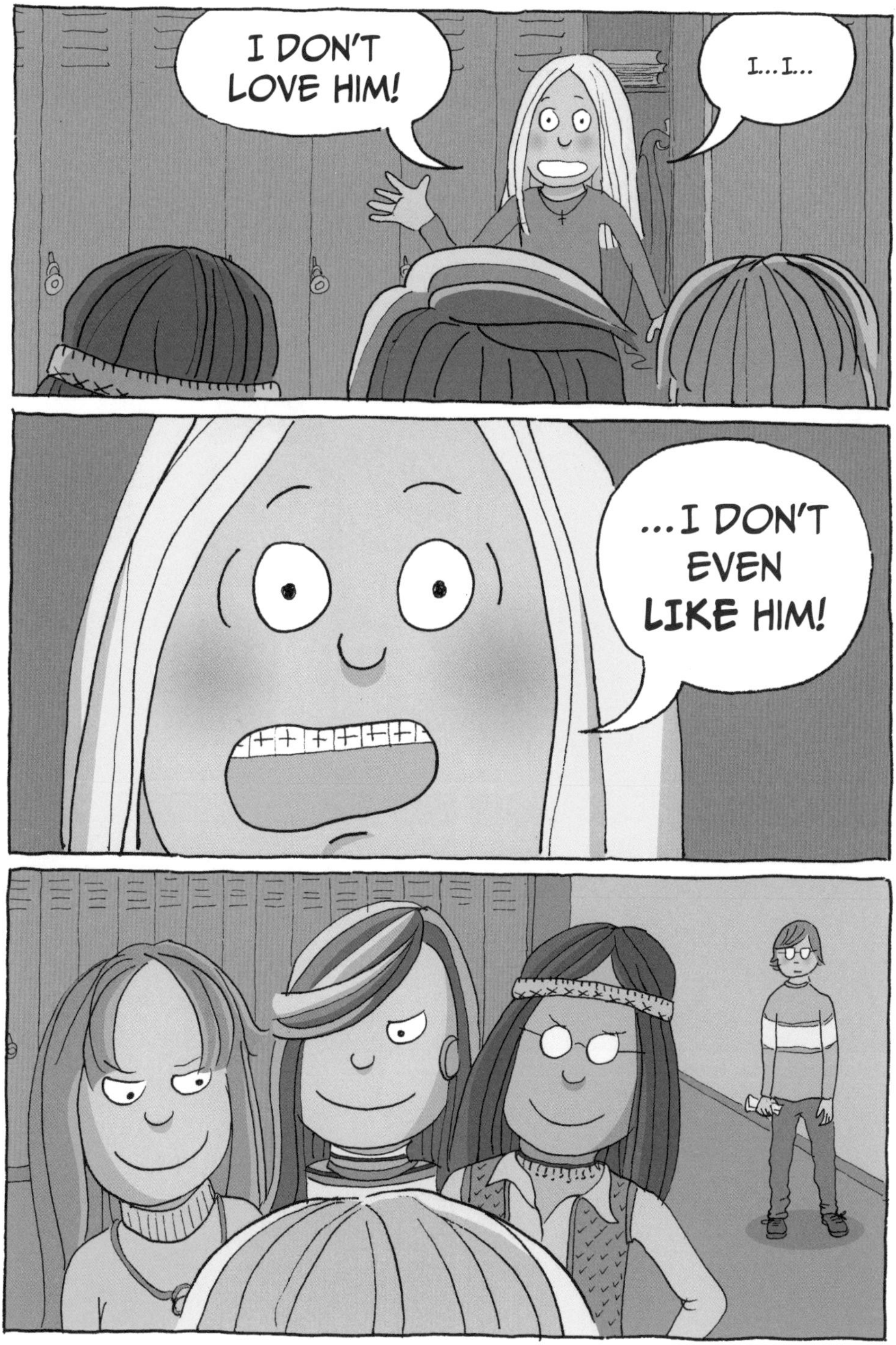
I DON'T LOVE HIM!
I...I...
...I DON'T EVEN LIKE HIM!

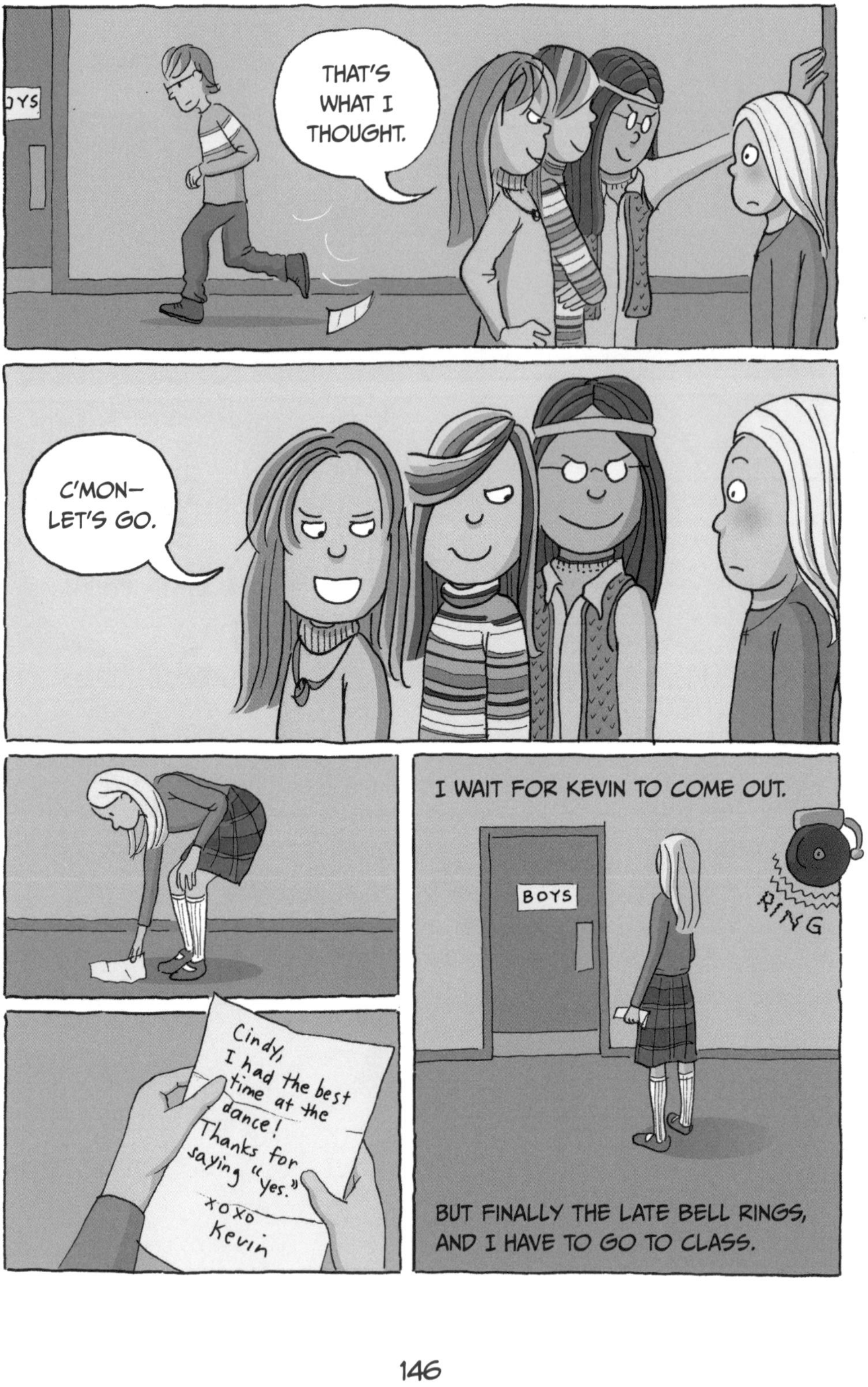
THAT'S WHAT I THOUGHT.
C'MON— LET'S GO.
Cindy, I had the best time at the dance! Thanks for saying "yes." xoxo Kevin
I WAIT FOR KEVIN TO COME OUT.
BOYS
RING
BUT FINALLY THE LATE BELL RINGS, AND I HAVE TO GO TO CLASS.

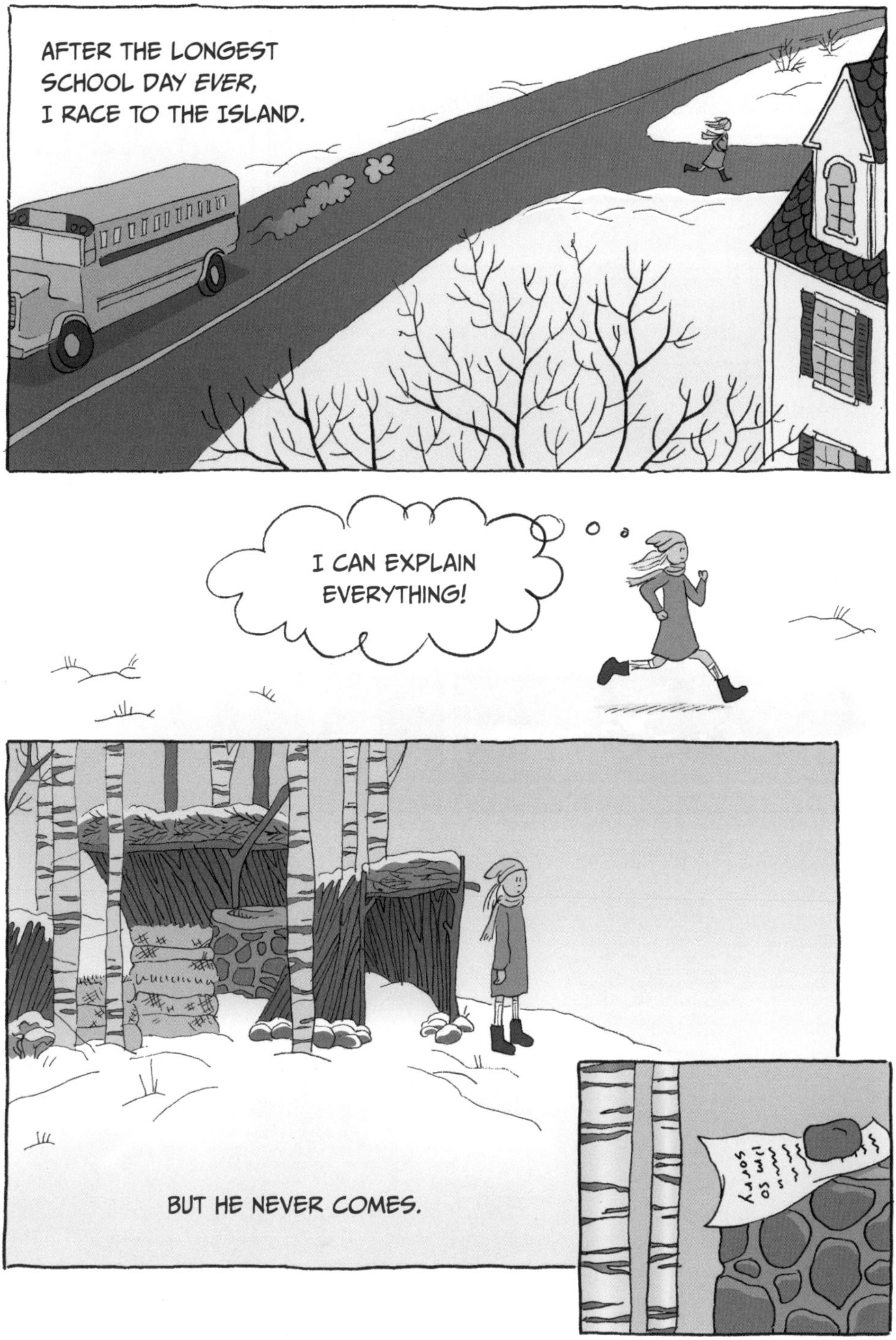
AFTER THE LONGEST SCHOOL DAY *EVER*, I RACE TO THE ISLAND.
I CAN EXPLAIN EVERYTHING!
BUT HE NEVER COMES.
I'm so sorry

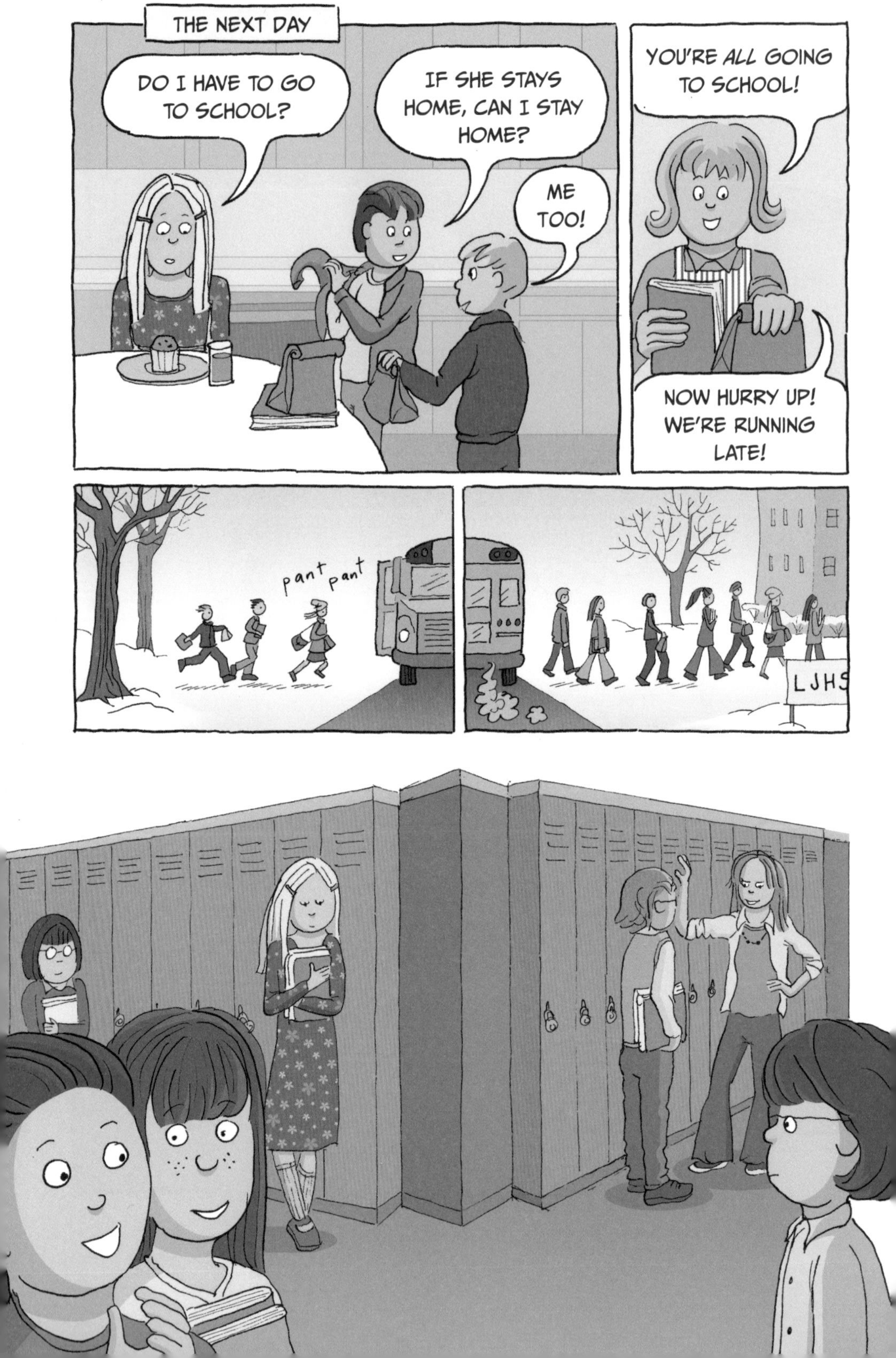
THE NEXT DAY
DO I HAVE TO GO TO SCHOOL?
IF SHE STAYS HOME, CAN I STAY HOME?
ME TOO!
YOU'RE *ALL* GOING TO SCHOOL!
NOW HURRY UP! WE'RE RUNNING LATE!
pant pant
LJHS

LUNCH PERIOD IS EVEN WORSE THAN I IMAGINED IT WOULD BE.

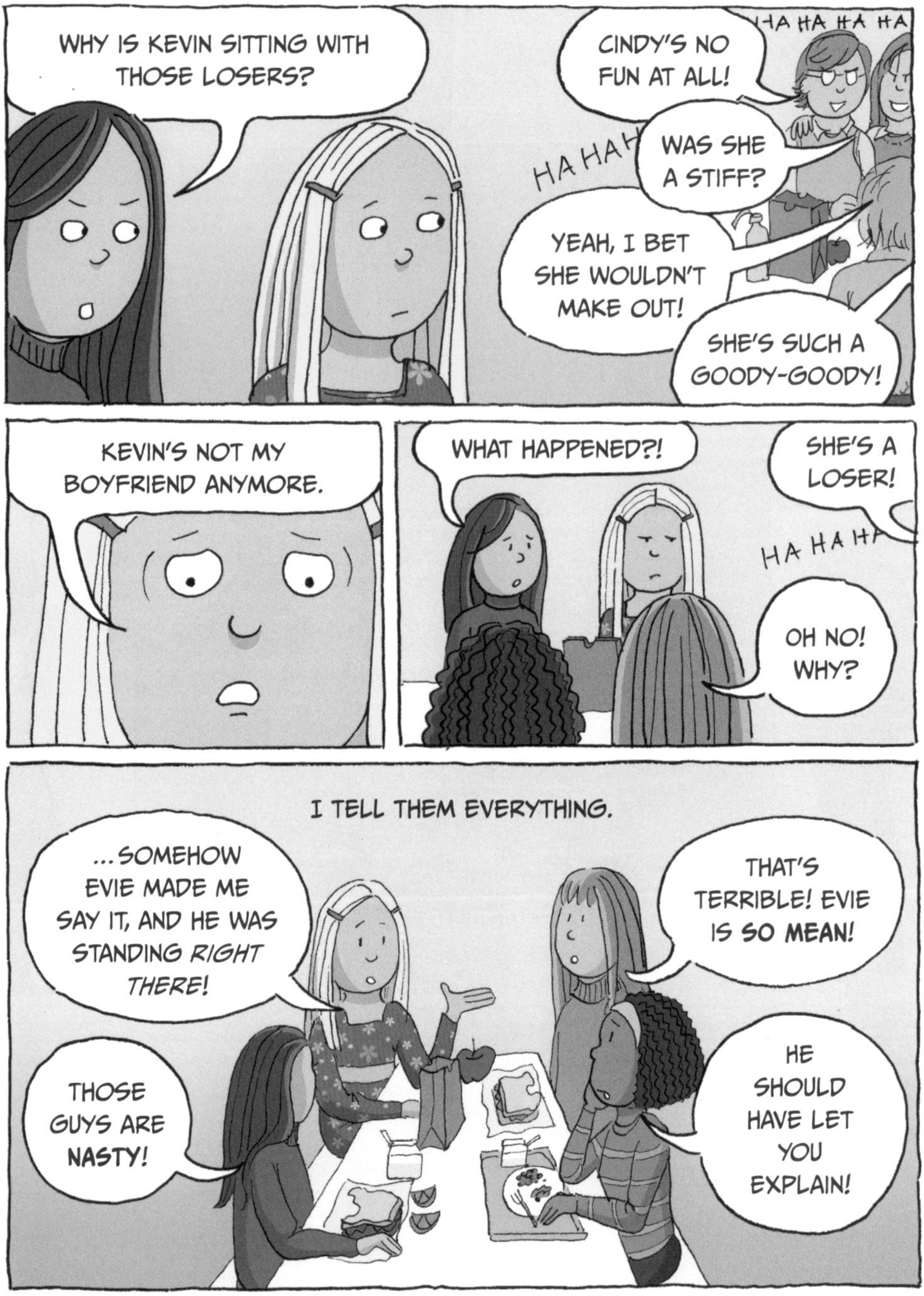
WHY IS KEVIN SITTING WITH THOSE LOSERS?
CINDY'S NO FUN AT ALL!
HA HA HA HA
HA HAH
WAS SHE A STIFF?
YEAH, I BET SHE WOULDN'T MAKE OUT!
SHE'S SUCH A GOODY-GOODY!
KEVIN'S NOT MY BOYFRIEND ANYMORE.
WHAT HAPPENED?!
SHE'S A LOSER!
HA HA HA
OH NO! WHY?
I TELL THEM EVERYTHING.
...SOMEHOW EVIE MADE ME SAY IT, AND HE WAS STANDING *RIGHT THERE!*
THAT'S TERRIBLE! EVIE IS **SO MEAN!**
THOSE GUYS ARE **NASTY!**
HE SHOULD HAVE LET YOU EXPLAIN!

SAYING IT OUT LOUD MAKES ME FEEL A LITTLE BETTER.

AT LUNCH THE NEXT DAY, MY FRIENDS AREN'T SITTING AT OUR REGULAR TABLE.

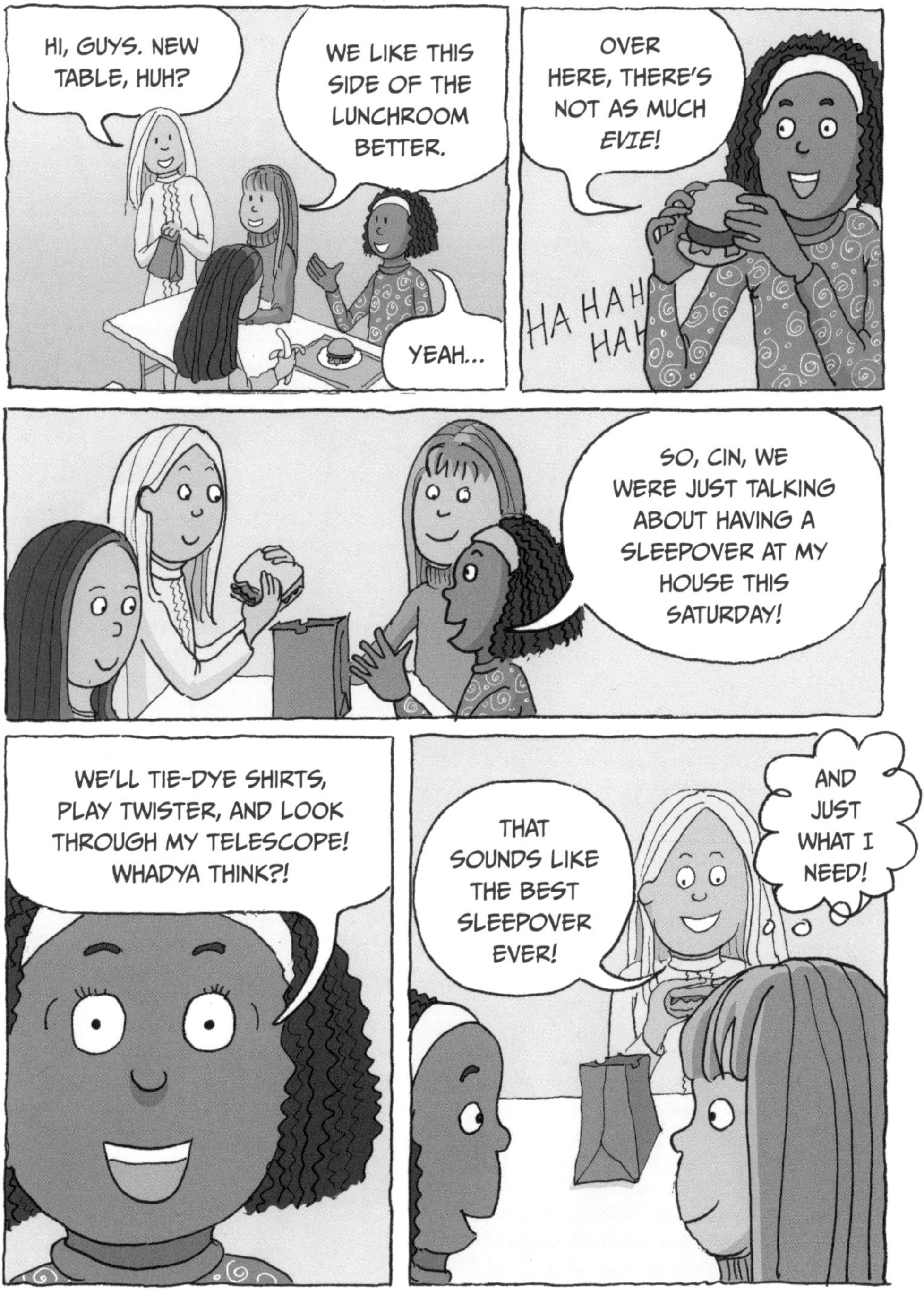
HI, GUYS. NEW TABLE, HUH?
WE LIKE THIS SIDE OF THE LUNCHROOM BETTER.
YEAH...
OVER HERE, THERE'S NOT AS MUCH *EVIE!*
HA HA
HA
SO, CIN, WE WERE JUST TALKING ABOUT HAVING A SLEEPOVER AT MY HOUSE THIS SATURDAY!
WE'LL TIE-DYE SHIRTS, PLAY TWISTER, AND LOOK THROUGH MY TELESCOPE! WHADYA THINK?!
THAT SOUNDS LIKE THE BEST SLEEPOVER EVER!
AND JUST WHAT I NEED!

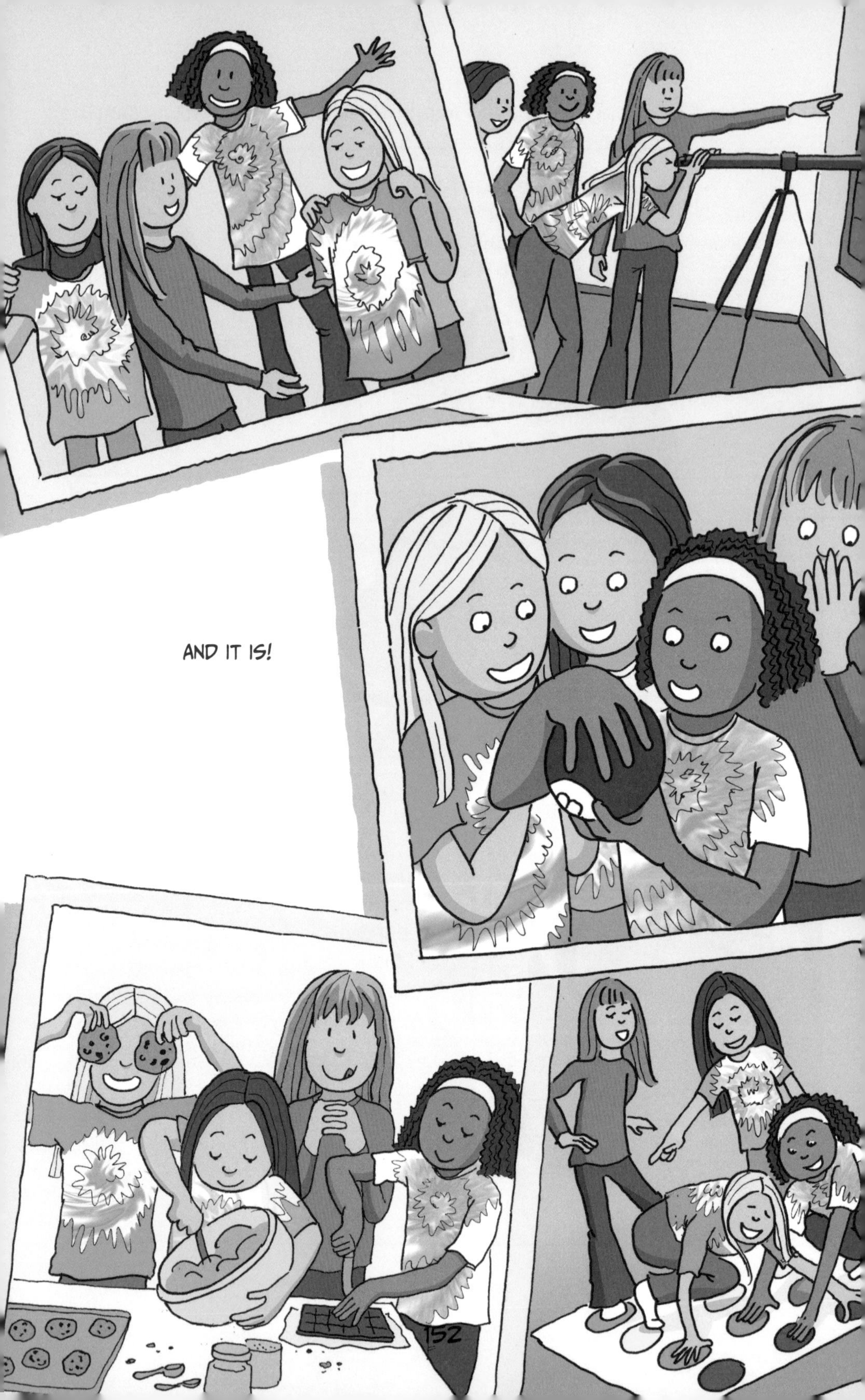
AND IT IS!

NO ONE TALKS ABOUT BOYS *AT ALL* UNTIL JUST BEFORE MIDNIGHT. PENNY PULLS A OUIJA BOARD FROM HER DUFFEL BAG AND SETS IT UP ON MOLLY'S BED.

KEVIN IS THE WORST

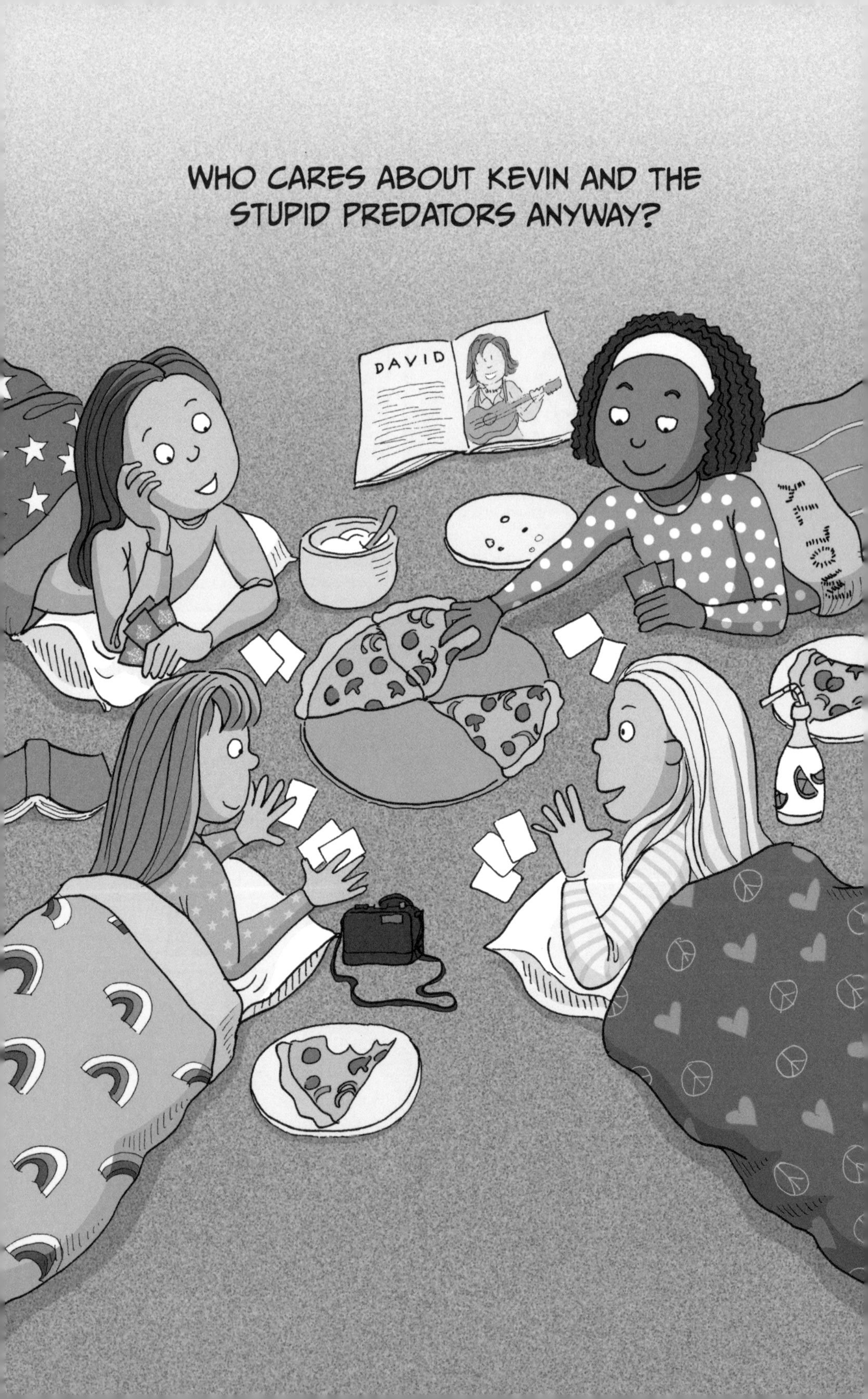
WHO CARES ABOUT KEVIN AND THE
STUPID PREDATORS ANYWAY?
DAVID

THERE'S *ONE* GOOD THING ABOUT WHAT HAPPENED WITH KEVIN: I DON'T HAVE TO WORRY ABOUT HIM BEING ANNOYED WHEN I HAVE A PLAN WITH LESLIE. AND RIGHT NOW, WE HAVE A **FULL SCHEDULE!**

THE PEREGRINE FALCON IS ALSO CALLED THE DUCK HAWK...

NATURE PROGRAM

THERE IS A NATIONAL HEALTH FOOD MOVEMENT RIGHT NOW...

LECTURE

PLAY

WHEN WE DON'T HAVE AN EVENT TO ATTEND, WE DRIVE AROUND TOWN, LOOKING FOR GREAT PHOTOS.

IT'S FINE. I'M ~~TOTALLY~~ MOSTLY OVER HIM.

JUST AS MR. KRAMER TURNS TOWARD ME, A GIRL WE'VE NEVER SEEN BEFORE WALKS INTO THE ROOM. (NO ONE REALLY MOVES IN OR OUT OF LITCHFIELD, SO NEW KIDS ARE PRETTY RARE.)

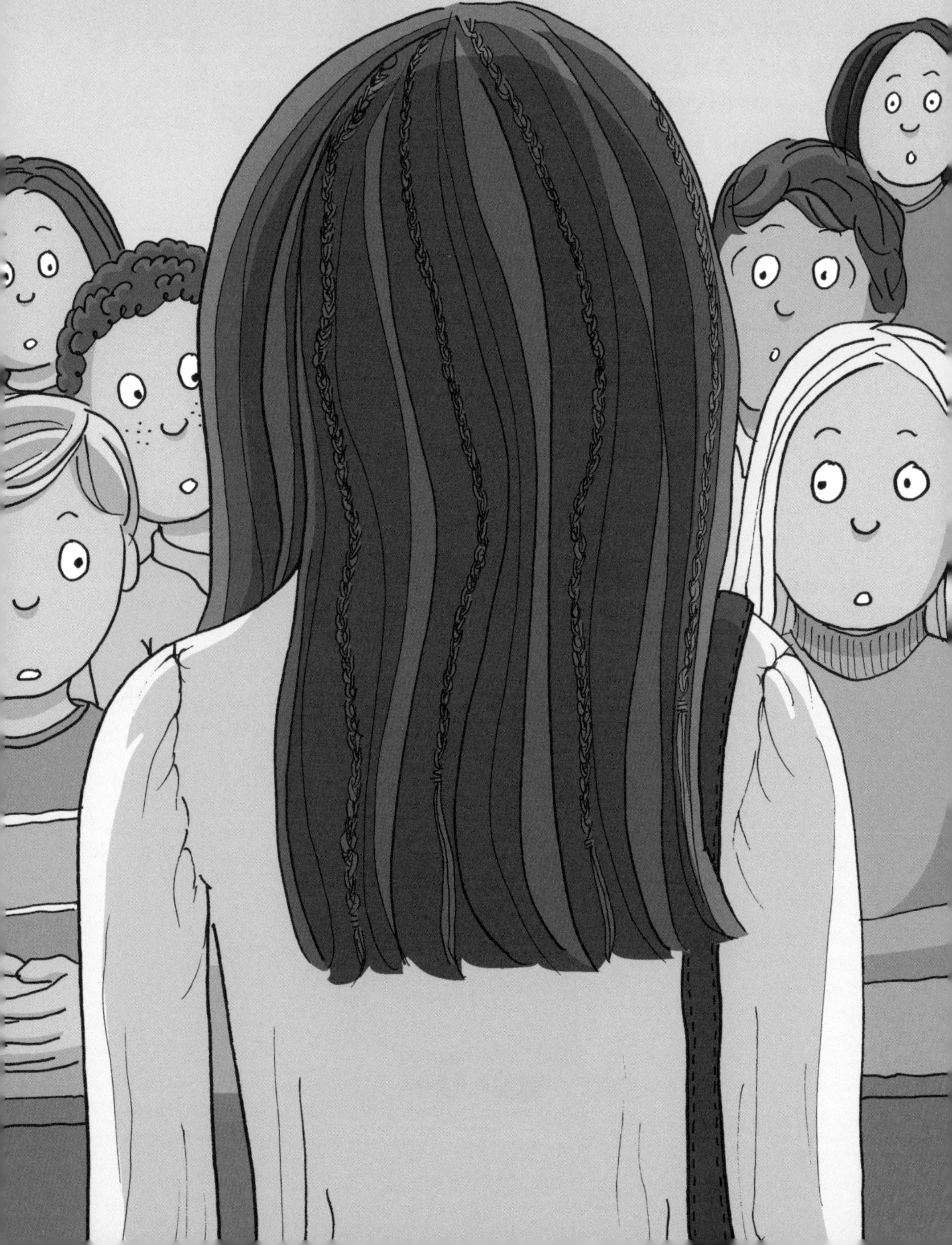

The New Girl

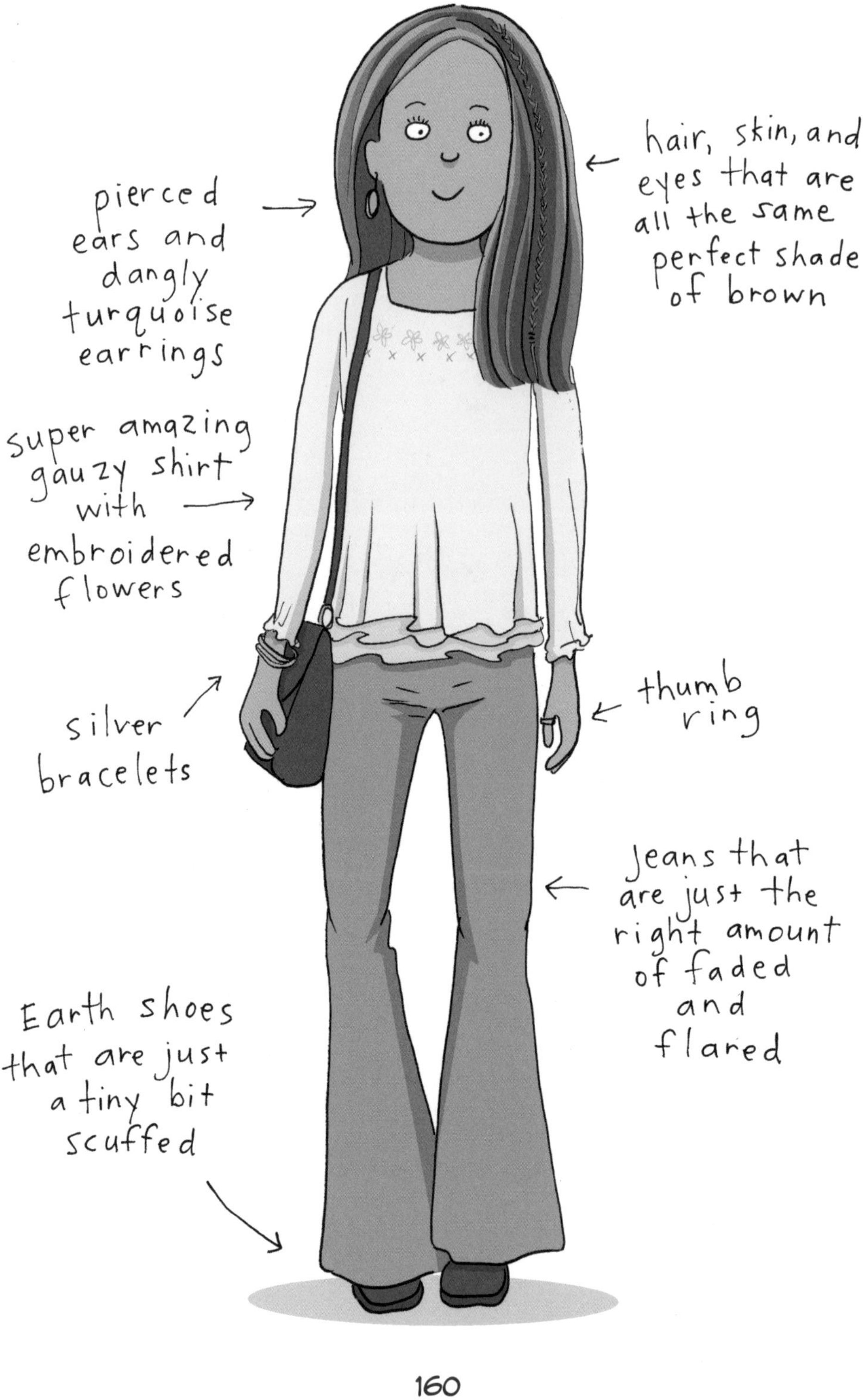

hair, skin, and eyes that are all the same perfect shade of brown
pierced ears and dangly turquoise earrings
super amazing gauzy shirt with embroidered flowers
silver bracelets
thumb ring
jeans that are just the right amount of faded and flared
Earth shoes that are just a tiny bit scuffed

LISA SEEMS TO UNDERSTAND THAT SHE NEEDS TO HELP HIM OUT.

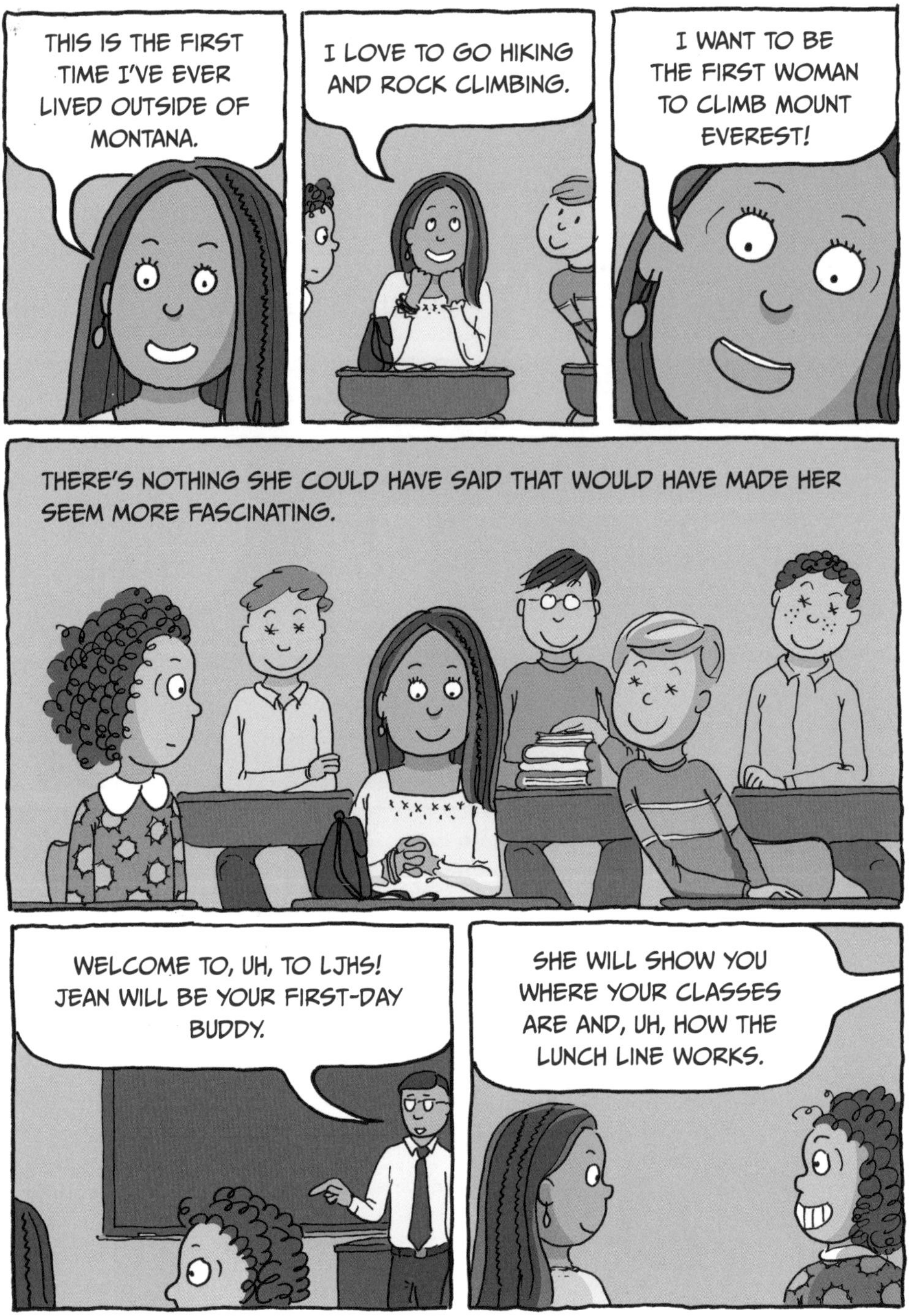
THIS IS THE FIRST TIME I'VE EVER LIVED OUTSIDE OF MONTANA.
I LOVE TO GO HIKING AND ROCK CLIMBING.
I WANT TO BE THE FIRST WOMAN TO CLIMB MOUNT EVEREST!
THERE'S NOTHING SHE COULD HAVE SAID THAT WOULD HAVE MADE HER SEEM MORE FASCINATING.
WELCOME TO, UH, TO LJHS! JEAN WILL BE YOUR FIRST-DAY BUDDY.
SHE WILL SHOW YOU WHERE YOUR CLASSES ARE AND, UH, HOW THE LUNCH LINE WORKS.

THE NEXT DAY, LISA WALKS INTO THE LUNCHROOM ALONE AND PAUSES.

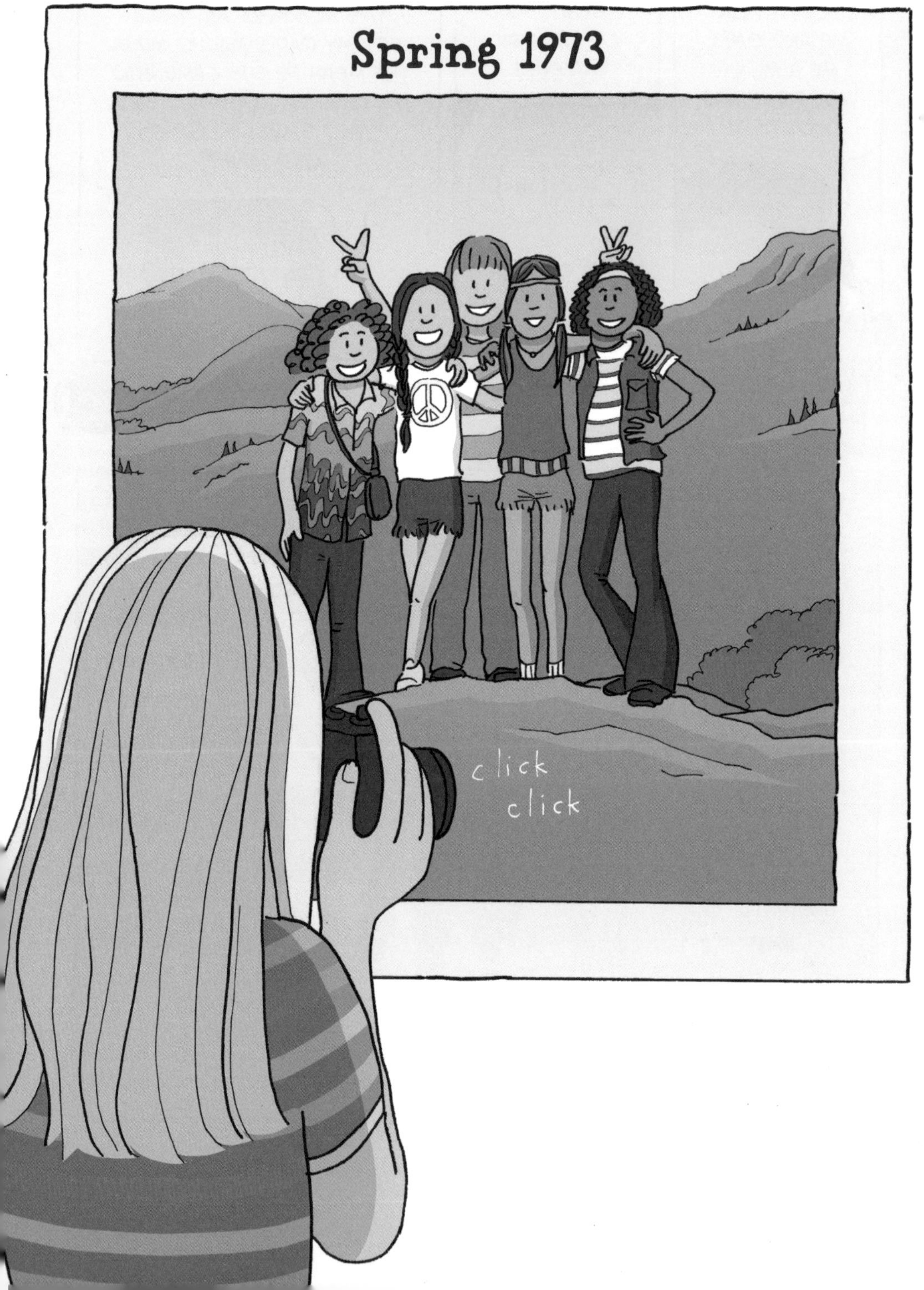
Spring 1973
click
click

Chapter 14

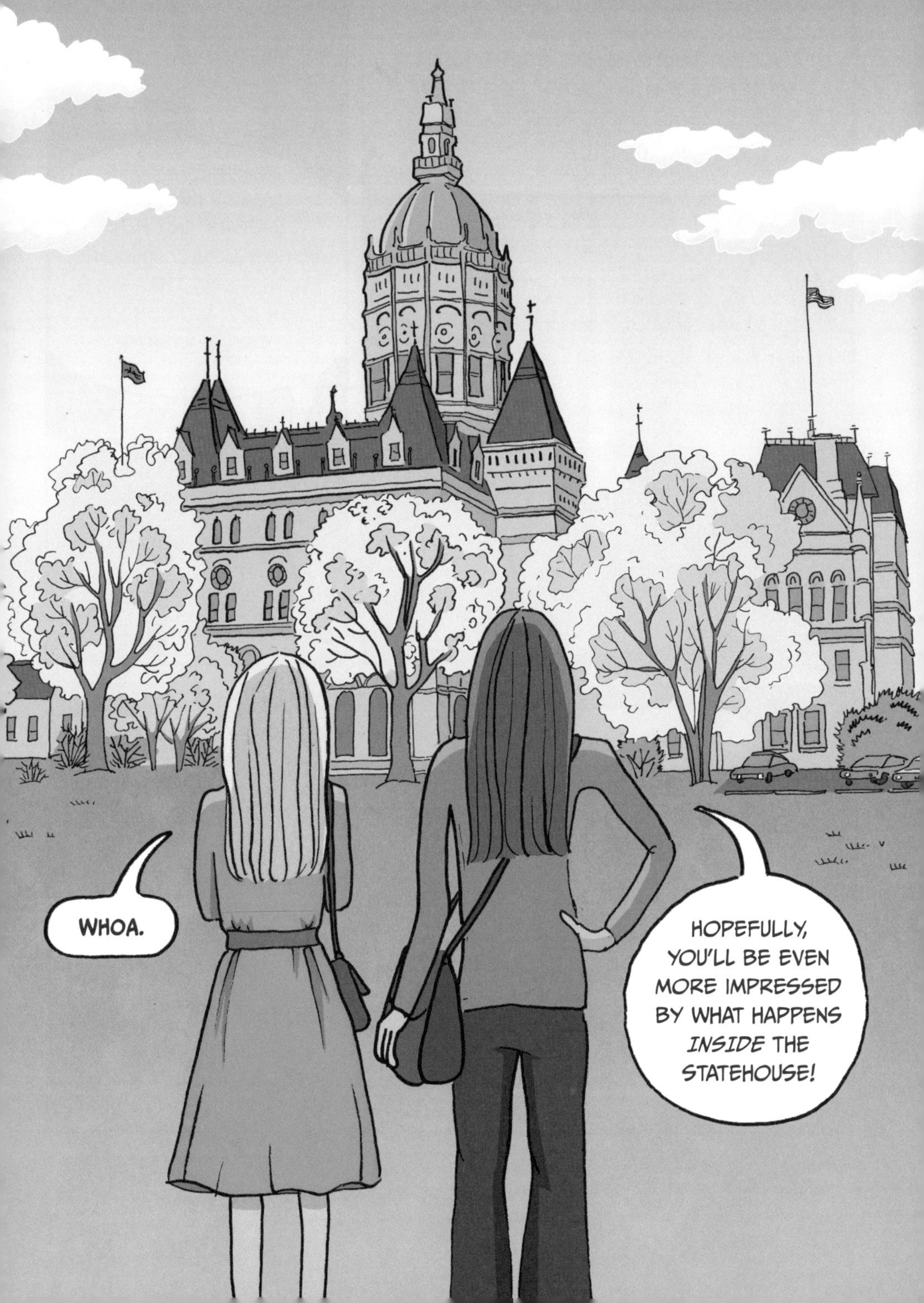
WHOA.
HOPEFULLY, YOU'LL BE EVEN MORE IMPRESSED BY WHAT HAPPENS *INSIDE* THE STATEHOUSE!

170

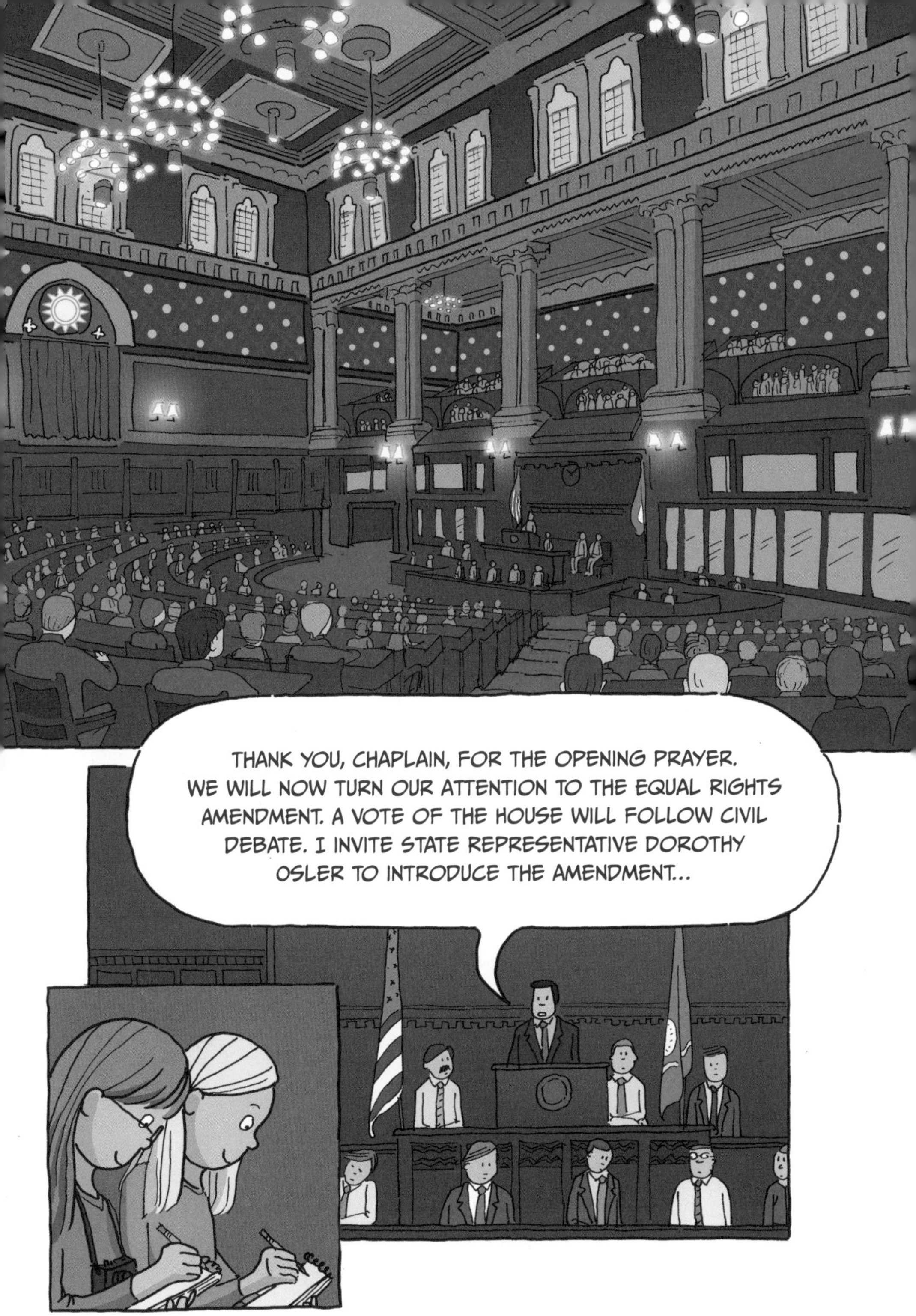
THANK YOU, CHAPLAIN, FOR THE OPENING PRAYER. WE WILL NOW TURN OUR ATTENTION TO THE EQUAL RIGHTS AMENDMENT. A VOTE OF THE HOUSE WILL FOLLOW CIVIL DEBATE. I INVITE STATE REPRESENTATIVE DOROTHY OSLER TO INTRODUCE THE AMENDMENT...

Torrington Register

TORRINGTON, CONNECTICUT   FRIDAY, MARCH 9, 1973   VOL 99   NO 58   10 CENTS

State House passes ERA after heated debate

Senate approval still needed

by Leslie Jacobs

Following a lengthy, emotional debate, the State House of Representatives voted 99–47 in favor of ratifying the Equal Rights Amendment to the US Constitution.

Cheers rang out from the public gallery, crowded to capacity by women who had come to witness the historic vote.

According to State Rep. Dorothy Osler (R-Greenwich), the amendment will simply prohibit discrimination on the basis of a person's equa

Osler insisted that men will also reap benefits if the amendment is adopted.

The amendment does not mean that housewives will be discriminated against or that men's rights will be weakened, Osler stated.

173

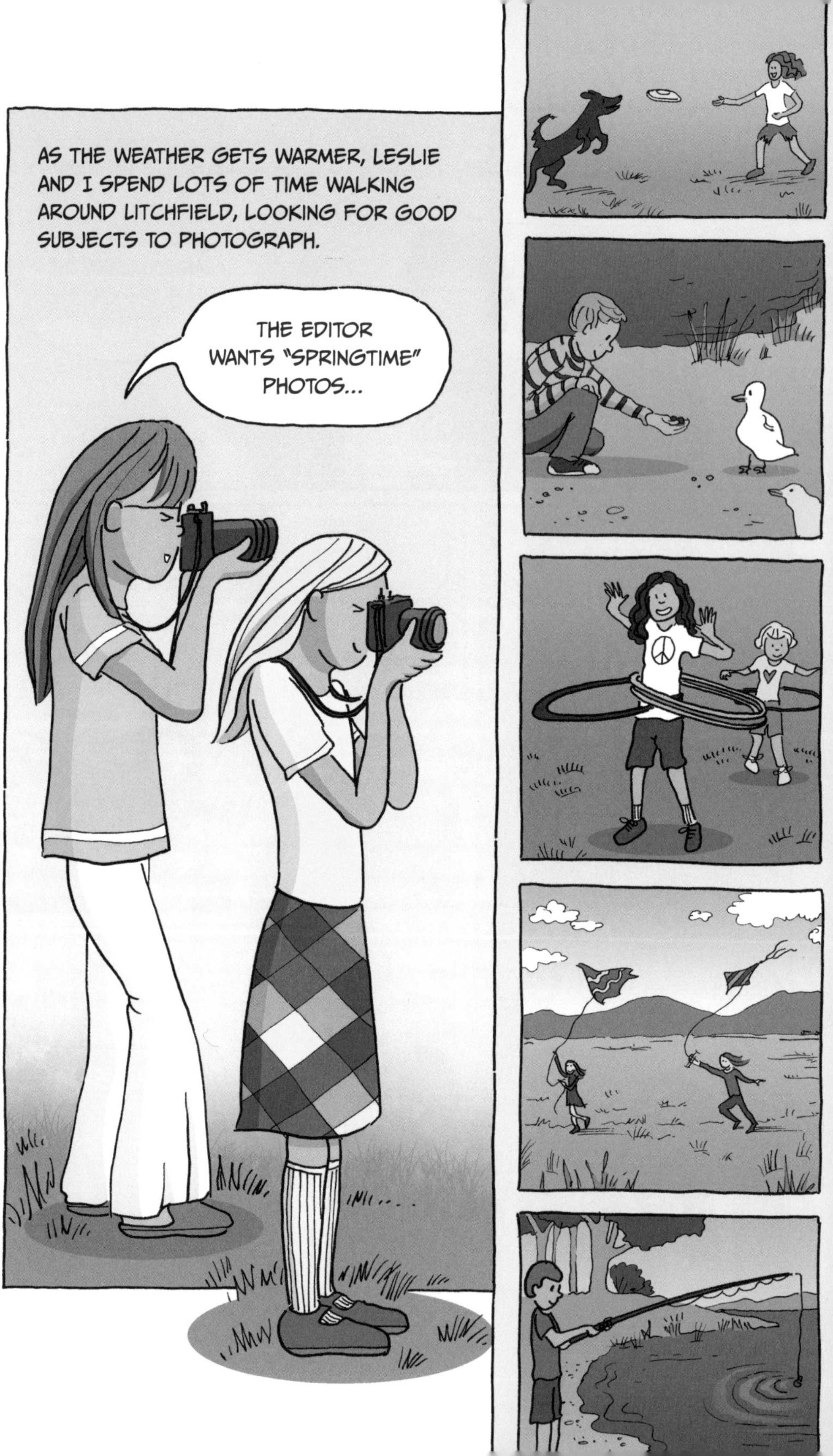
AS THE WEATHER GETS WARMER, LESLIE AND I SPEND LOTS OF TIME WALKING AROUND LITCHFIELD, LOOKING FOR GOOD SUBJECTS TO PHOTOGRAPH.
THE EDITOR WANTS "SPRINGTIME" PHOTOS...

175

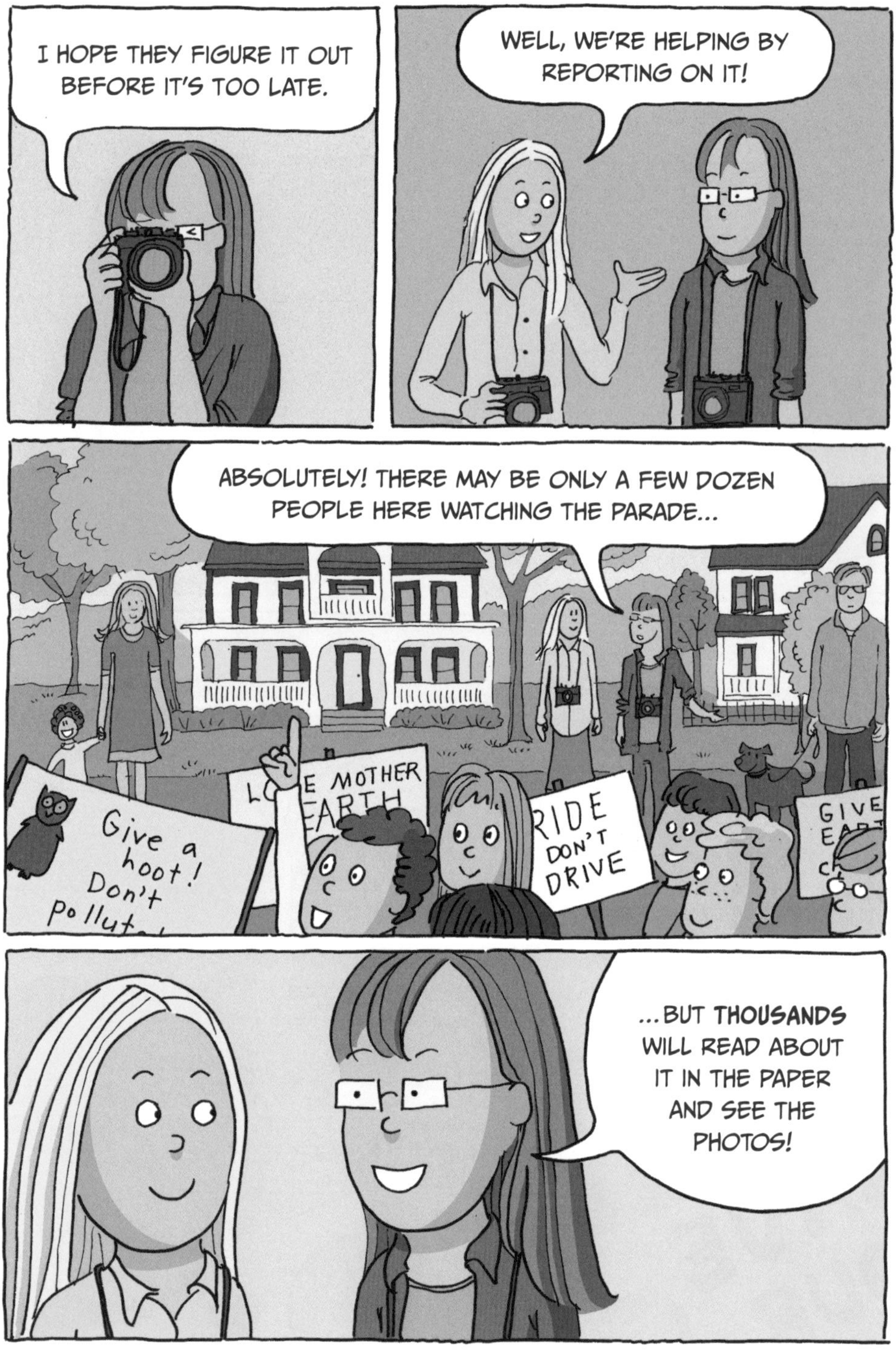
I HOPE THEY FIGURE IT OUT BEFORE IT'S TOO LATE.
WELL, WE'RE HELPING BY REPORTING ON IT!
ABSOLUTELY! THERE MAY BE ONLY A FEW DOZEN PEOPLE HERE WATCHING THE PARADE...
Give a hoot! Don't
MOTHER
RIDE DON'T DRIVE
GIVE
...BUT THOUSANDS WILL READ ABOUT IT IN THE PAPER AND SEE THE PHOTOS!

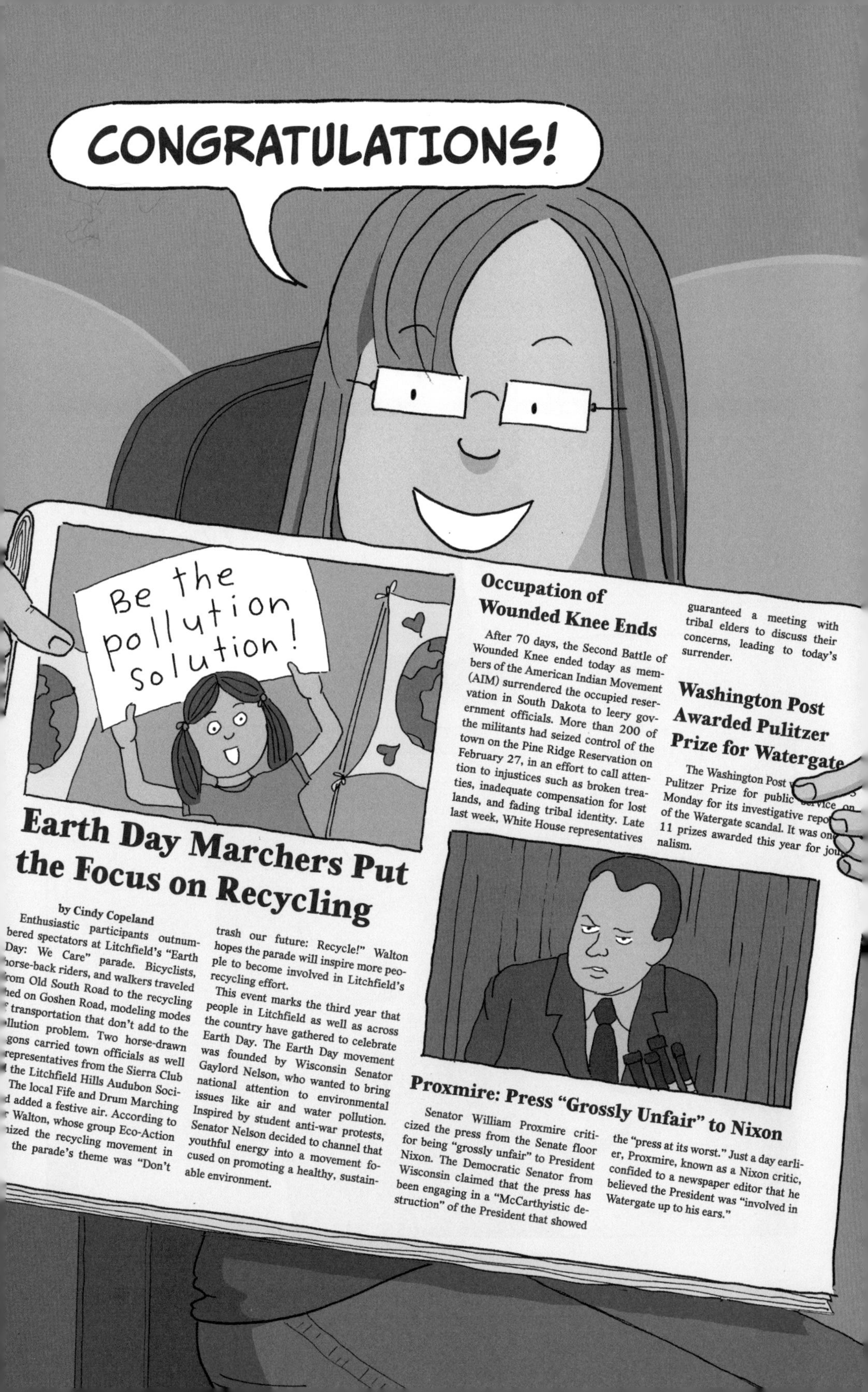
CONGRATULATIONS!
Be the pollution solution!
Earth Day Marchers Put the Focus on Recycling
by Cindy Copeland
Enthusiastic participants outnum-bered spectators at Litchfield's "Earth Day: We Care" parade. Bicyclists, horse-back riders, and walkers traveled rom Old South Road to the recycling hed on Goshen Road, modeling modes transportation that don't add to the llution problem. Two horse-drawn gons carried town officials as well representatives from the Sierra Club the Litchfield Hills Audubon Soci- The local Fife and Drum Marching d added a festive air. According to Walton, whose group Eco-Action nized the recycling movement in the parade's theme was "Don't trash our future: Recycle!" Walton hopes the parade will inspire more peo-ple to become involved in Litchfield's recycling effort.
This event marks the third year that people in Litchfield as well as across the country have gathered to celebrate Earth Day. The Earth Day movement was founded by Wisconsin Senator Gaylord Nelson, who wanted to bring national attention to environmental issues like air and water pollution. Inspired by student anti-war protests, Senator Nelson decided to channel that youthful energy into a movement fo-cused on promoting a healthy, sustain-able environment.
Occupation of Wounded Knee Ends
After 70 days, the Second Battle of Wounded Knee ended today as mem-bers of the American Indian Movement (AIM) surrendered the occupied reser-vation in South Dakota to leery gov-ernment officials. More than 200 of the militants had seized control of the town on the Pine Ridge Reservation on February 27, in an effort to call atten-tion to injustices such as broken trea-ties, inadequate compensation for lost lands, and fading tribal identity. Late last week, White House representatives guaranteed a meeting with tribal elders to discuss their concerns, leading to today's surrender.
Washington Post Awarded Pulitzer Prize for Watergate
The Washington Post Pulitzer Prize for public Monday for its investigative repo of the Watergate scandal. It was on 11 prizes awarded this year for jo nalism.
Proxmire: Press "Grossly Unfair" to Nixon
Senator William Proxmire criti-cized the press from the Senate floor for being "grossly unfair" to President Nixon. The Democratic Senator from Wisconsin claimed that the press has been engaging in a "McCarthyistic de-struction" of the President that showed the "press at its worst." Just a day earli-er, Proxmire, known as a Nixon critic, confided to a newspaper editor that he believed the President was "involved in Watergate up to his ears."

Chapter 15

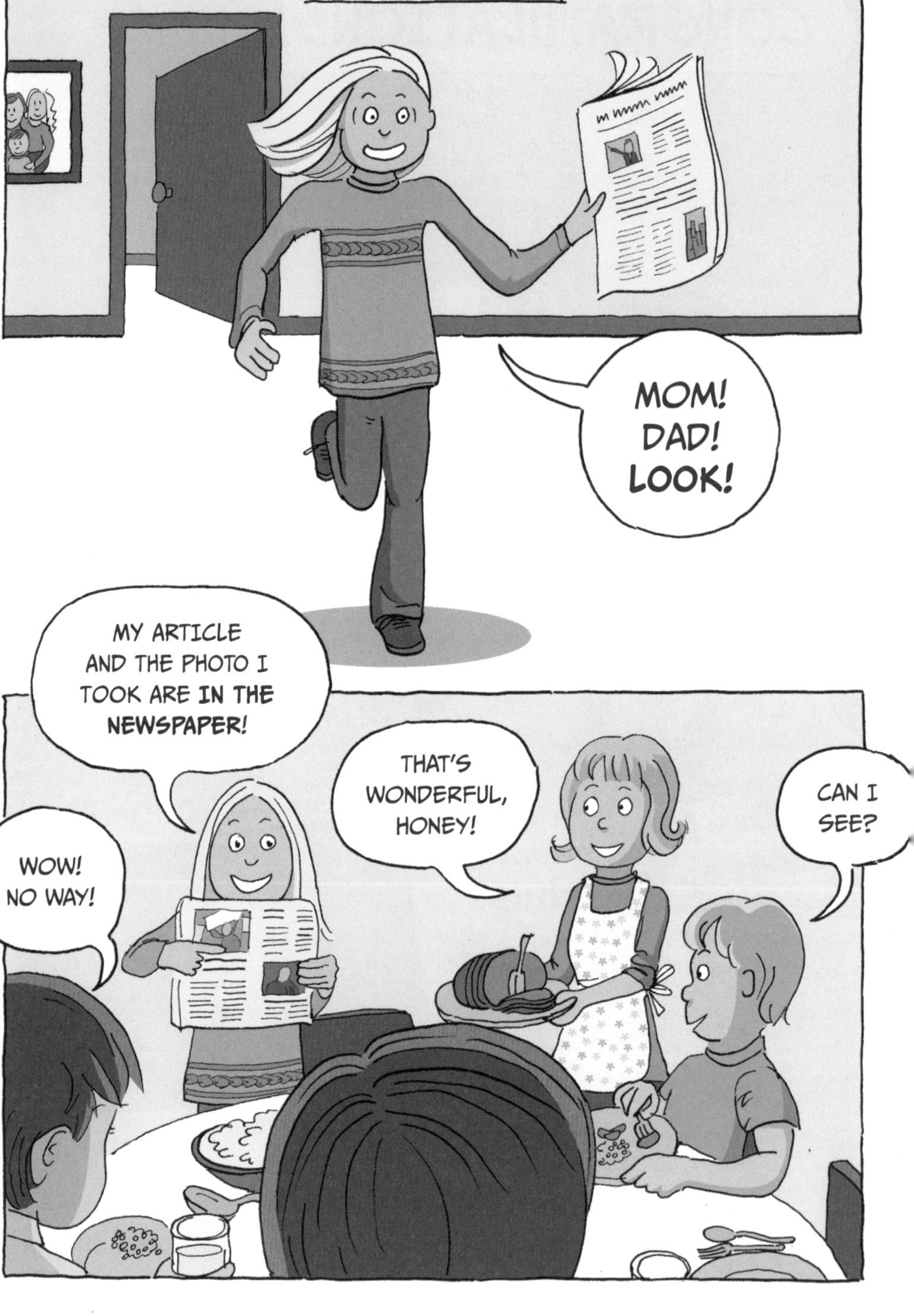
MOM! DAD! LOOK!
MY ARTICLE AND THE PHOTO I TOOK ARE IN THE NEWSPAPER!
WOW! NO WAY!
THAT'S WONDERFUL, HONEY!
CAN I SEE?

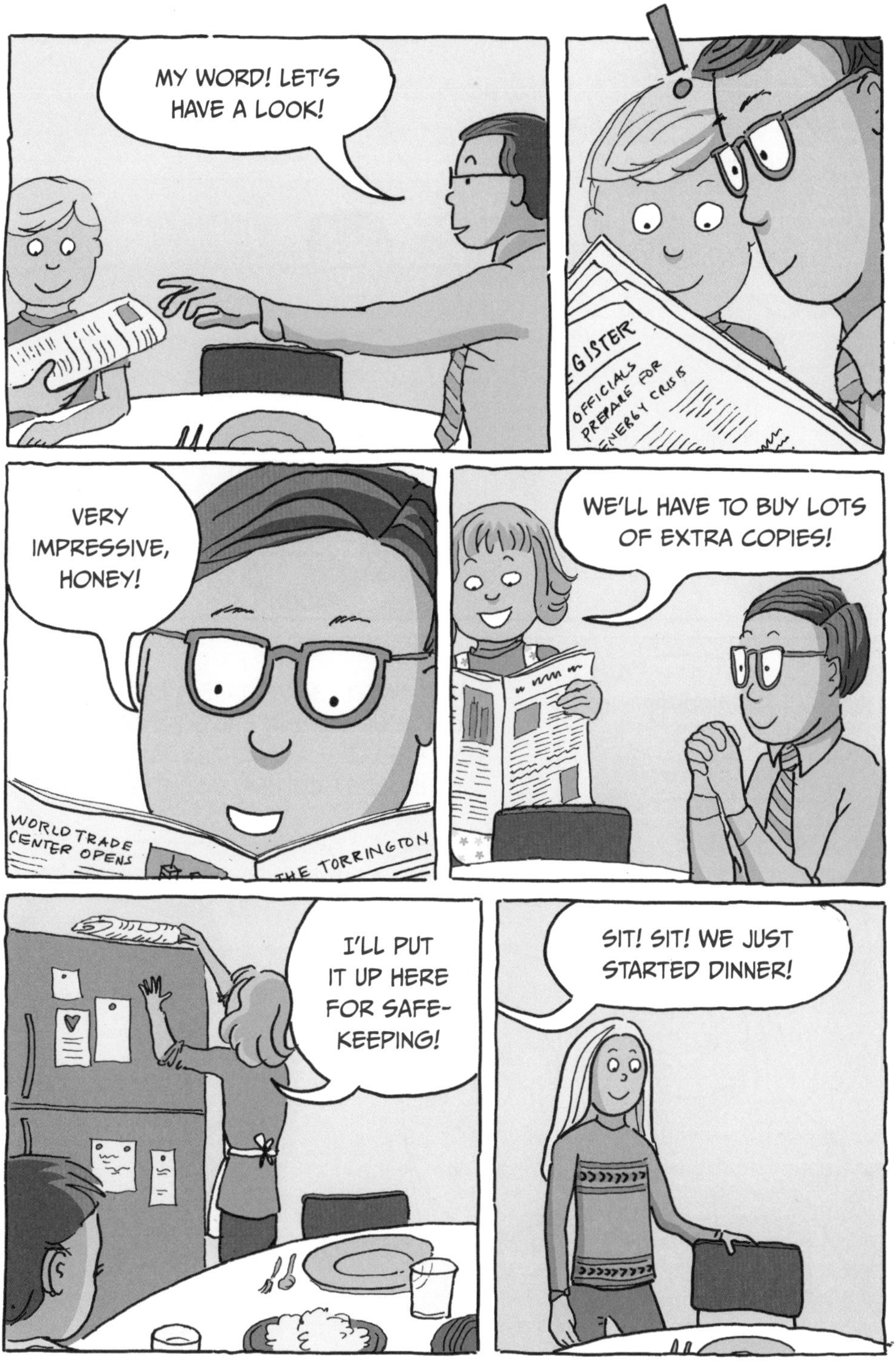
MY WORD! LET'S HAVE A LOOK!
-GISTER
OFFICIALS PREPARE FOR ENERGY CRISIS
VERY IMPRESSIVE, HONEY!
WORLD TRADE CENTER OPENS
THE TORRINGTON
WE'LL HAVE TO BUY LOTS OF EXTRA COPIES!
I'LL PUT IT UP HERE FOR SAFE-KEEPING!
SIT! SIT! WE JUST STARTED DINNER!

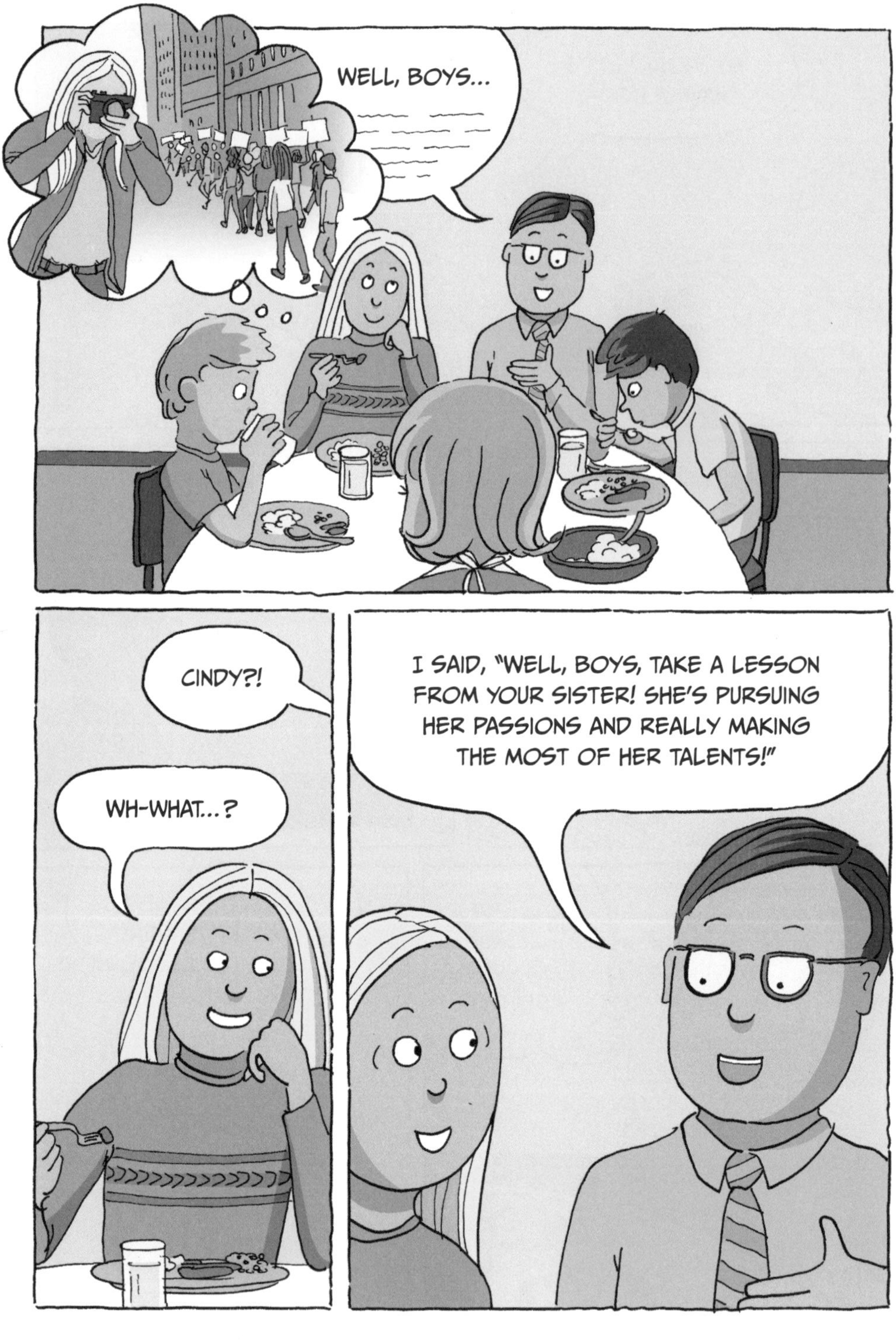
WELL, BOYS...
CINDY?!
WH-WHAT...?
I SAID, "WELL, BOYS, TAKE A LESSON FROM YOUR SISTER! SHE'S PURSUING HER PASSIONS AND REALLY MAKING THE MOST OF HER TALENTS!"

*THE SECRET PLACE IS A HUGE STORAGE CLOSET IN THE BACK OF THE HOUSE.

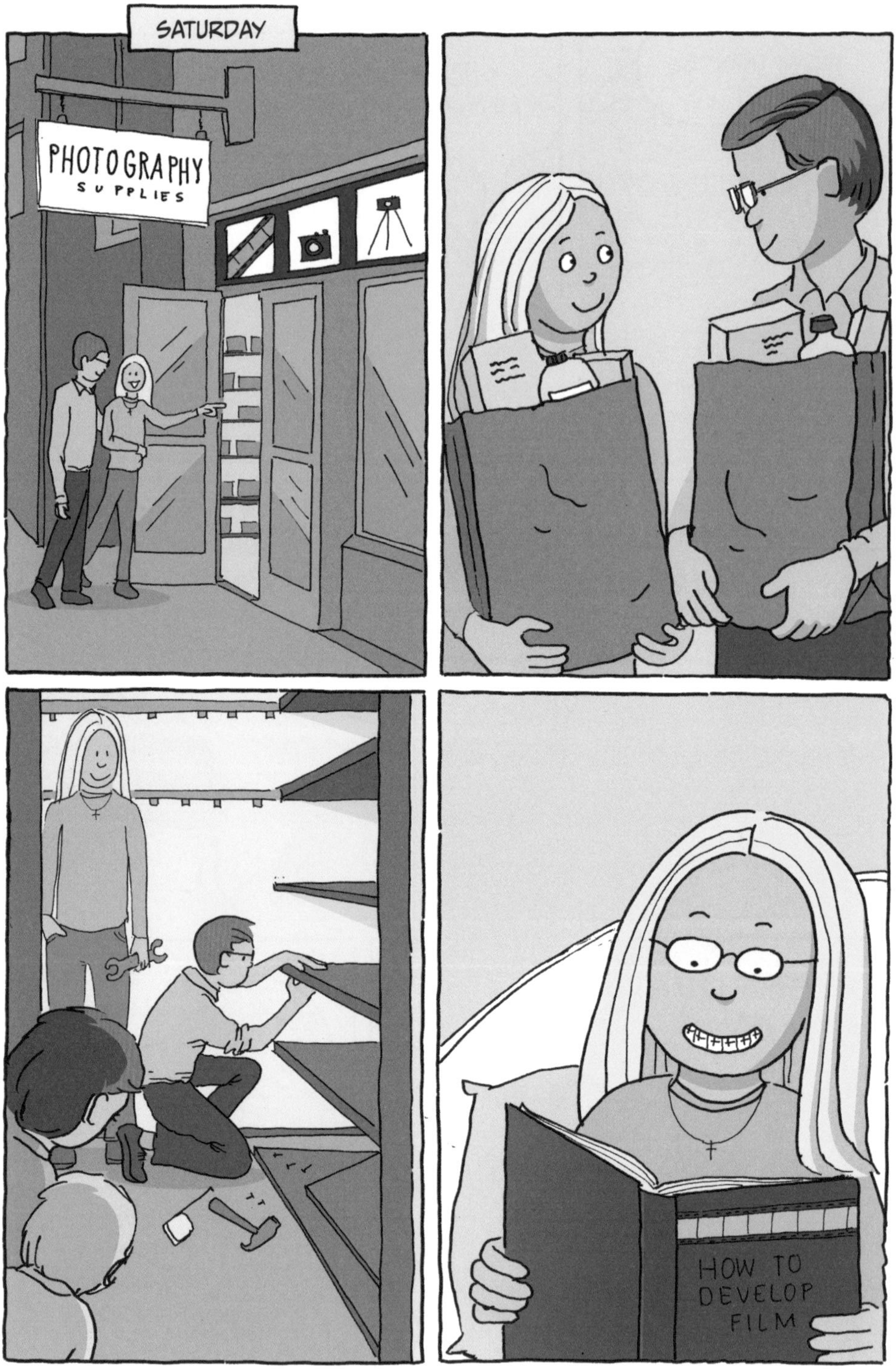
SATURDAY
PHOTOGRAPHY
SUPPLIES
HOW TO
DEVELOP
FILM

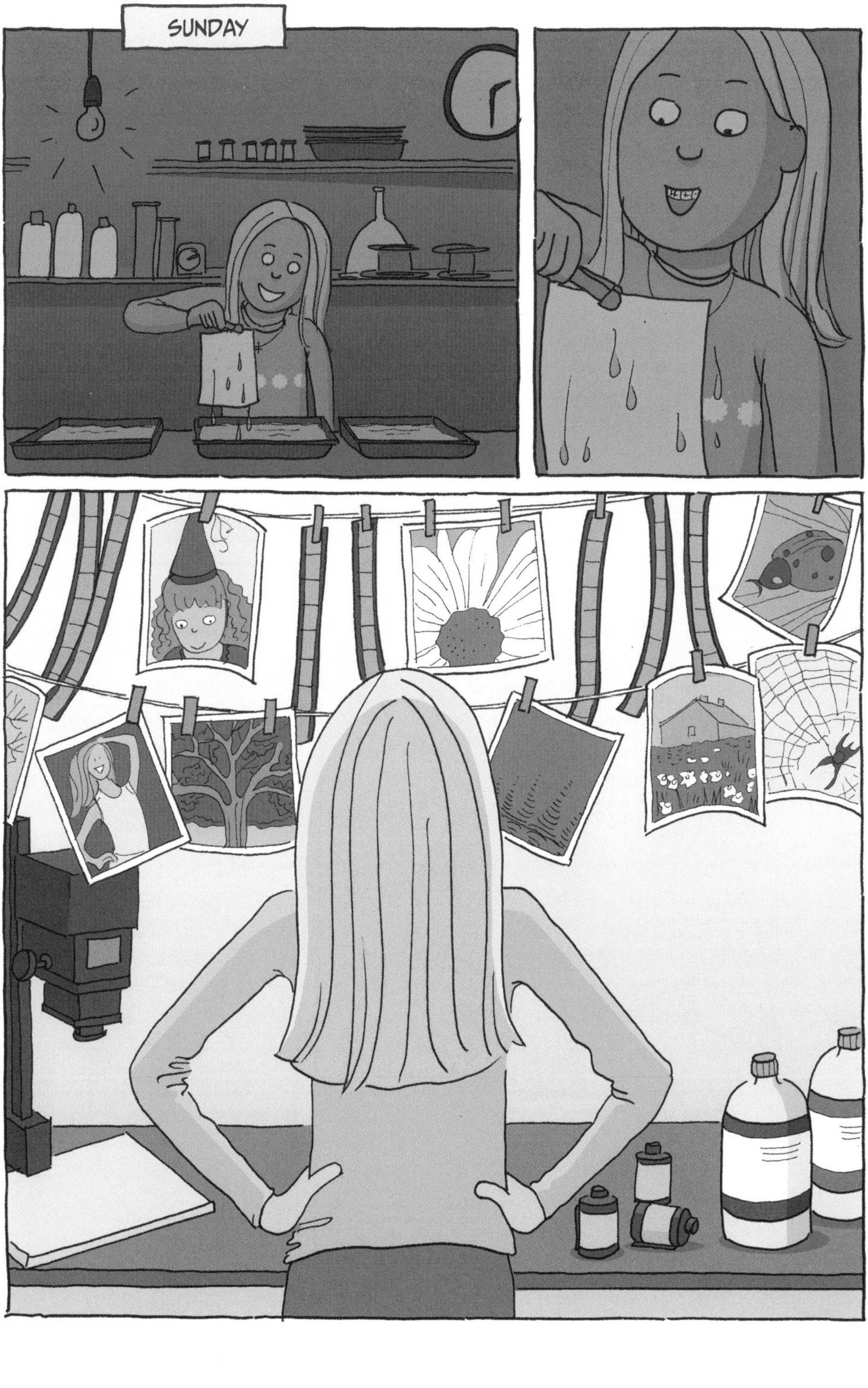
SUNDAY

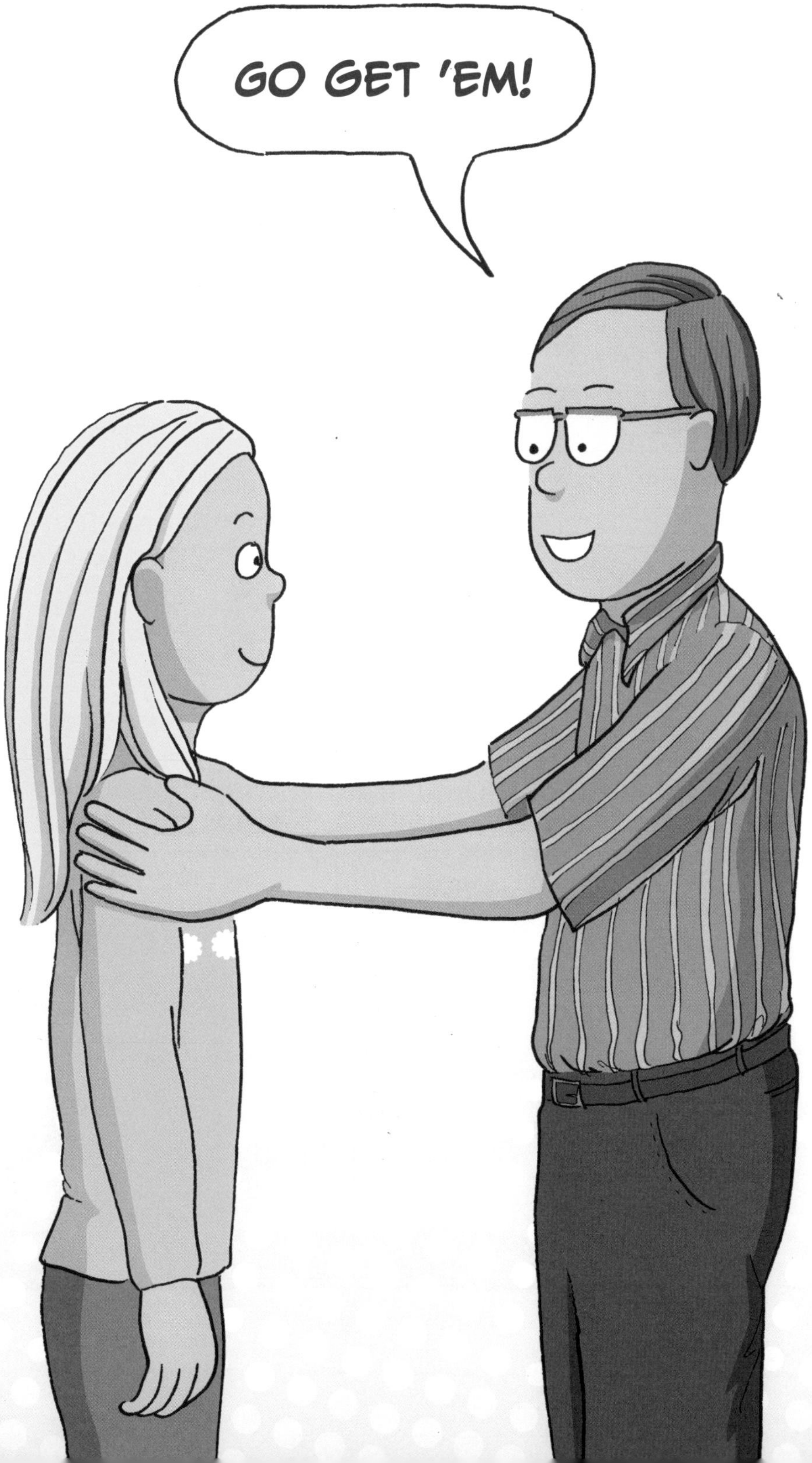
GO GET 'EM!

Chapter 16

189

AFTER I DELIVER THE FLYERS, I STAY NEAR THE PHONE. I DON'T WANT TO MISS A CALL!

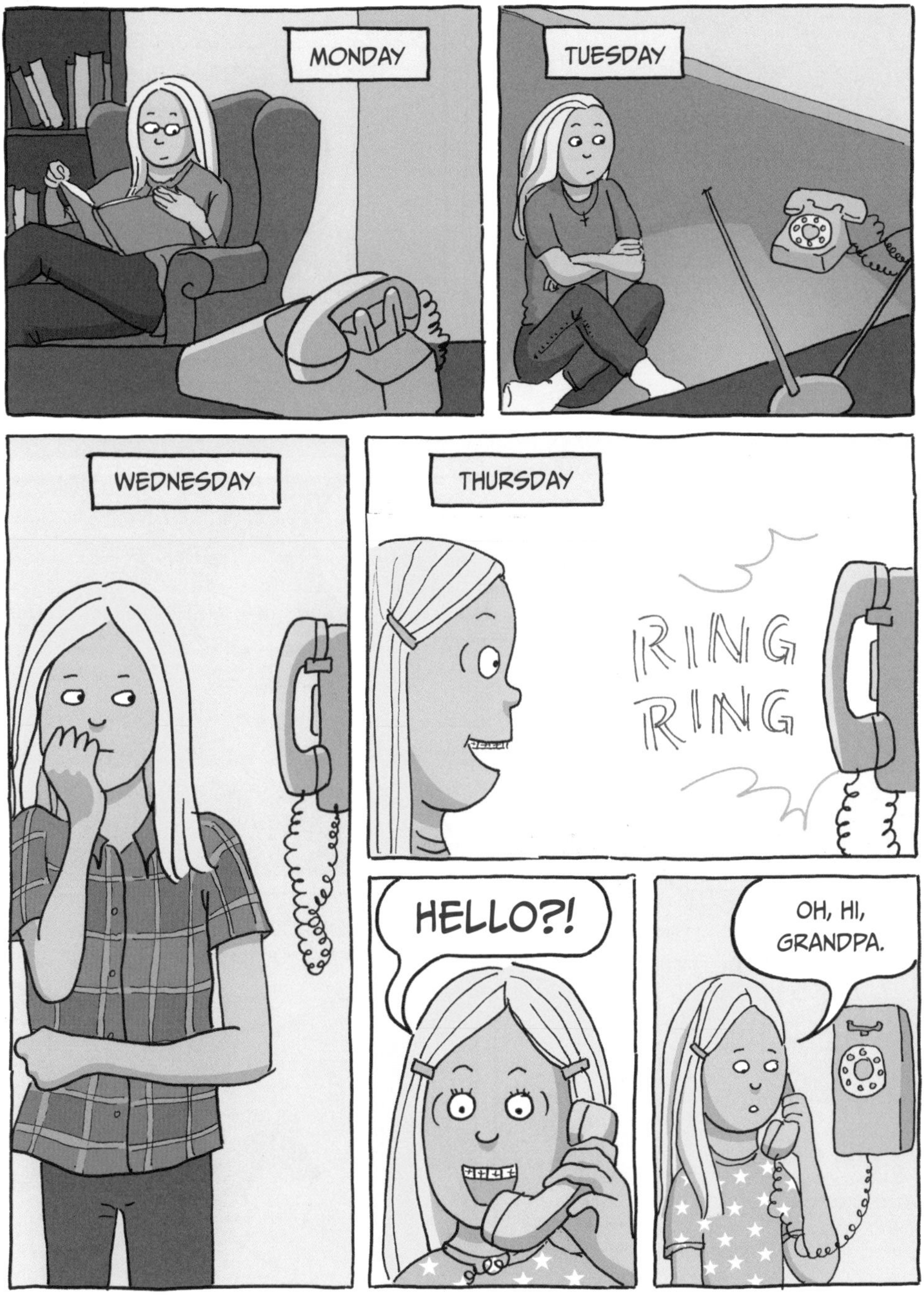
MONDAY
TUESDAY
WEDNESDAY
THURSDAY
RING
RING
HELLO?!
OH, HI, GRANDPA.

EVERYONE'S DISTRACTED BY SUMMER PLANS. THE TEACHERS TRY ALL SORTS OF TRICKS TO KEEP US "ENGAGED."

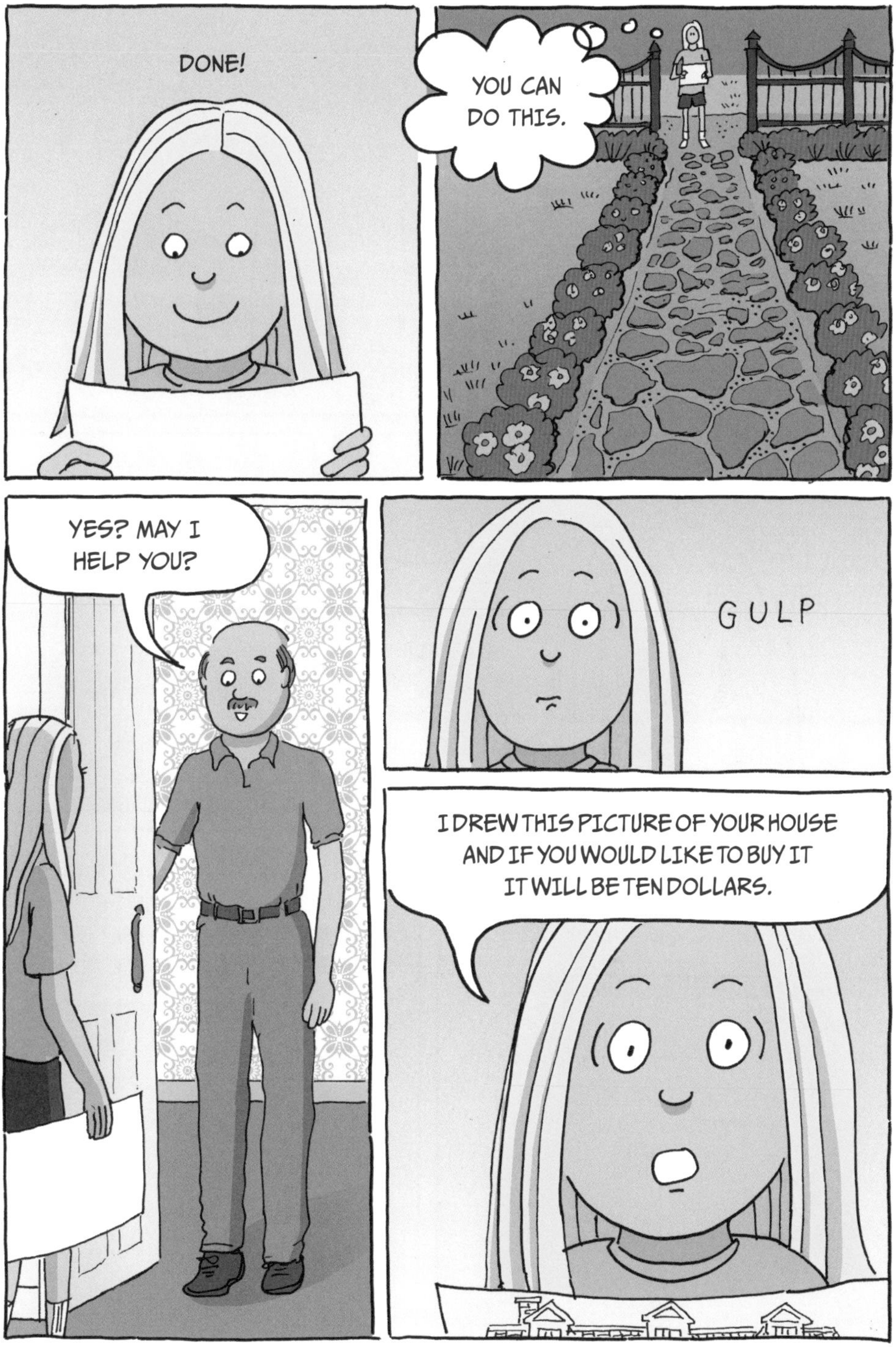
DONE!
YOU CAN DO THIS.
YES? MAY I HELP YOU?
GULP
I DREW THIS PICTURE OF YOUR HOUSE AND IF YOU WOULD LIKE TO BUY IT IT WILL BE TEN DOLLARS.

SUDDENLY, SEVENTH-GRADE PROBLEMS SEEM VERY FAR AWAY... AND VERY INSIGNIFICANT.

Chapter 17

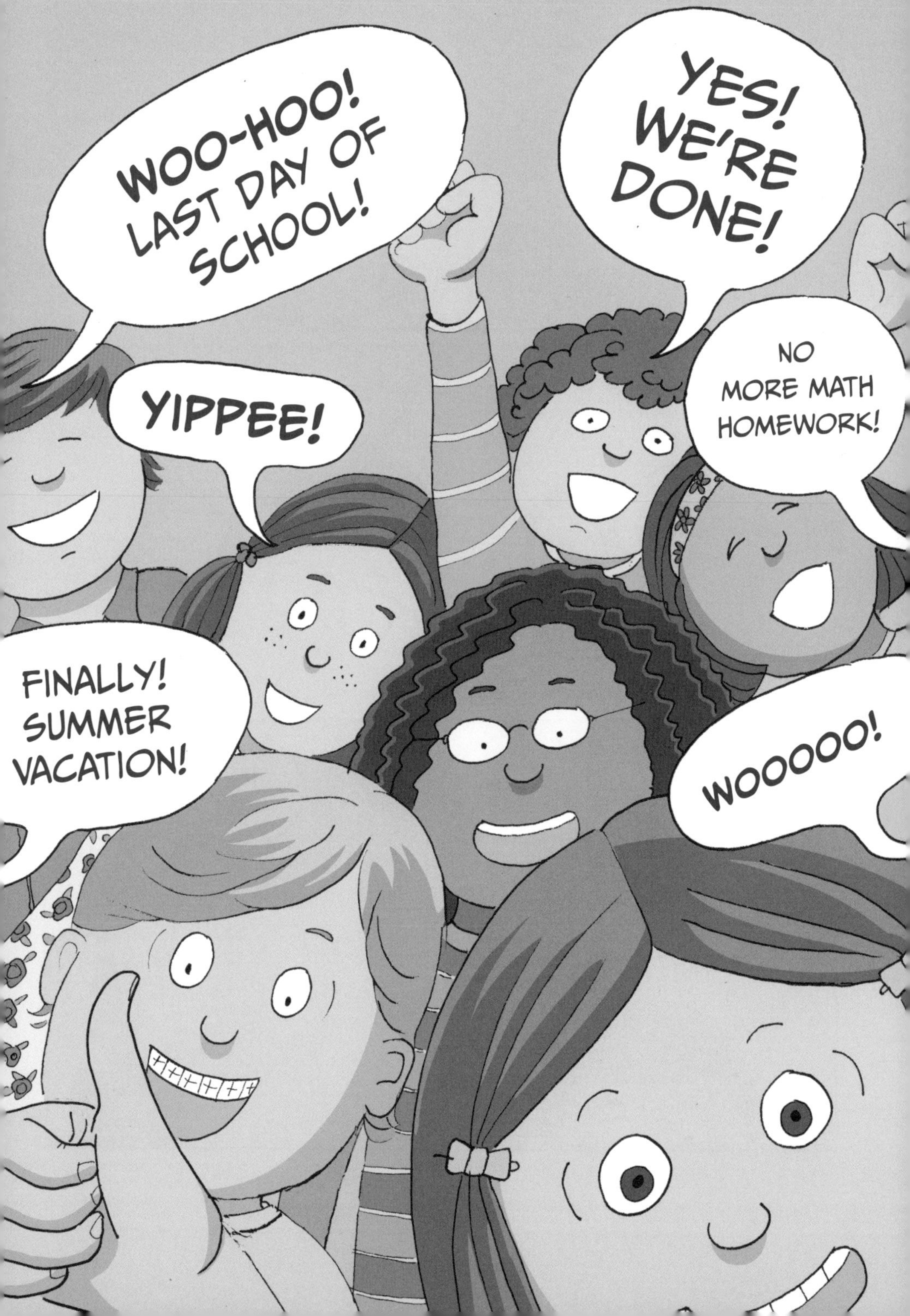
WOO-HOO! LAST DAY OF SCHOOL!
YES! WE'RE DONE!
YIPPEE!
NO MORE MATH HOMEWORK!
FINALLY! SUMMER VACATION!
WOOOOO!

207

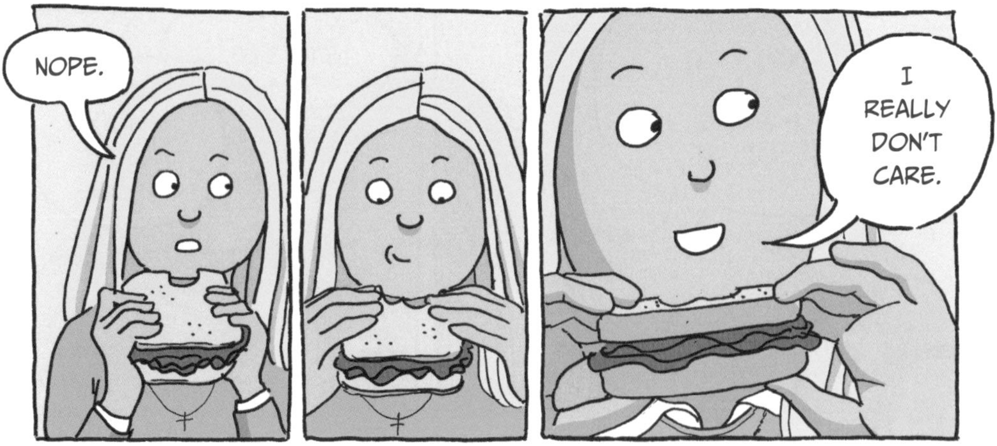
NOPE.
I REALLY DON'T CARE.

I KNOW HOW IT'S SUPPOSED TO WORK IN SEVENTH GRADE:
YOU ARE WHO THE OTHER KIDS SAY YOU ARE.
BUT I'M NOT OK WITH THAT.
I'LL SAY WHO I AM.

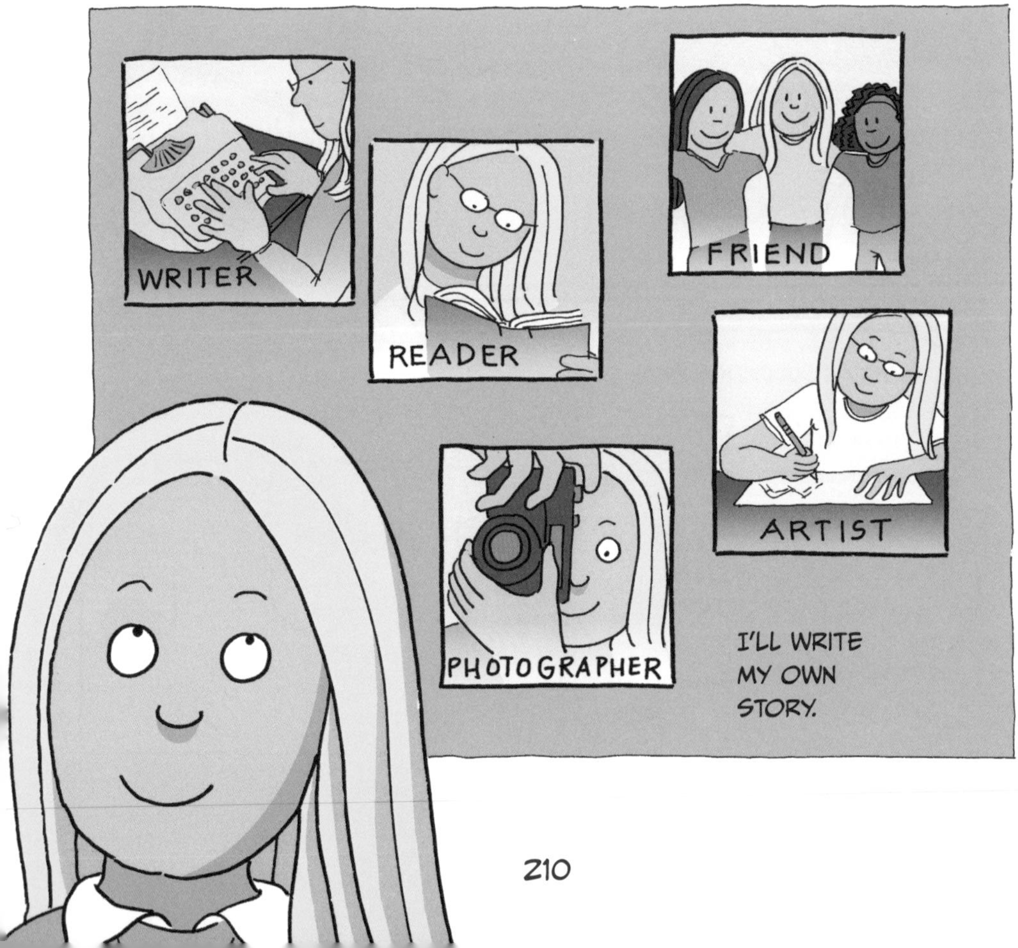
WRITER
READER
FRIEND
ARTIST
PHOTOGRAPHER
I'LL WRITE MY OWN STORY.

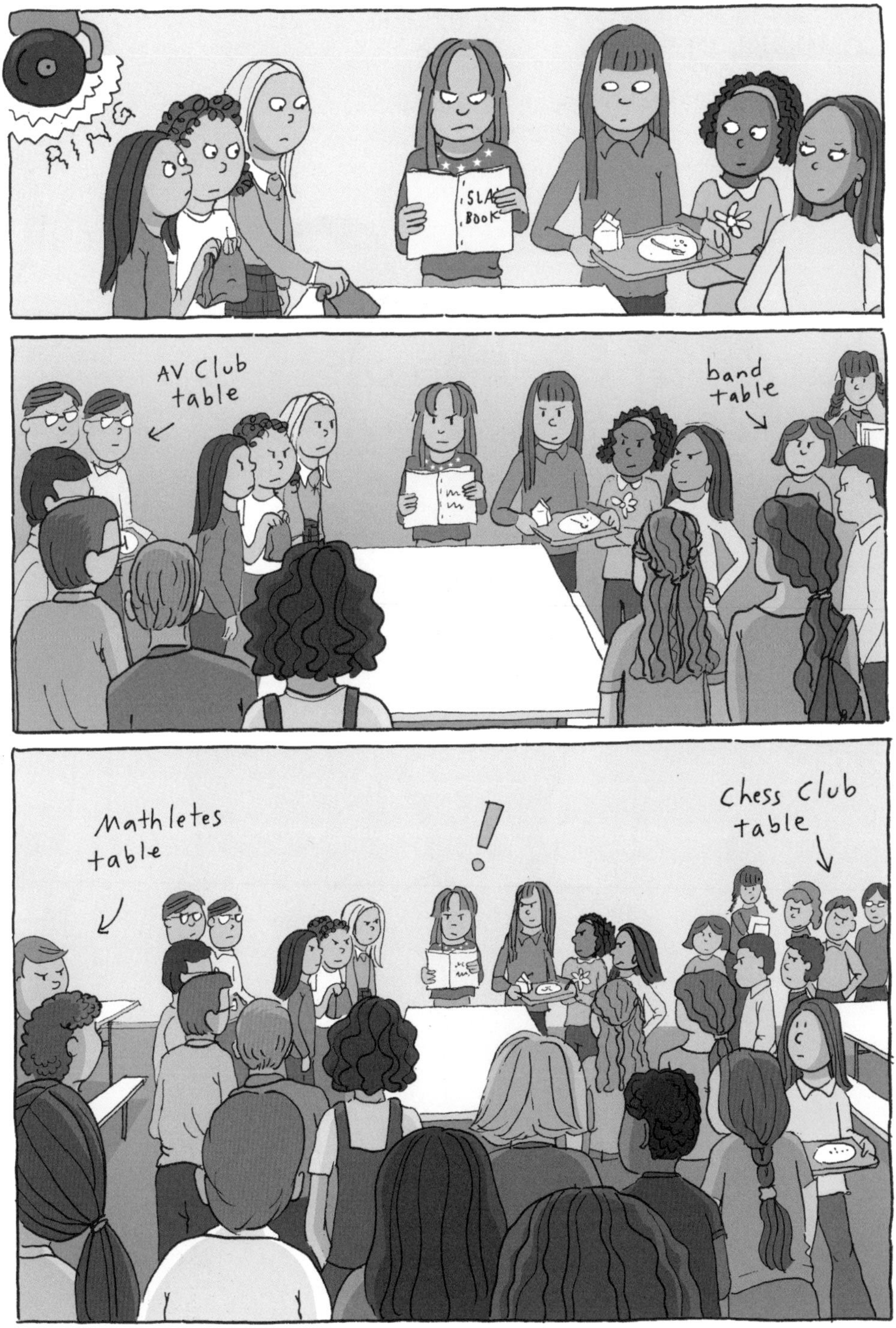
RING
SLAM BOOK
AV Club table
band table
Mathletes table
!
Chess Club table

THERE IS *ONE MORE* DEFENSE PREY CAN USE:
COMMUNAL DEFENSE.

A PREY GROUP DEFENDS ITSELF BY STICKING TOGETHER AND MOBBING A PREDATOR RATHER THAN RUNNING AWAY.

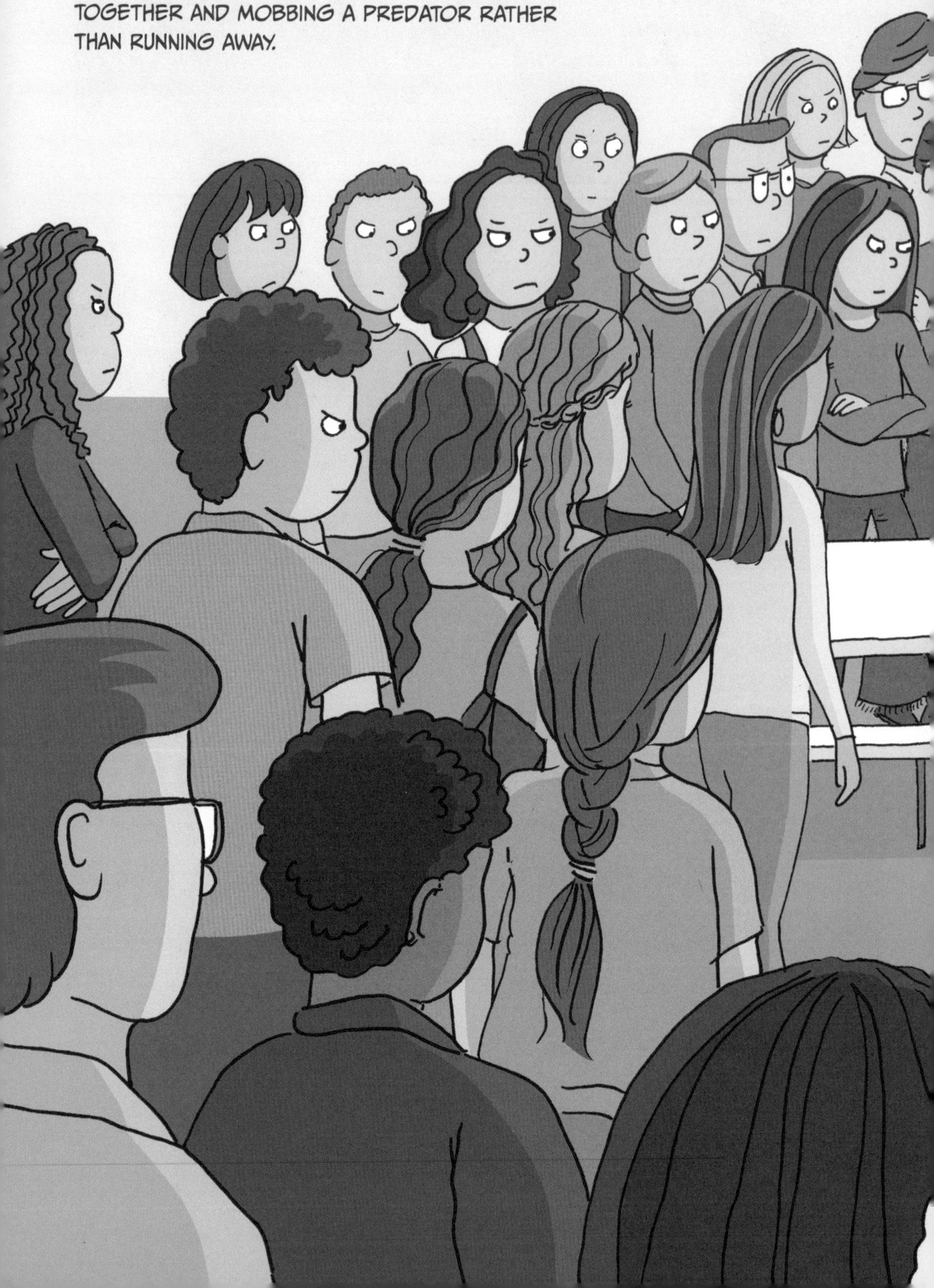

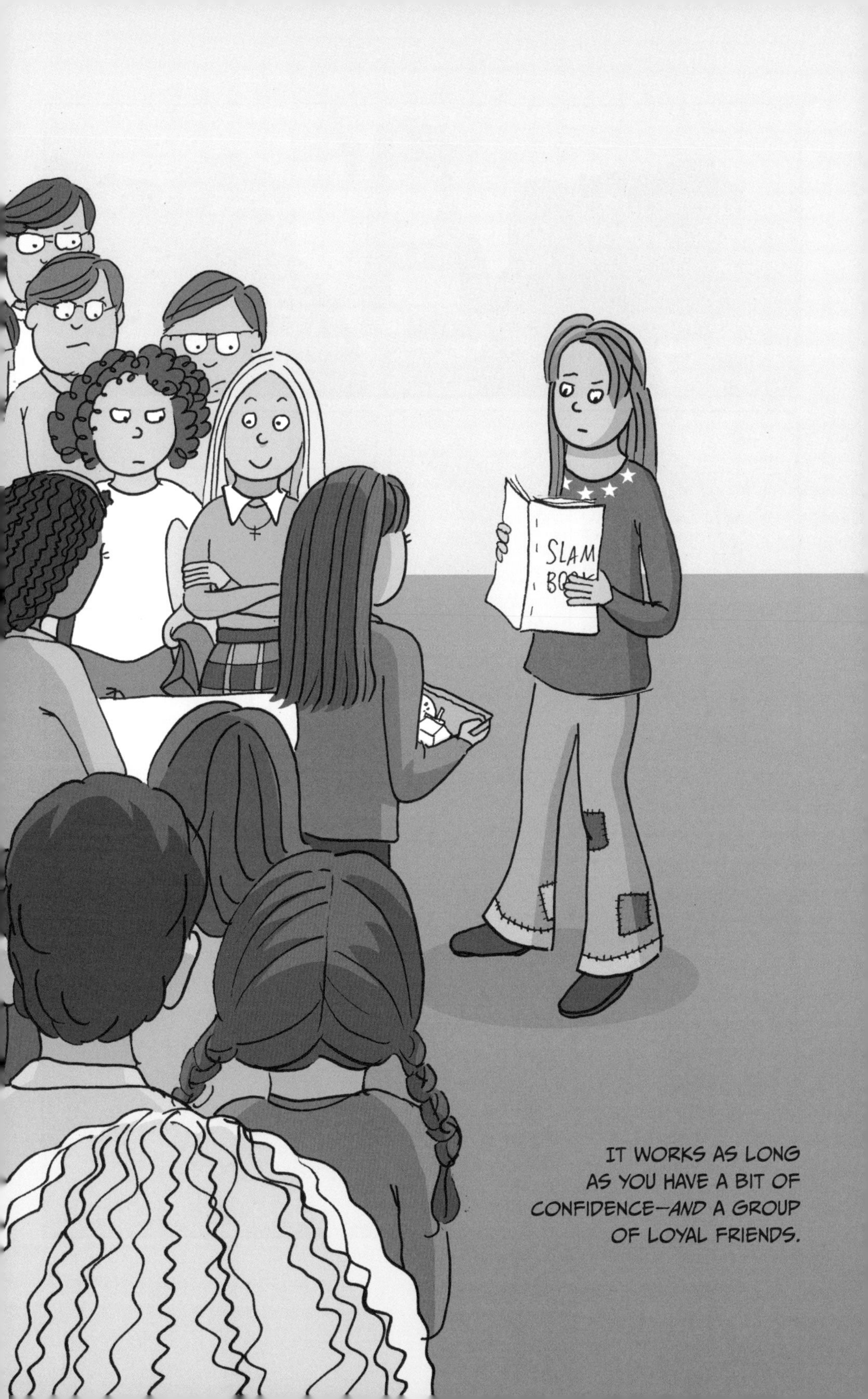
SLAM BO
IT WORKS AS LONG AS YOU HAVE A BIT OF CONFIDENCE—*AND* A GROUP OF LOYAL FRIENDS.

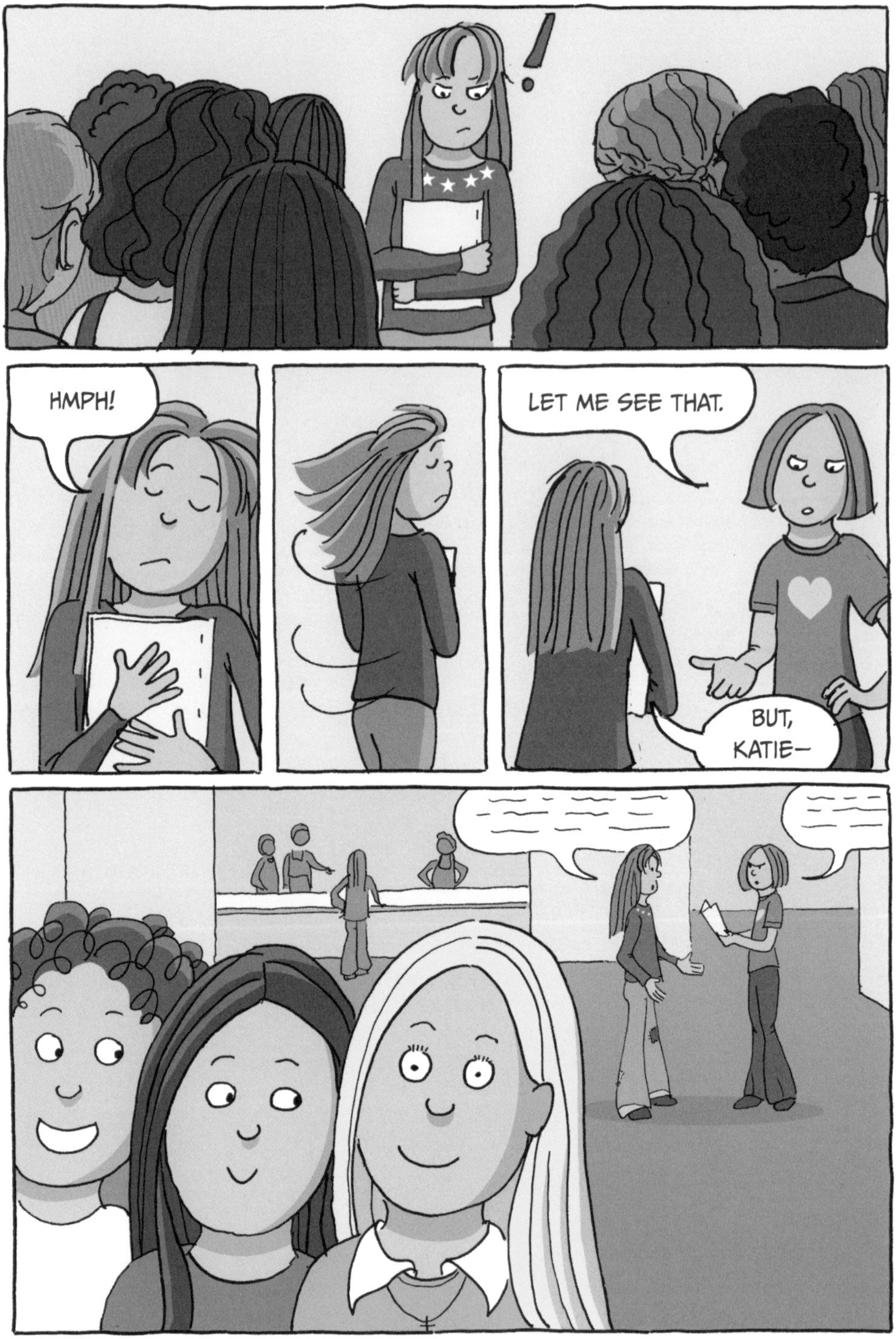
!
HMPH!
LET ME SEE THAT.
BUT, KATIE—

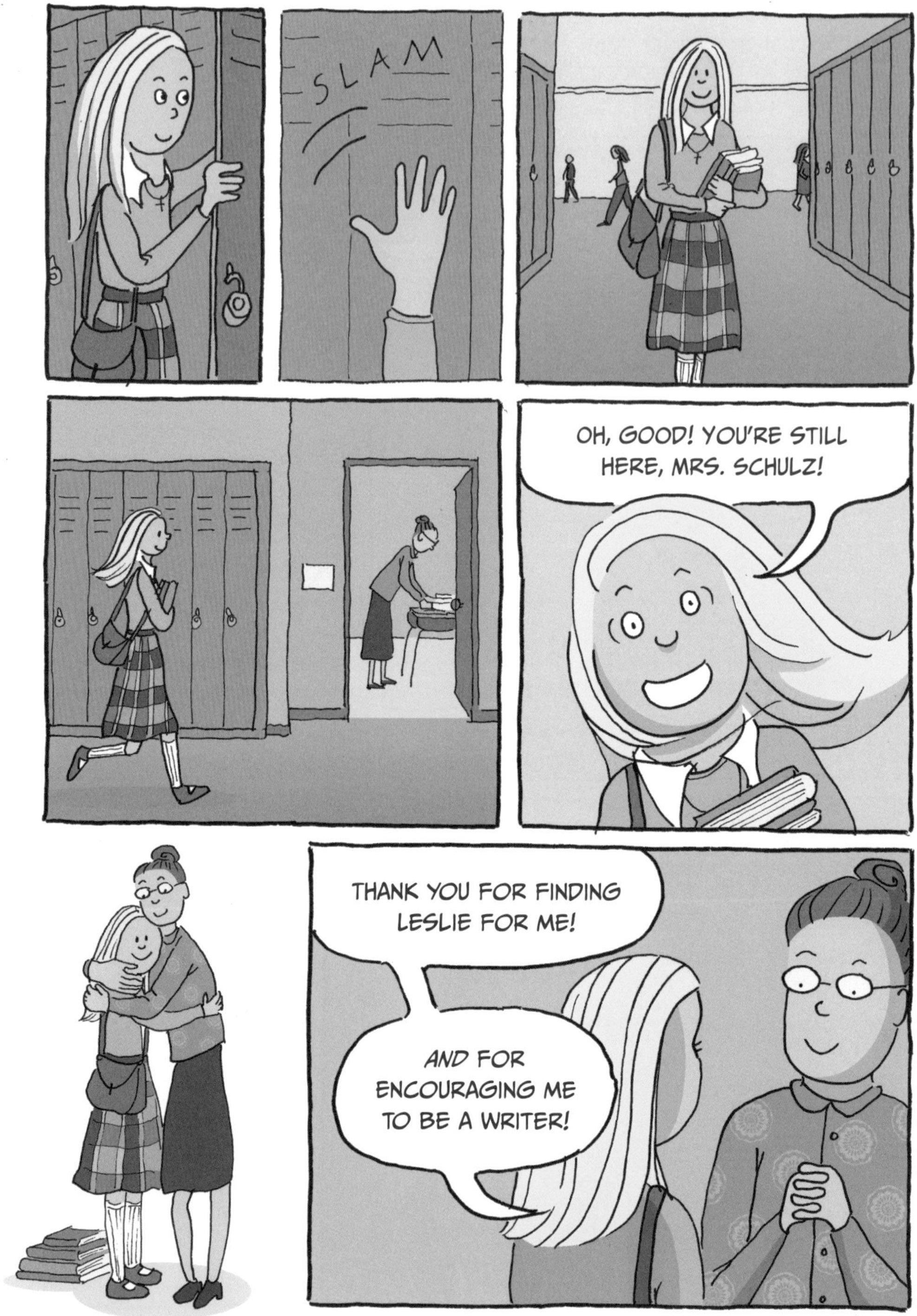
SLAM
OH, GOOD! YOU'RE STILL HERE, MRS. SCHULZ!
THANK YOU FOR FINDING LESLIE FOR ME!
AND FOR ENCOURAGING ME TO BE A WRITER!

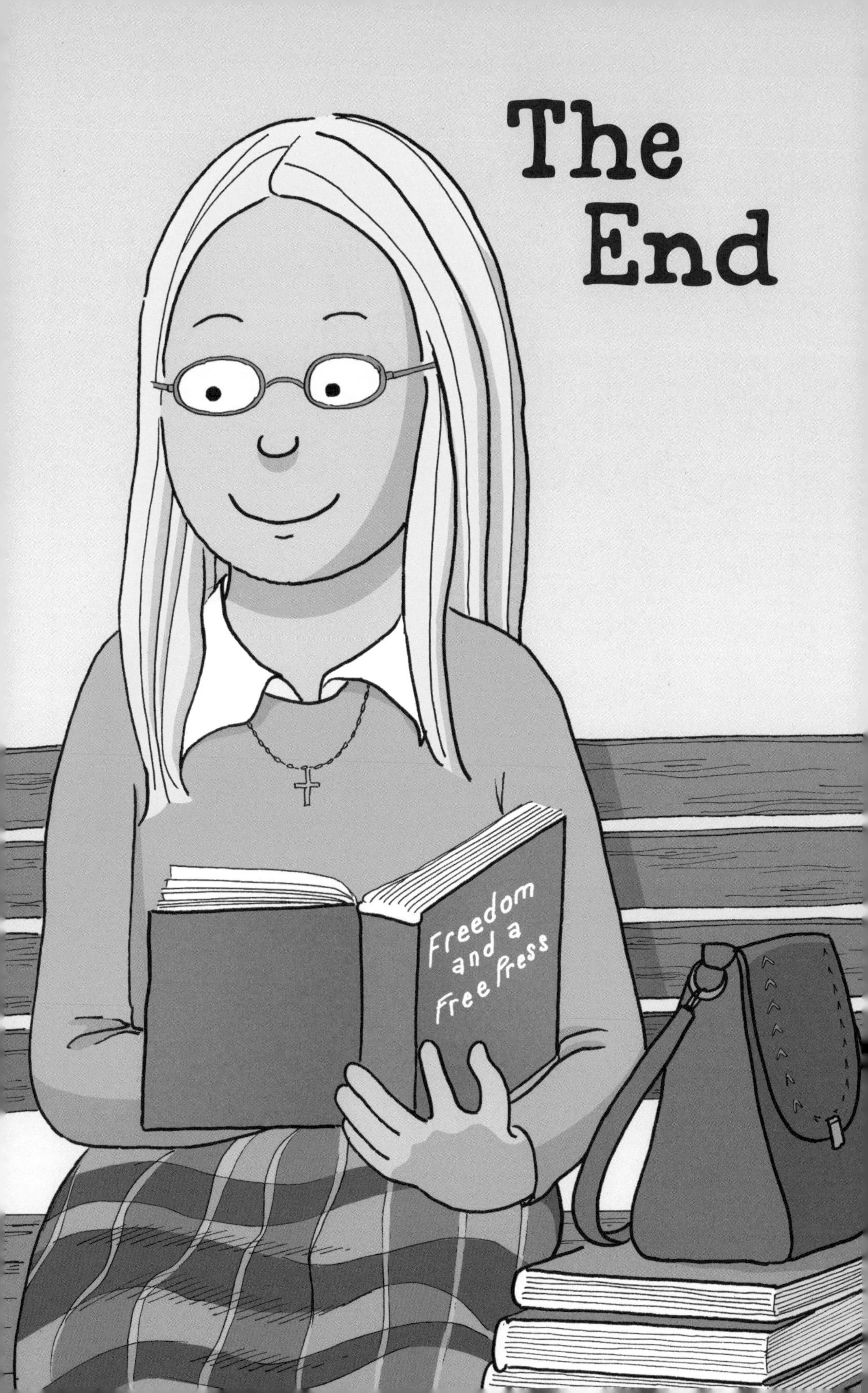
The End
Freedom and a Free Press

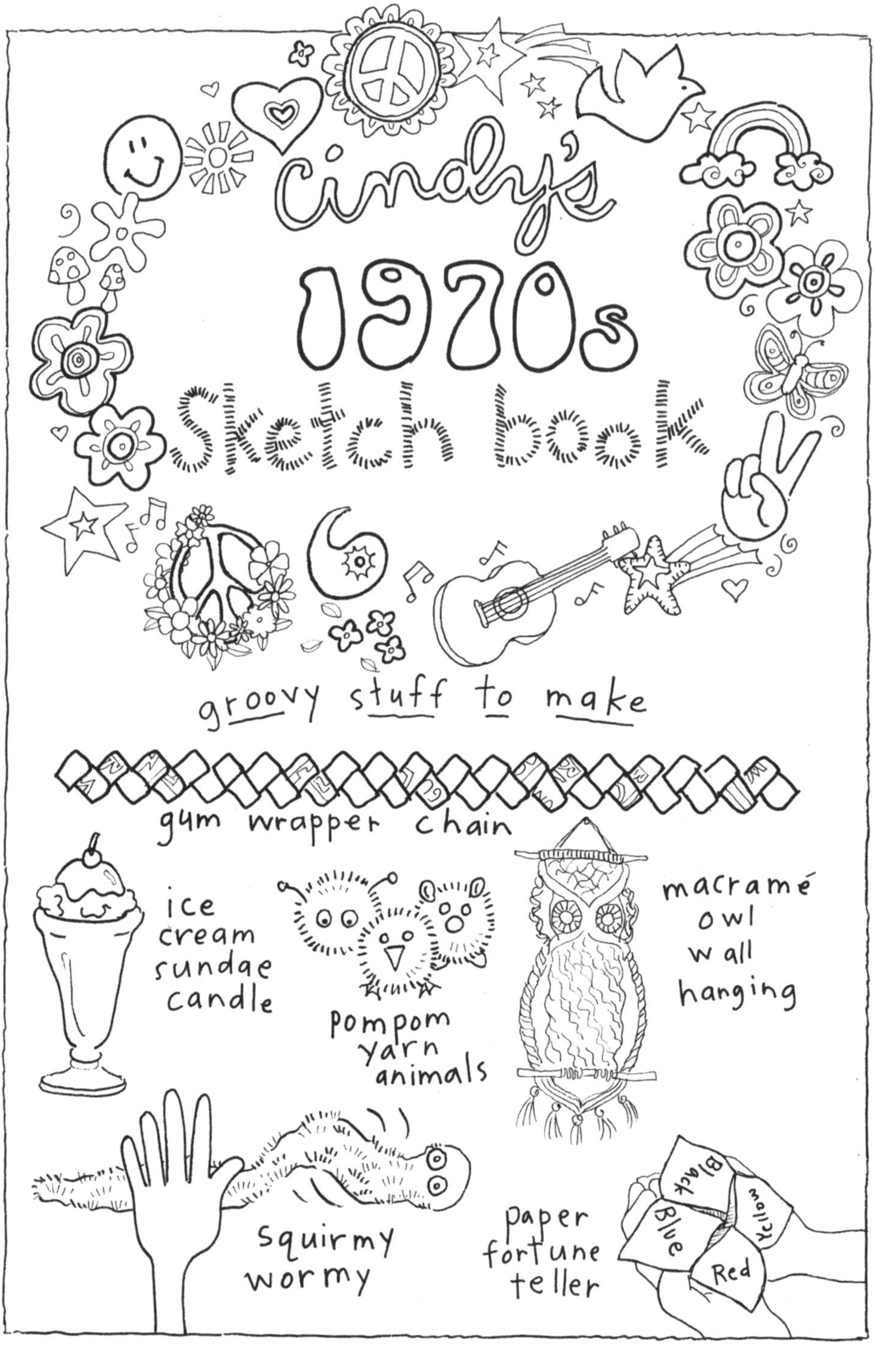
cindy's
1970s
Sketch book
groovy stuff to make
gum wrapper chain
ice cream sundae candle
pompom yarn animals
macramé owl wall hanging
squirmy wormy
paper fortune teller
Black
Yellow
Blue
Red

Nice Threads!

crafty fashion fun

tie-dye a shirt

macramé a belt

jazz up your bell-bottoms with...

auto-graphs

patches

a little bleach

add pieces of fabric

Crochet a vest

string love beads

fringe the bottoms

make a beaded headband

Then add...

leather ponytail holder

mood ring

suede purse

platform shoes

plaid poncho

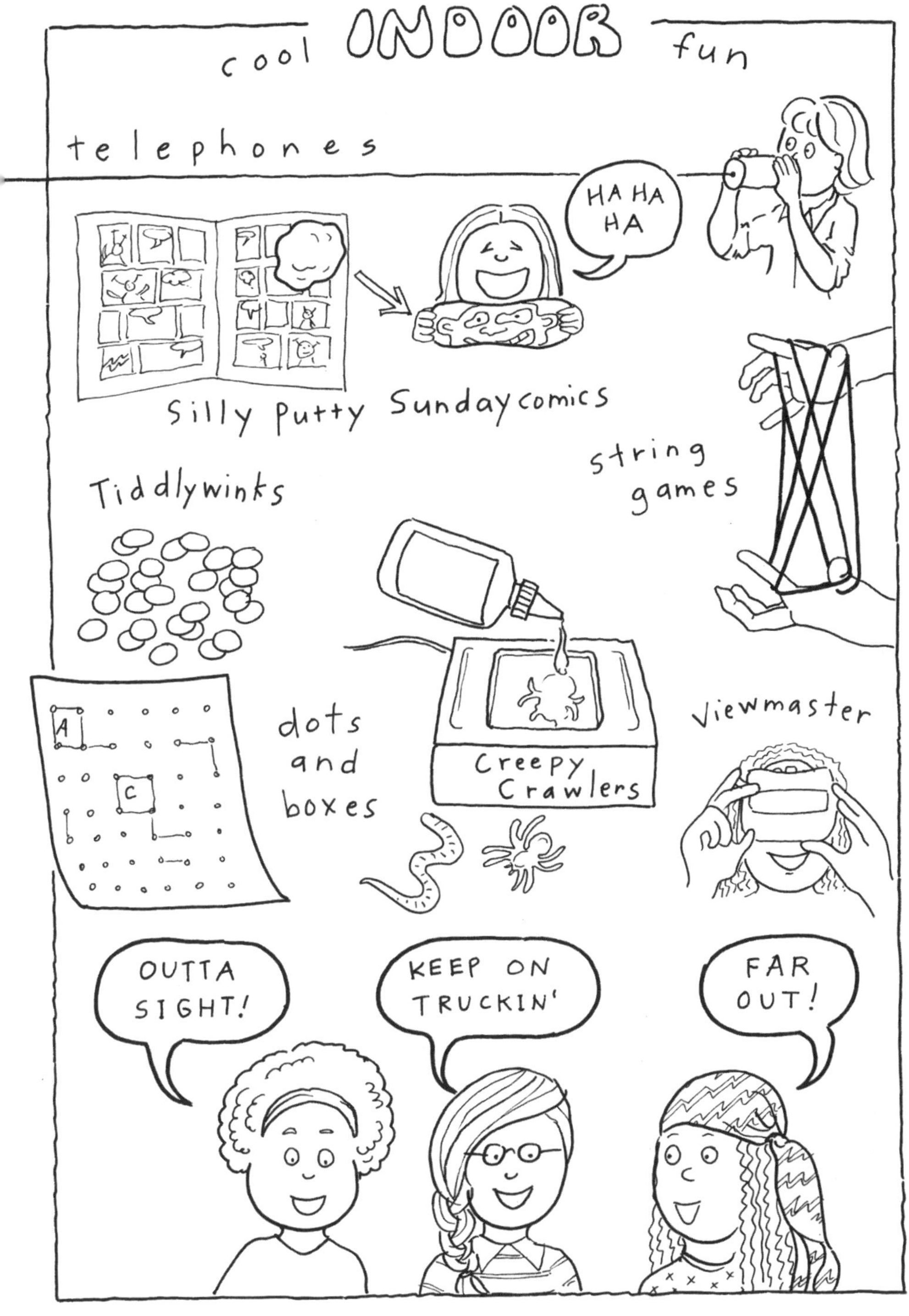

cool INDOOR fun
telephones
HA HA HA
Silly Putty
Sunday comics
string games
Tiddlywinks
dots and boxes
A
C
Creepy Crawlers
Viewmaster
OUTTA SIGHT!
KEEP ON TRUCKIN'
FAR OUT!

AUTHOR'S NOTE

Cub is based on the true story of my time as a cub
reporter for a regional Connecticut newspaper, beginning
when I was in seventh grade. Many of the details
are true; for example, my work was published in the
newspaper, my dad built me a darkroom, and my drawings of
historic buildings appeared on crockery sold in town. I
lost my childhood best friend to a cool (and cruel) crowd
for a time and frequently hung out with my crush at the
secret fort we made on "the Island."

But real life rarely, if ever, unfolds in a way that
creates a perfect story. Like many memoirs, this one is
inspired by real events and maintains the essence of
what happened in my life, but incorporates changes for a
better reading experience. Some of the changes are mine,
and others were suggested by my editors.

I compressed the timeline in *Cub*, for instance, so
it would occur within one school year; in reality, I
continued to work with Leslie Jacobs into my high school
years. The newspaper headlines and articles in the book
are based on real ones that were published at that time,
and a lot of the meetings and events that Leslie and I
attend in the book were informed by the articles Leslie
wrote for the *Torrington Register* that year. Specific
details of meetings and interviews, however, are largely
fictional.

The challenge in writing about a historical time period—
especially for younger readers—is how authentically to
represent it. Is the book a time capsule, with language
and culture frozen in 1972 and accurately portrayed? Or
is it a modernized version, seen through a twenty-first-
century filter?

Cub is a bit of both. I hope that readers will notice
and discuss details like the all-boy AV club, kids riding

bikes without helmets, the number of adults smoking cigarettes, and the relatively homogeneous population, as well as the positive aspects of life in the seventies: lots of family meals and togetherness, the freedom (and free time) to explore the outdoors, the absence of intrusive social media, and the valued role of the town library. I also hope readers will notice how many of the issues we worried about all those years ago—equality for all, protecting the environment, corrupt politicians, attacks on a free press—are still topics of concern today.

Other than Mrs. Schulz, Leslie Jacobs, and my family members, I changed all the names and identifying details of characters in the book. Many of my classmates in *Cub* are composites of my friends from that time. The character called Katie remains a close friend to this day. In her childhood bedroom, the pencil lines where we—and yes, "Evie"—charted our growth are etched into the doorframe; the chalkboard in her attic still has the faintest markings from when we played school.

My beautiful hometown of Litchfield looks much as it did when this story took place. Kids still ride their bikes to Murphy's Pharmacy for candy, meet up at the cannon on the town green, and (I'm guessing) build secret forts on the Island.

It was a marvelous place to grow up. I was a lucky girl.

ACKNOWLEDGMENTS

Every book is a collaboration, and I'm deeply grateful to the talented and dedicated people on my team at Algonquin Young Readers, Workman Publishing, and Writers House.

My extraordinary agent, Dan Lazar, was instrumental in helping me shape and expand this story early on. His guidance—from the project's inception to its conclusion—was invaluable. I trust his instincts and always welcome his input.

Elise Howard, publisher of Algonquin Young Readers, provided wise and thoughtful edits. Her vision for *Cub* inspired and guided me, and I (gratefully) took every piece of advice she offered. I would have been lost without associate editor Sarah Alpert, who had a ready answer for every question I asked (and there were many!).

I was very fortunate to have had Neil Swaab design *Cub*; his was the calm voice of reason and reassurance over many months, and his subtle (delightful!) touches punctuate the book.

The contribution of Eisner-nominated colorist Ronda Pattison to the visual appeal of *Cub* can't be overstated. Ronda's talent and creative instincts brought my inked pages to life.

My daughter, Alex Carley, provided valuable feedback on the cover art and design and offered wisdom and encouragement throughout the many years it took to create *Cub*.

Many other exceptional people worked behind the scenes, playing important roles in *Cub*'s development: Laura Williams, Ashley Mason, Steve Godwin, Julie Primavera, and Janice Lee. Thanks to Megan Harley, Caitlin Rubinstein, and Carla Bruce-Eddings for seeing that young readers everywhere have a chance to discover *Cub*.

I've been part of the Workman Publishing family since 1993, when Peter Workman offered me my first significant book contract. I've always appreciated the support, respect, and attention the Workman group gives every one of its authors.

As for the experiences that inspired *Cub*, I'm indebted to Leslie Jacobs, who seemed so grown up when she was mentoring me, but was actually in her twenties. Idealistic and inspirational, she expanded my idea of what women's lives could look like, encouraging me to dream big.

Maureen Schulz, the exceptional English teacher whose phone call to the newspaper started it all, retired from teaching long ago. I recently wrote to her about *Cub*. She said that she read my note with tears in her eyes, having always wondered if she'd "left any positive mark" during her many years of teaching. I hope caring, compassionate teachers everywhere—including my beloved Mrs. Schulz—realize just how much of a lasting impact they have on their students.

I'm grateful most of all to my family, for providing me with my best memories and the happiest possible start in life. Growing up, my brothers made every day more fun (even when they were pestering me); now they are among my biggest supporters. My sweet mom, the family cheerleader, is still a whirlwind of happy energy. I'm thrilled that she was able to have a fulfilling career after we all left home—and has continued working into her eighties!

I dedicated *Cub* to my dad, who died before this book was finished. I hope his kind and gentle manner and devotion to his family come through in these pages. He was my fierce protector and biggest fan. I miss him every single day.

CYNTHIA L. COPELAND IS THE *NEW YORK TIMES* BESTSELLING AND AWARD-WINNING AUTHOR/ILLUSTRATOR OF MORE THAN 25 BOOKS FOR ADULTS AND CHILDREN. A GRADUATE OF SMITH COLLEGE, SHE LIVES IN NEW HAMPSHIRE WITH HER FAMILY. *CUB* IS HER FIRST GRAPHIC MEMOIR FOR YOUNG READERS.